Sri Lanka is blessed with a beautiful climate and abundant natural resources. It is also ideally positioned at the southernmost point of the Indian Sub-Continent for the maritime trade which brings people, products and ideas from all over the world. Alas, the coin has two sides. Sri Lanka's endowments naturally attract unwelcome external interest and big power rivalry. When the country is united, the external elements can be kept in balance. When the country is divided, the divisions are made worse by external forces. In 70 years of independence, Sri Lanka has had to confront interconnected internal and external challenges. Abeyagoonasekera's book describes and analyses these challenges and points a way forward to a happier future for this gem of an island in the Indian Ocean.

George Yeo, Former Foreign Minister of Singapore

As the Indo-Pacific theatre takes center stage in geopolitics, Sri Lanka has been cast in a central role. This timely and important collection sheds light on scenarios for the future of the country and region that open a window into forecasting the future power balance in Asia.

Parag Khanna, author of Connectography *(2016) and* The Future is Asian *(2019)*

This is one of the best books to understand the dilemma Sri Lanka is facing. Currently, the 'Japan-U.S.-India-Australia versus China' confrontation has been intensifying. In such a situation, what should Sri Lanka do? The importance of Sri Lanka is rising and geographically speaking, the country has an advantage. Thus, Sri Lanka needs a strategy for surviving as a rising independent country, by using this geographical advantage. In this book, Asanga Abeyagoonasekera explains the right course with his in-depth knowledge of the country, allowing us to learn about the new, bright future of Sri Lanka.

Satoru Nagao, Visiting Fellow at Hudson Institute and expert on Japan-U.S.-India security cooperation

Asanga Abeyagoonasekera offers a unique perspective on a broad range of political, economic, and cultural trends as they impact and relate to Sri Lanka. With a focus on geopolitical influences, he offers great insight into the contemporary issues facing this relatively young island nation.

Karen S. Miller
Chair, Political Science, Criminal Justice, and Organizational Leadership
Northern Kentucky University

This book is an interesting, important, and useful read for those who are to shape Sri Lanka's foreign policy. I share most of the author's views. Sri Lanka has indeed an exceptional geopolitical position and will continue to be exposed to the interests and ambitions of great powers, China and India in particular. Sri Lanka will have to find, as Asanga suggests in the book, the appropriate balance between their own and foreign interests to assure its own security and development and the wellbeing of its people.

The special value of this book is its chapters dealing with the domestic situation in Sri Lanka. It is important to emphasise the successful endeavours for reconciliation and rehabilitation that have been implemented in Sri Lanka after three decades of war. Sri Lanka should serve as a positive example of how to re-establish a national society after a conflict. Unfortunately, these endeavours have been too long ignored outside the country.

This book will significantly contribute not only to a better understanding of Sri Lanka's unique geopolitical position and its foreign policy choices, but also its great development potential based in particular on its geopolitical position, and on its domestic resources, including the current high level of education of its population, and consequently, the capacity for innovation, which is becoming the most important driving force of development.

Ernest Petrič
Professor of International Law and International Relations, University of Ljubljana, Slovenia
Judge, Former Diplomat and President of the Constitution Court of Slovenia

This is a great project linking Sri Lanka's geopolitics (as a backdrop) to examine the country's national security, foreign policy, relations, national development, regional affairs, etc., in a globalised world — namely involving China, India, and the U.S. It is an in-depth study connecting all these aspects defining Sri Lanka's geopolitics, security, and development.

Runa Das
Professor of Political Science, University of Minnesota Duluth

Abeyagoonasekera's book discusses the shift of power from the Asia-Pacific to the Indo-Pacific. With its unique geographic position, its human and natural resources, Sri Lanka is resuming its geostrategic and geopolitical significance.

The book describes the decline of the west and how the epicenter of global development is shifting to Asia. After 450 years of colonial domination, the western civilization is on the decline. The world is witnessing the Fourth Industrial Revolution. In his admirable study, Abeyagoonasekera makes an appreciable contribution towards understanding our region's future!

Rohan Gunaratna
Head of the International Centre for Political Violence and Terrorism Research
S. Rajaratnam School of International Studies, NTU

Asanga Abeyagoonasekera has written a wide-ranging and frank set of essays setting out a Sri Lankan point of view on the country's geopolitical and internal political challenges and opportunities. Coming when the centrality and importance of the Indian Ocean and its littoral to Asian and world developments is increasing rapidly, this volume is a welcome addition to the literature. It is a realistic portrayal of Sri Lanka's pivotal position, of her intertwined relations with India and China, and of her options for the future. It should therefore be of considerable interest to the foreign policy community and all those interested in the future development of this critical country and region.

Shivshankar Menon
Former Foreign Secretary and National Security Advisor to the
Indian Prime Minister

This book provides solid impetus to the work of dedicated and determined, contemporary leaders who are optimistic of a better world. Through a compendium of essays, this work provides readers with in-depth analyses about issues ranging from geopolitics in the Indo-Pacific to the changing role of world order, foreign policy to reconciliation and peace building, and democracy to cyber security. This scholarly work is a timely contribution to the existing literature, and undoubtedly supports the advancement of knowledge and the understanding of geopolitics and allied fields.

Eugene de Silva
CEO, Virginia Research Institute, USA

Asanga Abeyagoonasekera skilfully and meticulously guides the reader to a clearer understanding of the thinking and decision-making within the highest echelons during various periods of Sri Lanka's recent past, and also offers a trenchant analysis as to the country's aspirations (including in the wider geopolitical and strategic context) into the future.

Shashi Jayakumar
Head, Centre of Excellence for National Security,
S. Rajaratnam School of International Studies, NTU

For those interested in the future of Sri Lanka and its position in the region and the world, this book shares many insights for a serious overview of prospects and strategies that must be considered.

Jerome C. Glenn, CEO and Co-Founder, The Millennium Project

This book provides keen insights into Sri Lanka´s political and economic future by looking at key aspects that have shaped this country's past and present. Sri Lanka is "at crossroads" in multiple ways, most importantly because it lies squarely in the middle of an extremely strategic position geographically. Asanga Abeygoonesekera, using his considerable experience as an academic and political insider, addresses the promises and perils of being sandwiched between two rising superpowers, India and China. The book is for those concerned about which economic, political and diplomatic paths this island nation should follow in order to secure peace and prosperity for its people. It is certainly a 'must read' for academics interested in Sri Lanka and the region.

Indra de Soysa
Professor of Political Science
Norwegian University of Science and Technology

There are at least three thrusts of crosswinds that virtually every nation is having to grapple with today: a shift away from the unipolar world order (and its ideological consensus) of the past two and a half decades, a technology-led industrial revolution that has far-reaching consequences, and a resurgence of domestic politics based on identity and polarisation. Sri Lanka faces these challenges with a unique history and geo-strategic location that could afford it significant advantages. In this excellent anthology, Asanga provides a framework and a nautical chart that is not only relevant to Sri Lanka but to many others seeking to future-proof their nations with deliberate geo-economic strategy. From the World Economic Forum in Davos to the Shangri La Dialogue in Singapore and sometimes the flights in between, Asanga draws on personal observations and debates across domains and disciplines. *Sri Lanka at Crossroads* is a timely and practical reference for governments and businesses alike.

Lutfey Siddiqi
Visiting Professor-in-Practice, London School of Economics and Political Science
Adjunct Professor, National University of Singapore

This is an insightful work both in its scope and specificity, weaving intelligently the text and context into a coherent narrative of a country, Sri Lanka, that has been largely undercovered and whose importance cannot be ignored in the coming decades.

Uttam Kumar Sinha
Fellow, Institute of Defence Studies and Analyses (IDSA),
Senior Fellow, Nehru Memorial Museum and Library, New Delhi

SRI LANKA AT CROSSROADS

Geopolitical Challenges and National Interests

SRI LANKA AT CROSSROADS

Geopolitical Challenges and National Interests

Asanga Abeyagoonasekera

Institute of National Security Studies Sri Lanka (INSSSL), Sri Lanka

NEW JERSEY · LONDON · SINGAPORE · BEIJING · SHANGHAI · HONG KONG · TAIPEI · CHENNAI · TOKYO

Published by

World Scientific Publishing Co. Pte. Ltd.
5 Toh Tuck Link, Singapore 596224
USA office: 27 Warren Street, Suite 401-402, Hackensack, NJ 07601
UK office: 57 Shelton Street, Covent Garden, London WC2H 9HE

Library of Congress Cataloging-in-Publication Data
Names: Abeyagoonasekera, Asanga, author.
Title: Sri Lanka at crossroads : geopolitical challenges and national interests /
  Asanga Abeyagoonasekera.
Description: New Jersey : World Scientific, 2019. | Includes bibliographical references and index.
Identifiers: LCCN 2018041493 | ISBN 9789813276727
Subjects: LCSH: Sri Lanka--Politics and government--21st century. | Sri Lanka--
  Foreign relations--21st century. | Geopolitics--Sri Lanka. | Peace-building--Sri Lanka. |
  Reconciliation--Political aspects--Sri Lanka. | Democracy--Sri Lanka. |
  Institution building--Sri Lanka. | Computer security--Sri Lanka.
Classification: LCC JQ655 .A74 2019 | DDC 320.95493--dc23
LC record available at https://lccn.loc.gov/2018041493

British Library Cataloguing-in-Publication Data
A catalogue record for this book is available from the British Library.

ISBN: 978-981-120-142-4 (pbk)

Copyright © 2019 by World Scientific Publishing Co. Pte. Ltd.

All rights reserved. This book, or parts thereof, may not be reproduced in any form or by any means, electronic or mechanical, including photocopying, recording or any information storage and retrieval system now known or to be invented, without written permission from the publisher.

For photocopying of material in this volume, please pay a copying fee through the Copyright Clearance Center, Inc., 222 Rosewood Drive, Danvers, MA 01923, USA. In this case permission to photocopy is not required from the publisher.

For any available supplementary material, please visit
https://www.worldscientific.com/worldscibooks/10.1142/11167#t=suppl

Desk Editor: Shreya Gopi

Typeset by Stallion Press
Email: enquiries@stallionpress.com

Printed in Singapore

To
Avish and *Arya*

From the silent sky
where the half-moon becomes pronounced
by and by
there drips the milk
for a child's heart;
the infant son smiles
dreaming of the new world
that will come up tomorrow

In the motherland
where a nation of giants
who built the thousand reservoirs
are now reborn
new freedoms emerge
in a myriad of color
elegantly polished
by his smile;
I wipe my tears
and see
the little boy reigning
in a debt-free fear-free tomorrow...

Excerpt from Sri Lankan poet Mahagama Sekera's narrative poem "Prabuddha" (1977). Translated by Malinda Senaviratne from the original work in Sinhala.

Contents

List of Abbreviations	xix
Acknowledgement	xxiii

Introduction   1

Chapter 1   Geopolitics   3

The Geopolitics of Floating Bases and the New World Order	4
Sri Lanka: Leveraging the Politics of Geography	7
Steering Co-operation Across Oceans	9
Oceans of (Dis)trust	12
Geo-strategy in the Indo-Pacific	16
Sri Lanka Facing the Geopolitical Game in the Indian Ocean	24

Chapter 2   Political Landscape   43

Changing Political Horizons in Sri Lanka?	44
Monuments Over Mortality?	46
Sri Lanka: National Interests in a Globalized World	49
Securing Sri Lanka's National Interests	51
The Role of Independence in an Interchanging World Order	53
Politics of Promise: Between Sirisena and Rajapaksa	56
Sri Lanka: Moving Towards a Higher Collective Outcome	58
The Importance of Electing the Best to Our Nation's Parliament	61
Sri Lanka: Brain Drain, 'Connection Culture', and National Development	64

Chapter 3 Foreign Relations   67

Sri Lankan Foreign Policy: Diaspora and Lobbying   68
The Island and the Mainland: Impact of Fisheries on
    Indo-Lanka Relations   70
New Delhi-Tamil Nadu Relations and India's
    Sri Lanka Policy   73
Remembering Tagore in Turbulent Times   75
Trumpism and the Diplomatic Dragon: Balancing
    Interests in the New Year   77
Sri Lanka: The New Regime and the Revolution   81
Maritime Security in the Indian Ocean —
    A Geopolitical Perspective from Sri Lanka and
    the Role of the EU in the Indian Ocean Region (IOR)   83

Chapter 4 Peace Building and Reconciliation   91

Racism, Riots, and the Sri Lankan State   92
Re-building Sri Lanka: An Island at a Crossroads   94
Understanding Our 'Blind Spot' to Make Peace Building
    Comprehensive   97
The Darkest Day in the City of Lights   99
Sri Lanka and the World: Terrorism and Effective
    Reconciliation   102
Sri Lanka: Toward a Diaspora Re-Engagement Plan   104
Countering Youth Radicalisation in South Asia: A Sri Lankan
    Perspective   107
The Role of Youth in Reconciliation   112
Remembering General Denzil Kobbekaduwa   114

Chapter 5 Democracy and Institution Building   117

Death and Democracy   118
Riot and Responsibility: Governance   120
New Year Kokis to Luxury Permits   122
Disasters & Democracy: Facing Up To Reality in Following
    New Year Tragedy   124
The Forgotten Professions: The Plight of a Nation   128

Parliamentary Blows & the South Asian Buddha: The Case
  of Dignity in Sri Lanka 130
Economic Crime — A Sri Lankan Perspective 133

Chapter 6 Cyber Security and Foresight **141**

Unified Mechanism to Improve Cyber Security 142
A Collaborative Venture in the Age of 'Information
  Wars': Japan and Sri Lanka 146
Cyber Security Threats to Sri Lanka 149
Forecast 2016: A Roadmap for Sri Lanka 152
Crisis and Foresight Analysis 156
Forecast 2017: Sri Lanka 158

Endnotes 169
Index 197
About the Author 200

List of Abbreviations

ADB	—	Asian Development Bank
AIIB	—	Asian Infrastructure Investment Bank
AML	—	Anti-Money Laundering
APTA	—	Asia-Pacific Trade Agreement
ASEAN	—	Association of Southeast Asian Nations
B&R	—	The Belt and Road
BIMSTEC	—	The Bay of Bengal Initiative for Multi-Sectoral Technical and Economic Cooperation
BRI	—	Belt and Road Initiative
BRICS	—	Brazil, Russia, India, China and South Africa
CALMIT	—	Chinese Aerospace Long–March International Trade
CEIEC	—	China National Electronics Import and Export Corporation
CERT	—	Computer Emergency Readiness Teams
CFT	—	Combating the Financing of Terrorism
CIABOC	—	Commission to Investigate Allegations of Bribery or Corruption
CICA	—	Conference on Interaction and Confidence-building in Central Asia
CKD	—	Chronic Kidney Disease
CMC	—	Colombo Municipal Council
COP	—	Conference of Parties
COPE	—	Committee on Public Enterprises
CPA	—	Committee on Public Accounts
CPEC	—	China-Pakistan Economic Corridor

CPI	—	Corruption Perception Index
CTFRM	—	The Consultation Task Force on Reconciliation Mechanisms
EEZ	—	Exclusive Economic Zone
EUISS	—	European Union Institute for Security Studies
EXIM	—	Chinese Export-Import Bank
FDI	—	Foreign Direct Investment
FTA	—	Free Trade Agreement
GCI	—	Global Competitiveness Index
GDP	—	Gross Domestic Product
GOSL	—	Government of Sri Lanka
GPS	—	Global Positioning System
GTF	—	Global Tamil Forum
HNDE	—	Higher National Diploma in Engineering
IAT	—	The Race Implicit Association Test
ICC	—	International Criminal Court
ICJ	—	International Court of Justice
ICT	—	Information and Communication Technology
ICU	—	Intensive Care Unit
ICWA	—	Indian Council of World Affairs
IMBL	—	International Maritime Boundary Line
IMF	—	International Monetary Fund
INSSSL	—	Institute of National Security Studies Sri Lanka
IONS	—	Indian Ocean Naval Symposium
IOR	—	Indian Ocean Region
IORA	—	Indian Ocean Rim Association
IPKF	—	Indian Peace Keeping Force
IS	—	Islamic State
ISIS	—	Islamic State of Iraq and the Levant
ISRI	—	Instituto Superior de Relaciones Internacionales "Raul Roa Garcia"
ITJP	—	International Truth and Justice Project
IUU	—	Illegal, Unreported and Unregulated (Fishing)
JVP	—	Janatha Vimukthi Peramuna
LKYSPP	—	Lee Kuan Yew School of Public Policy
LLRC	—	Lessons Learnt and Reconciliation Commission

LSE	—	London School of Economics
LTTE	—	Liberation Tigers of Tamil Eelam
MOU	—	Memorandum of Understanding
MP	—	Member of Parliament
MRIA	—	Mattala Rajapaksa International Airport
MSR	—	Maritime Silk Road
MW	—	Molecular Weight
NAM	—	Non-Aligned Movement
NATO	—	North Atlantic Treaty Organization
NGO	—	Non-Governmental Organizational
NHS	—	National Health Service
NIDS	—	National Institute for Defence Studies
NITC	—	National Information Technology Conference
NSA	—	National Security Agency
OBOR	—	One Belt, One Road
OHCHR	—	Office of the United Nations High Commissioner for Human Rights
ORF	—	Observer Research Foundation
PARCS	—	Protective Accommodation and Rehabilitation Centres
PHI	—	Public Health Inspector
PLA	—	People's Liberation Army of China
PLAN	—	People's Liberation Army Navy
QMS	—	Quota Management System
RAW	—	Research and Analysis Wing
RTI	—	Right to Information Act
SAARC	—	South Asian Association for Regional Cooperation
SAFTA	—	South Asian Free Trade Area Agreement
SAGAR	—	Security and Growth for All in the Region
SAR	—	Synthetic Aperture Radar
SCO	—	Shanghai Cooperation Organisation
SDF	—	Self-Defence Force
SFM	—	Soros Fund Management
SGBV	—	Sexual and Gender Based Violence
SLFP	—	The Sri Lankan Freedom Party
SLOC	—	Sea Lines of Communication
SREB	—	Silk Road Economic Belt

STEM	—	Science, Technology, Engineering and Mathematics
TNA	—	Tamil National Alliance
TOR	—	Terms of Reference
TPA	—	Tamil Progressive Alliance
TRO	—	Tamil Rehabilitation Organization
UNDP	—	United Nations Development Programme
UNESCO	—	United Nations Educational, Scientific and Cultural Organization
UNFCCC	—	United Nations Framework Convention on Climate Change
UNFGG	—	United National Front for Good Governance
UNHCR	—	United Nations High Commissioner for Refugees
UNHRC	—	United Nations Human Rights Council
UNP	—	United National Party
UNSC	—	United States Security Council
UPFA	—	United People's Freedom Alliance
USPACOM	—	United States Indo-Pacific Command
VAT	—	Value Added Tax
VIP	—	Very Important People
WEF	—	World Economic Forum
WHO	—	World Health Organization
WMD	—	Weapons of Mass Destruction

Acknowledgement

An author rarely works alone and I am deeply grateful for all the help that others have given me. It is a pleasure to acknowledge their assistance.

This book began life as a thought from conversations with my students to compile a volume of my writings for the 70th Independence of Sri Lanka.

I thank Juliana Chan for her support from the inception to introduce me to the publisher. I thank World Scientific for publishing this book and for all the support they have offered to make this book reach a wide audience.

I thank all academics, government officers, researchers and everyone for their support. I thank all the scholars and teachers who has guided me, I would have not made it and thus would never have written without their support, advice, opportunities offered to me and the institutions where they taught me. For all the help I am forever grateful.

Malinda Seneviratne's translation of the poem "Prabuddha" by the Sri Lankan poet Mahagama Sekera was excerpted with Ravinda Mahagamasekera's permission. I thank Malinda and Ravinda for giving me the permission. The great poet Mahagama Sekara's words have been a mirror to pause, reflect and view myself in this busy world. I thank Prof. Vini Vitharana for his kind advice and guidance which I have treasured.

My effort were aided by researchers, specially I thank Ms. Ramla Wahab Salman who has assisted me so much and IPCS editors for their time and dedication. The initial copy edit was done by Priyanka Moonasinghe and the final copy edit was completed by Jayamini Rathna

Kumari and Shreya Gopi, editor of World Scientific, who worked tirelessly and I am grateful for their time and dedication.

I would also like to acknowledge long-standing debt to my mentors. Specially Prof. G.L. Peiris, the former foreign minister of Sri Lanka, who introduced me to the foreign policy think tank (Kadirgamar Institute) where I began my journey of writing and research in international relations and geopolitics.

Finally, I thank my wife Kumudu, to whom I owe so much. This book is dedicated to my children Avish and Arya.

Note

The chapters in this book include speeches and essays that have previously been delivered/published, and which refer to events at the time of writing. Refer to the Endnotes to learn when each article was written, to better understand the context. Certain examples or points are repeated across the articles. These repeats have been retained in the chapters of this book for the benefit of readers who may prefer not to read the chapters in order. Furthermore, people's names in the index have been retained in the form they are most commonly referred to, for easy, quick reference for general readers.

The pattern on the inside of the covers of this book (hardcover version) is from the beautifully painted ceiling of a hall at the Temple of the Sacred Tooth Relic in Kandy, Sri Lanka.

Introduction

Sri Lanka is at crossroads and we still have the option to choose the right path towards prosperity.

This book is a compilation of essays on themes intended to provoke thought in making our society and world a better place. It intertwines the unfolding of a new world order driven by geopolitical tensions with the journey of Sri Lanka as an island nation celebrating 70 years of independence.

The rise of regional and extra-regional great powers in the Indian Ocean Region, as well as their sphere of influence on Sri Lanka, is elucidated in this book. In this context, many of the essays focus on the rise of China as a geopolitical influencer. A trillion-dollar initiative by the name of *One Belt, One Road* (OBOR) signifies the awakening of a sleeping giant from the ancient past to create a new Asian world order. While observing that the centre of gravity of the world order is shifting from West to East, this book attempts to root Sri Lanka's place in it as a '*super connector*' at the centre of the Maritime Silk Road (MSR).

Within this overarching world context, Sri Lanka has embarked upon its own internal journey of rehabilitation, reconstruction, and reconciliation in the years after the long war. On 4 February 2018, this journey culminated in Sri Lanka's 70th year of independence. After an era of colonial rule, nearly 30 years of civil war, and two youth insurrections, the nation has lost many lives and sacrificed the potential of so many youths. The book looks at the twin dimensions of Sri Lanka, existing in the international arena whilst securing her own safety as a proud and sovereign nation.

I decided to compile this book as a sequel to my first book, *Towards a Better World Order* (2015), in the hopes that it would draw from both global and local context to illuminate Sri Lanka's strategic position as well as its potential in this new world order. The book consists of essays written for a New Delhi based think tank, *Institute for Peace and Conflict Studies* (IPCS), as well as lectures delivered at the University of Cambridge, Lee Kuan Yew School, and many places around the world. In addition, articles written to the Sri Lankan media are also included in this book.

I believe the collection of essays, lectures, and articles will have some relevance to and can shed some light on the nation-building process that Sri Lanka has currently embarked upon. The chapters consist of the following thematic areas: *Geopolitics, Political Landscape, Foreign Relations, Peace Building and Reconciliation, Democracy and Institution Building*, and *Cyber Security and Foresight*.

After serving for 13 years in the Sri Lankan Government administration, I have garnered extensive knowledge in the aforementioned thematic areas and therefore this book represents an imparting of that knowledge to better prescribe policy and a vision for the future of my beautiful island, Sri Lanka.

I thank everyone who has supported me throughout my journey.

Asanga Abeyagoonasekera

Chapter 1

Geopolitics

"Because the Indian Ocean is sort of the world's energy interstate and China will have a maritime presence, perhaps even a naval presence in some distant morrow. So the opening of this port in south Sri Lanka is of real geopolitical significance."

Robert D. Kaplan[a]

---

[a] Robert D. Kaplan, 29 June 2012, on China's port expansion in the Indian Ocean (Agenda), Stratfor interview.

The Geopolitics of Floating Bases and the New World Order[1]

"Those far distant, storm-beaten ships, upon which the Grand Army never looked, stood between it and the dominion of the world." — *Alfred Thayer Mahan*[2]

US naval officer and strategist Alfred Thayer Mahan's advice in 1890,[3] for the US to push outwards to rule the oceans, is still heeded by US maritime forces in the present day. The *USS Nimitz* aircraft carrier, standing 23 stories high and 333 metres long with 5,000 personnel on board, arrived in Sri Lanka in October 2017,[4] 32 years since the last arrival of a US aircraft carrier. Aircraft carriers are sea-faring air bases equivalent to floating geographical land masses with significant firepower which have been proven as key strategic war machines in the recent past.

The visit of the *USS Nimitz*[b] is a clear indication of the military and economic might that the US projects through floating bases, not only in the Indian Ocean Region (IOR) but globally. Floating bases are indicative of the US world order — one that is predominantly unilateral, save for '*collective security*'[c] partnerships, and one that seeks hegemony. Nevertheless, the presence of *USS Nimitz* in the IOR was meant to symbolise the strong cooperation between the US and Sri Lanka during the regime of President Maithripala Sirisena. Back in 1985, the US aircraft carrier visit would have raised concerns for Sri Lanka's immediate neighbour, India. However, today, the US and India enjoy a different relationship than in the past. The US has clearly cemented strong '*collective security*' relations with India, Japan, and Australia.

In this context, countries with a geostrategic advantage such as Sri Lanka are seen as ideal sites to further strengthen these lateral ties.

---

[b] USS Nimitz (CVN-68) is a super carrier of the United States Navy, and the lead ship of her class. One of the largest warships in the world, the ship was named for World War II Pacific fleet commander Chester W. Nimitz.

[c] Collective security: a system by which states have attempted to prevent or stop wars. Under a collective security arrangement, an aggressor against any one state is considered an aggressor against all other states, which act together to repel the aggressor. See: https://www.britannica.com/topic/collective-security

From 2010 onwards, there have been more than 200 foreign naval visits to Sri Lanka, including India's *INS Vikramaditya*,[5] another aircraft carrier that visited the Colombo Port in 2016. Sri Lanka strives to balance all major powers' interests in the country and thus accommodates these warships as friendship visits. The prevalent counter-argument is that some major powers, most notably China, are aggressively and one-sidedly pursuing their own self-interest by setting up military bases in the IOR. However, one could also contend that aircraft carriers as floating bases (such as the US') in the deep oceans are trying to showcase and achieve a similar military strategy and projection of power.

President Sirisena's Government is enacting this balancing act for Sri Lanka and creating equidistant foreign relations with the US, India, and China. In the region, India has also engaged in joint military exercises, the most recent being '*Mitra Shakti 2017*'[6] with Sri Lanka in October of 2017. According to the *Indian Express*[7] the joint military exercise was India's response to China's growing influence in South Asia and the IOR. However, this author's opinion is that the article is speculative since the military exercise clearly falls short of limiting China's growing power in the region. In this vein, many speculative media stories will raise similar questions with regard to Sri Lanka's relationship with its neighbour, India.

President Trump visited China[8] against the backdrop of all these geopolitical events in the IOR. Chinese leader Xi Jinping has arguably presided over more domestic stability and economic prosperity in his country than Angela Merkel, Theresa May, Vladimir Putin, and Donald Trump combined. President Xi, in his speech[9] to the 19th National Congress in October, highlighted the founding aspirations of Chinese communist values. This included moving 80 million people from rural to urban areas, boosting the country's GDP from 54 trillion to 80 trillion yuan, projecting China as the world's second largest economy, and contributing to 30 per cent of global economic growth in a span of only five years.[10] While propelling innovation and scientific advancement, China has also made more than 1,500 reforms of a socialist nature to pursue modernisation, including fighting corruption. On the latter point, President Xi remarked, "*We have taken out tigers, swatted flies and hunted down foxes*",[11] leaving no space for corruption.

At the 19th National Congress, China's external approach to the world was discussed. President Xi's gigantic One Belt, One Road (OBOR)[d] project has already altered the natural geography in many parts of the world. This includes the China–Pakistan Economic Corridor (CPEC),[e] connecting to Gwadar Port, as well as Hambantota Port,[f] which will change trading patterns in the region. The Asian Infrastructure Investment Bank (AIIB) and the Silk Road Fund are other economic initiatives working towards funding a new economic order. Thus, it is apparent that China has charted its own course in creating an Asian-led new world order that is geopolitically, economically, and militarily in direct contravention of the US' world order, renouncing the perceived Western view.

Today, China projects itself as a proud country, at a time when socialists around the world are celebrating the centennial of the great October Revolution of 1917,[12] spearheaded by Vladimir Ilyich Ulyanov, better known as Lenin. From its long history of struggle, China has set itself in the right direction to alter the existing world order (the one contravened by the US), by pursuing a strategy that is rooted in economic and geopolitical prowess. Much like the US, China's power projections are articulated through the amassing of land bases. Yet China's world vision is far broader, in that it is striving to combine its economic and military might with its socialist-political orientation as well as the geostrategic interests of developing countries.

---

[d] The Silk Road Economic Belt and the 21st-Century Maritime Silk Road — better known as the One Belt and One Road Initiative (OBOR), The Belt and Road (B&R), and The Belt and Road Initiative (BRI) — is a development strategy proposed by China's President Xi Jinping that focuses on connectivity and cooperation between Eurasian countries, primarily the People's Republic of China (PRC), the land-based Silk Road Economic Belt (SREB), and the oceangoing Maritime Silk Road (MSR).

[e] China–Pakistan Economic Corridor (CPEC) is a collection of infrastructure projects that are currently under construction throughout Pakistan.

[f] The Hambantota Port (also known as the Port of Hambantota) is a maritime port in Hambantota, Sri Lanka. The first phase of the port was opened on 18 November 2010, with the first ceremonial berthing of the naval ship *Jetliner* to use the port facilities. It is named after former President Mahinda Rajapaksa. Hambantota Port is built inland and operated by the Sri Lanka Ports Authority.

Sri Lanka: Leveraging the Politics of Geography[13]

"The Village in the Jungle is different because it's not about Us, but wholly about Them. It was very advanced in 1913, when many people in Europe were racist." — Nick Rankin[14]

Rural Hambantota was first known for being featured in a book by Leonard Woolf[15] in the early 20th century, and now, as a port shaping Sri Lankan politics. Woolf's *Village in the Jungle* was the first novel in English literature to be written from an indigenous perspective rather than a coloniser's.

According to British author Nick Rankin, *"It's not a book about the white chaps at the club who run the show, but about those at the very bottom of the imperial heap, the black and brown fellows who don't even know they're part of an Empire, but who just survive day by day, hand to mouth, as slash-and-burn agriculturalists."*[16] If Woolf was alive today, he would probably be writing his second masterpiece, *Village that was Leased Out, Hambantota*.

After Chinese President Xi Jinping launched the Belt and Road Initiative (BRI), Sri Lanka signed an agreement with China for one of the key strategic projects of this initiative in May 2017. The agreement was to lease out Hambantota Port with a majority share to a Chinese company for three generations.

BRI is the *"project of the century"*, according to President Xi. This trillion-dollar initiative aims to integrate Eurasia through the development of infrastructure. It is unquestionably the most ambitious project ever launched in recent times, and it seeks to revisit and resurrect the global legacy of Zheng He, an admiral from the Ming dynasty.[g] A century ago, a British geopolitical thinker Sir Halford Mackinder[h] argued that whoever controls the Eurasian heartland will control the world.[17] US strategy looks further into Alfred Mahan's maritime power; after World War II, George Kennan[18] incorporated Mahan's geostrategic focus on rim lands, rather

---

[g] Zheng He was a Chinese mariner, explorer, diplomat, fleet admiral, and court eunuch during China's early Ming dynasty.

[h] Sir Halford Mackinder was an English geographer, academic, and politician, who is regarded as one of the founding fathers of both geopolitics and geo-strategy.

than heartlands, to his Cold War strategy of containment of the Soviet Union to create a favourable balance of power.

As Washington rebalances to Asia, relations between the US and China have become increasingly contentious and zero-sum oriented. According to Wang Jisi,[19] a Chinese foreign policy scholar, China must avoid a head-on military confrontation with the US. Instead, it should fill in the gaps left by the US retreat from the Middle East. By doing so, China will be able to decisively influence regions that are free from a US-dominated security order or a pre-existing economic integration mechanism. BRI was conceived from Wang Jisi's initial inputs and strategy to have a significant Chinese footprint in Eurasia, especially to recalibrate the existing world order. According to the World Economic Forum,[20] by 2030 the US will no longer be the only superpower, and China will be well positioned among the many countries to become one of the big powers.

With its geostrategic position at the centre of the Maritime Silk Road, Sri Lanka is a *'super-connector'* linking the east–west sea lanes. The Sri Lankan people should reap the benefits of the country's participation in this initiative, and it is important that all strategic projects in this regard are carefully calibrated. However, the process of determining the content of the agreement has not been discussed in Parliament, in consultation with think-tanks, or the public. As a democracy with its sovereignty vested in the people by the Constitution, it is important to get input from as many quarters as possible when determining strategic projects for the country. Sri Lankan President Sirisena pointed out that the debate should go to Parliament, an argument which Minister Wijedasa Rajapaksa[i] further expounded, and this is absolutely correct. The failure of such public consultations has triggered much internal destabilisation; in the past, the hurried nature of the 13th Amendment[21] to the Constitution — the Indo-Sri Lankan Accord[22] — triggered the southern insurrection.

China is Sri Lanka's second largest trading partner, surpassing the US and just behind India. Sino–Lankan trade remains at more than

---

[i] Wijeyadasa Rajapaksa is a Sri Lankan lawyer and politician. He is a Member of Parliament for the Colombo District, a former Minister of Justice and Buddasasana from 2015 to 2017, and Minister of State Banking Development from 2005 to 2006.

US$ 3 billion.[23] This position will change significantly with the Chinese economic zone and Hambantota Port's full operationality. By 2025, China will become Sri Lanka's largest trading partner due to the significant investments in the island.[24] In the geopolitical context, while the global hegemon — the US — is strengthening its ties with India, other South Asian countries are strengthening ties with the regional hegemon, China, to counterbalance this. India's role and China's aspirations in the Indian Ocean remain a topic of debate among scholars. India fears encirclement by China and China feels the same vis-à-vis the US.

Tensions at the lines of intersection are highest at geostrategic hotspots like Sri Lanka. The Government's consideration to lease out the new Chinese-built Mattala Rajapaksa International Airport[j] (MRIA) to India is a measure to counterbalance China. While India, the US, and Japan will strengthen the rules-based order of the world, China will be the peace-loving explorer set on transforming the world on a self-proclaimed *"win-win"* basis.

In this strained geopolitical environment, Sri Lanka should design a plan, not based on the process of leasing, but rather chart a path within the interests of emergent and existing powers. It must seek to develop a value-added export basket to strengthen its economy.

Steering Co-operation Across Oceans[25]

"We should not develop a habit of retreating to the harbour whenever we encounter a storm, for this will never get us to the other side of the ocean." — *President Xi Jinping*[26]

The nuclear-powered aircraft carrier USS Carl Vinson,[k] which is the size of three football fields and holds the capacity to launch 75 fighter jets

---

[j] Mattala Rajapaksa International Airport (MRIA) is an international airport serving southeast Sri Lanka. It is located in the town of Mattala, 18 km from Hambantota. It is the first greenfield airport and the second international airport in the country, after Bandaranaike International Airport in Colombo.

[k] USS Carl Vinson (CVN-70) is the United States Navy's third Nimitz-class super-carrier and is named after Carl Vinson, a Congressman from Georgia, in recognition of his contributions to the US Navy. The ship was launched in 1980 and undertook her maiden voyage in 1983.

at any given time, sailed to the Korean peninsula several weeks ago. US President Donald Trump speaking to the media claimed, *"We are sending an armada. Very powerful, we have submarines. Far more powerful than the aircraft carrier. That I can tell you."*[27] It looks like Trump has taken a leaf out of Kissinger's[l] limited war strategy.

In a 1958 interview, Kissinger advocated the importance of *"limited warfare"*[28] and why the US should adopt it. What we are witnessing today is significantly different from 1958 when nuclear deterrence was at the top of the agenda with the erstwhile Soviet Union.

Asia is going through profound transformations. China is in the process of expanding its blue-water navy[m] and seeks domination of the Indian and Pacific Oceans. This strikes a familiar chord with the US, which had a similar two-ocean strategy in the past that sought US domination over the Pacific and Atlantic Oceans.

US Vice President Mike Pence's first visit to Asia[29] took place against the background of mounting tensions. Its objectives included reaffirming the US commitment to the region. Pence also wanted to clarify and ensure that the US is compensated as the arbiter of regional security and stability. Finally, the visit was also conducted with the intention of discussing China's continued effort to expand its maritime capability in the region, especially in the South China Sea.

Pence described the Pacific situation as *"just a very serious time"*[30] during his discussion with Australian Prime Minister Malcolm Turnbull. He further explained that *"The US and Australia face this threat and every other one together, because we know that our security is the foundation of our prosperity."*[31] Both nations agreed to raise pressure on North Korea and seek China's support.

The author, as a participant at 2016's Shangri-La Dialogue,[n] raised a question for the Indian Minister of Defence regarding the circumstances

---

[l] Henry Alfred Kissinger is an American diplomat and political scientist who served as the United States Secretary of State and National Security Advisor under the Presidential administrations of Richard Nixon and Gerald Ford.

[m] A blue-water navy is a maritime force capable of operating globally, essentially across the deep waters of open oceans.

[n] The IISS Shangri-La Dialogue is Asia's premier defence summit, a unique meeting of ministers and delegates from over 50 countries. See: https://www.iiss.org/en/events/shangri-la-dialogue/about-s-shangri-la-s-dialogue

of another Chinese submarine's visit to Sri Lanka. Although defence strategies should be considered keeping broader strategic implications in mind, the Indian defence minister replied that they would take this up on a case-by-case basis.

As China witnesses geopolitical developments, there is a high probability of a sudden appearance of another Chinese submarine in the future. In October 2006,[32] when *USS Kitty Hawk*[o] was sailing through the East China Sea between southern Japan and Taiwan, a Chinese submarine surfaced without prior warning. The Americans were amazed when the Song-class attack submarine surfaced at a torpedo distance. The same sentiment applied when the last Chinese submarine's appearance in Sri Lanka created tensions between Colombo and New Delhi. According to some experts, Indians exaggerated the event for political purposes to remove the pro-Chinese Rajapaksa government of that time.

Indian Prime Minister Narendra Modi[p] visited Sri Lanka for the UN international Vesak celebrations,[q] a day recognised by the UN after the tremendous efforts of late Lakshman Kadirgamar, Sri Lanka's truly visionary former foreign minister. Modi's second visit is a clear indication of the friendship between the leaders of India and Sri Lanka.

After the celebration, Sri Lankan Prime Minister Ranil Wickremesinghe headed to China for the country's largest One Belt, One Road (OBOR) conference.[33] Sri Lanka's strategic role in the Maritime Silk Road is an important area, which will be addressed. This is occurring at a time when the Sri Lankan government is in discussions with India to lease out the tank farm in the east coast harbour of Trincomalee.

---

[o] The super carrier *USS Kitty Hawk* (CV-63) was the second naval ship named after Kitty Hawk, North Carolina, the site of the Wright brothers' first powered airplane flight. Kitty Hawk was both the first and last active ship of her class, and the last oil-fired aircraft carrier in service with the United States Navy.

[p] Narendra Modi is an Indian politician who is the 16th and current Prime Minister of India, in office since May 2014. He was the Chief Minister of Gujarat from 2001 to 2014, and is the Member of Parliament for Varanasi. Modi is a member of the Bharatiya Janata Party (BJP) and a Hindu nationalist.

[q] International Day of Vesak is a national holiday declared by the United Nations in 1999. Vesak is an important Buddhist holiday that celebrates the birth, enlightenment, and passing of Gautama Buddha.

136 countries and 28 heads of states are in Beijing for this large-scale high powered summit.[34] Of the South Asian countries, India will not participate. It is a clear indication of India's reservations. As explained by Indian Finance Minister Arun Jaitley, *"I have no hesitation in saying that we have some serious reservations about it, because of sovereignty issues."*[35] In an expert commentary written for the Institute for National Security Studies Sri Lanka, Swaran Singh explained tensions within India's neighbourhood, especially the US$ 62 billion China–Pakistan Economic Corridor, in his article titled *'OBOR: Getting India On-board as a Partner'*.[36]

With such developments, Sri Lanka's geopolitical role in the Indian Ocean remains crucial and essential to regional and extra regional nations. The OBOR could be seen by some as a platform to side with China. While China is promoting OBOR, the US is seeking to demonstrate to the whole region that it is in China's best interest to side with Washington. In 1907, US President Theodore Roosevelt sailed his 16 battleships as *'the great white fleet'*[r] to 20 ports, a mixture of hard and soft power — depicting the military term *'force projection'*[s] — a factor proven even today from the visit of USS Carl Vinson.

The OBOR project will be welcomed by many countries, particularly to uplift the economies and social conditions of third world states. Countries absent from the processes and events of OBOR could limit global benefits of the Chinese state-led initiative, and as explained by Chinese President Xi Jinping: *"perhaps we will not see the other side of the ocean".*[37]

Oceans of (Dis)trust[38]

"No cause justifies the deaths of innocent people" — Albert Camus[39]

---

[r] The Great White Fleet was the popular nickname for the powerful United States Navy battle fleet that completed a journey around the globe from 16 December 1907 to 22 February 1909, by order of United States President Theodore Roosevelt.

[s] Power projection (or force projection) is a term used in military and political science to refer to the capacity of a state *"to apply all or some of its elements of national power — political, economic, informational, or military — to rapidly and effectively deploy and sustain forces in and from multiple dispersed locations to respond to crises, to contribute to deterrence, and to enhance regional stability."*

UN Secretary General Ban Ki-moon delivered a lecture at the Kadirgamar Institute, Colombo, on *'Sustainable Peace and Achieving Sustainable Development Goals'*.[40] Referring to the lack of UN intervention in Sri Lanka, the Secretary General said, "*Had we been more actively engaged, we could have saved much more, many more human lives.*"[41] The conflict in Sri Lanka has therefore had a ripple effect in many spheres.

On a visit to Singapore, Harvard University scholar Dr. Neelan Tiruchelvam's[t] son spoke about the death of his parents at the hands of the Liberation Tigers of Tamil Eelam (LTTE) over false promises on unattainable goals. Dr. N. Tiruchelvam was a peace loving man, who wanted nothing more than a political settlement, but he was (allegedly) assassinated by the LTTE leader Prabhakaran, like the late Hon. Lakshman Kadirgamar,[u] a Tamil lawyer and former Foreign Affairs Minister. The institute[42] where Ban Ki-moon delivered his lecture was named after Kadirgamar and the irony of his statement, under the late statesman's photograph, was not to be missed.

The Sri Lankan situation was clearly different from Rwanda[43] or Srebrenica[44] or other ethnic conflicts — and this has to be established and understood in the international arena. "*Sri Lankan Army lost 5,600 officers and soldiers with over 25,000 battlefield casualties during the last two years of the battle, thousands of soldiers are still lying on beds like vegetables. All Sri Lankans are happily and peacefully living today because of the sacrifices that they made to bring about a future with no bombs and blood,*" says Maj. Gen. Kamal Gunaratne (who fought the 45-minute final battle that killed LTTE leader Velupillai Prabhakaran), in an interview for his latest book *Road to Nandikadal*.[45] He further says,

---

[t] Neelakandan Tiruchelvam was a Sri Lankan Tamil lawyer, academic, politician, and Member of Parliament. Tiruchelvam was allegedly assassinated by the LTTE in 1999.

[u] Lakshman Kadirgamar was a Sri Lankan Tamil lawyer and statesmen. He served as Minister of Foreign Affairs of Sri Lanka from 1994 to 2001 and again from April 2004 until his assassination in August 2005. He achieved international prominence in this position due to his wide-ranging condemnation of the LTTE and his efforts to have them banned internationally. A distinguished lawyer and international humanitarian, he was assassinated by an LTTE sniper in August 2005. See: *Democracy, Sovereignty and Terror: Lakshman Kadirgamar on the Foundations of International Order*, for accounts of his views on politics and international relations.

"I wrote this book for the poor parents who sent their sons to fight with the ruthless LTTE, the elite people in Colombo and abroad and the human rights activists who were misled by a wrong picture."[46]

On 4 September 2016, a few LTTE sympathisers and supporters attacked the Sri Lankan High Commissioner to Malaysia,[47] Ibrahim Sahib Ansar, at the Kuala Lampur Airport. This clearly demonstrates how certain LTTE sympathisers can still be galvanised to act on what they subscribed to in the past. The disgraceful act of attacking Sri Lankans, including the Buddhist priest in South India,[48] cannot be ignored and speaks to the oceans of distrust that are still among us.

To counter such distrust, it is prudent that Sri Lanka use soft power as a coercive tool of diplomacy. 2 September 2016 concluded the two-day conference organised by the Sri Lankan Army. The central theme for this Colombo Defence Conference[49] was the importance of using soft power as a powerful tool in post-war Sri Lanka. To combat the rise in radical elements of society, soft power strategies need to be implemented on an urgent basis. Soft power as a tool has been used extensively in Sri Lanka in the past and has been an inherent part of Asian culture for many years. As a nation we have used soft power positively, yet there are times we have failed to use it to our advantage. Kadirgamar used soft power to ban the LTTE, and to promote art and culture as a means of uniting the country. In this regard, he commissioned the book *The World of Stanley Kirinde*;[50] however, he was killed a few days before the book launch. Soft power was also used by Sirimavo Bandaranaike[v] to position Sri Lanka in the global sphere. Another example of the use of soft power is when Michael J. Delaney,[w] Assistant US Trade Representative for South Asia, turned down the lecture at the Kadirgamar Institute at the last minute. This was symbolic of the political power plays at work behind the scenes and illustrated the fact

---

[v] Sirimavo Bandaranaike was a Sri Lankan stateswoman who was the modern world's first female head of government. She served as Prime Minister of Ceylon and Sri Lanka three times (1960–65, 1970–77, and 1994–2000) and was a long-time leader of the Sri Lanka Freedom Party.

[w] Chairman of the Trade Policy Staff Committee and Special Trade Representative for Post-Conflict Countries. Delaney was US Political Advisor to NATO Southern Regional Command at Kandahar in Afghanistan before assuming his latest post.

that there was a time when the Monitor overruled the Principal.[x] These incidents of soft power all amalgamate to create a negative narrative of Sri Lanka in the international arena.

During the Indian Ocean Conference in Singapore,[51] 1–2 September 2016, with 250 delegates from 21 nations, US Assistant Secretary of State Nisha Biswal explained the importance of soft architecture for the Indian Ocean nations and referred to Sri Lanka's ports with their impressive performance as an example. Prime Minister Wickremesinghe, who made the keynote speech at the conference, stated, *"Single power and duopoly appears to be a thing of the past and for the first time in five centuries economic power in the world is moving again towards Asia"*.[52] The Prime Minister was speaking about the twin engines of economic robustness as well as soft power in the international security context. He added, *"[the] US is proposing the furtherance of a single combined security strategy for the two Asian oceans — the Indian and Pacific"*,[53] thereby warning of implications for Asian security. Countries of the IOR have a strategic advantage due to geography. Asian soft power and Asian foreign policy today is interlocked with geography, thereby resulting in the geopolitical aspect of the IOR and the subject of this piece — *Oceans of (Dis)trust*. To counter the negative aspects of Sri Lanka's international image as well as the diffusion of distrust in the IOR, it is essential that countries in the region use soft power to bring together human capital in developing the Indian Ocean agenda.

To understand a polycentric Asia with no uniformity in terms of geopolitics and culture, understand that each country is a separate world unto itself,[54] according to Fukuyama.[y] Thus, it is important to understand

---

[x] External Affairs Minister G.L. Peiris had to give approval for this lecture to be held. There were several requests from the public to attend the lecture and a packed house was expected. However, at the last minute, the lecture was suddenly called off. A directive not to hold it has been given by Sajin Vass Gunawardena, Monitoring MP for the Ministry of External Affairs. The reason was that Mr. Delaney was an American. Therefore, he was not allowed to speak since the United States had moved a resolution against Sri Lanka at the UN Human Rights Council at the time. See: http://www.sundaytimes.lk/120325/Columns/cafe.html

[y] Francis Fukuyama is an American political scientist, political economist, and author. Fukuyama is known for his book *The End of History and the Last Man (1992)*, which argued that the worldwide spread of liberal democracies and free market capitalism of the

the multiple layers of dispute, historical backgrounds, and strategic mistrust before commenting and drawing parallels with other nations.

Geo-strategy in the Indo-Pacific[55]

"Indo-Asia-Pacific more accurately captures the fact that the Indian and Pacific Oceans are the economic lifeblood linking the Indian Subcontinent, Southeast Asia, Australia, Northeast Asia, Oceania, and the United States together. Oceans that once were physical and psychological barriers that kept us apart are now maritime superhighways that bring us together."— Admiral Harry Harris, Commander, U.S. Pacific Command

Abstract

The existing geopolitical order is threatened and a new world order is unfolding. This paper will present an analysis of two questions: *What is Sri Lanka's role in the Indo-Pacific considering its geo-strategic position? And how best could we apply President Sirisena's "Asia centric balanced" foreign policy to the Indo–Pacific for peaceful cooperation?*

Stratfor Global Intelligence,[56] one of the leading US security think tanks in the world, recently (2017) published an article about Sri Lanka which explained: *"Despite its small size Sri Lanka holds substantial strategic value by virtue of its geographic position: it is at the centre of Asia's busiest maritime routes and has a wealth of natural deep harbours"*.[57] Sri Lanka's geo-strategic position and its importance have been chronicled since ancient times. At the centre of China's modern Maritime Silk Road, Sri Lanka will play a pivotal role in global trade as a maritime hub. India as Sri Lanka's neighbour with deep-rooted, strong historical and cultural relationships will face many challenges to transform the region. The Indo–Lankan relationship, in this context, is vital. In addition, Japan regards Sri Lanka as a maritime security partner. Japan is promoting maritime security co-operation with India and thus a stronger Japan–Sri Lanka–India

---

West and its lifestyle may signal the end point of humanity's sociocultural evolution and become the final form of human government.

trilateral relationship will be an important factor in promoting peaceful cooperation in the IOR.

Indo-Pacific at the face of the volatile world order

The Indo-Pacific is a constructivist connotation of the spatial area which extends from the Eastern Coast of the African continent through the Indian Ocean and Western Pacific. In his Treatise of Maritime Power,[58] Alfred Mahan has outlined the primacy of the Indian and Pacific oceans as two oceans which will hedge the *"continental world island"*,[59] creating direct implications on geopolitical security and strategy. In contemporary times, Mahan's words are successively becoming a reality as the Indo-Pacific has attracted increasing geo-strategic significance, largely due to the shift of economic power from the West to the East; increasing integration between the Indian Ocean and the Pacific rim; and the elevating competition among rising and emerging powers in the region. As Nicholas Spykman asserts, *"the Indo-Pacific is the circumferential maritime highway which links the whole area together in terms of sea power."*[60]

Although the idea of the geo-strategic primacy of the Indo-Pacific has been discussed by scholars who lived centuries ago, the theorisation is still young and growing. Hence, it is imperative to understand the geopolitical backdrop of this herculean region prior to analysing the geo-strategy. It should be borne in mind that this vast region will be the most important and strategic region in the next few decades of the post-Westphalian world order.

In this light, the narrative of the power play in the Indo-Pacific should be discussed, from the time when the leader of the free world, the United States, deliberately set out to conquer a large piece of territory overseas, for the first time in the Pacific. Having conquered and occupied the Philippines,[z] US military power changed the geopolitics of the Pacific Ocean. With the recent military build-up of China and its naval power

---

[z] The US occupation lasted from 1898–1946. The Philippines was illegally ceded to the United States at the Treaty of Paris for US$20 million, together with Cuba and Puerto Rico. A Filipino–American War broke out as the United States attempted to establish control over the islands.

becoming truly demonstrable, China's geopolitical sway over Manila is becoming increasingly evident. Much has changed in the Indo-Pacific, due to the entrance of China in the present day.

The prevailing frozen relationship between the US and China, especially after the new President elect, is also at play in the region. The new US Secretary of State, Rex Tillerson, has openly questioned China's artificial islands[aa] in the South China Sea. China thus has emerged as a formidable player in the balance of power game. Ergo, a new world order has begun with interchanging roles between great powers. The US is advocating nationalism, despite being the great power architect; whilst China, praising globalisation, has idealised national values in the past. This was evident when President Xi, during his visit to Davos, clearly gave impetus toward the case of globalisation.[61] In this regard, understanding Chinese foreign policy in the Indo-Pacific is essential; remember that '*rising China*' and '*emerging India*' will play a pivotal role in the region.

It was the capture of the greater Caribbean by the US Navy after the Caribbean wars[ab] that unlocked the power of the US with regards to the Panama Canal, which was the most significant strategic project. Two oceans, the Atlantic and the Pacific, were controlled with US military strength and NATO was the platform to bring forward liberal democratic values via a coalition. In the same manner, one could examine the case of China who is seeking a historical claim of the South China Sea to unlock its power in the Indian Ocean. Just as the US held Panama in the greater Caribbean region in the past, today China has OBOR with an $890 billion investment with 900 projects along the Belt and Road.[62] This volatile yet

---

[aa] The South China Sea disputes involve both island and maritime claims among several sovereign states within the region, namely Brunei, the People's Republic of China (PRC), Malaysia, Indonesia, the Philippines, and Vietnam. An estimated US$ 5 trillion worth of global trade passes through the South China Sea.

[ab] The Battle of the Caribbean refers to a naval campaign waged during World War II that was part of the Battle of the Atlantic, from 1941 to 1945. German U-boats and Italian submarines attempted to disrupt the Allied supply of oil and other materials. They sank shipping in the Caribbean Sea and the Gulf of Mexico and attacked coastal targets in the Antilles. Improved Allied anti-submarine warfare eventually drove the Axis submarines out of the Caribbean region.

dynamic geopolitical milieu should be understood in comprehending the geo-strategic account of the Indo-Pacific.

Cooperation and competition in the ocean

Given that the Indo-Pacific is now turning into the centre of gravity in the eyes of the world's economic, political, and strategic interests, the security and stability of the oceans are two implications that should be the focus of the region. As Admiral Suresh Mehta[ac] states, *"the common link binding the diverse sub-systems within the Indo-Pacific is the sea."*[63] Hence, irrespective of the socio-cultural diversities that persist across the oceanic planes, the geo-strategic focus on the region should primarily be on protecting the oceans that interlink the Pacific communities. The ocean, in this regard, is both the foundation for cooperation as well as competition. Common threats of piracy and the war on drugs compound the persistent competition over a sea bed that is rich in hydrocarbons and which fuels the industrial engines of the world. We should view this situation through Prof. Lawrence W. Prabhakar's[ad] framework of the *"Indo-Pacific commons"*,[64] and see the Asia Pacific as two triangles: the inner triangle of countries in South East Asia that enclose the South China Sea; and the outer circle of India, South Korea, Japan, and Australia which have critical interests in the stability of the region.

What is Sri Lanka's role in the Indo-Pacific, considering its geo-strategic position?

It is apparent in this regard that the Indian Ocean will play the most important role due to its busy sea lanes and its rich resources. The South China Sea is clearly the most important sea to China as it unlocks a

---

[ac] Admiral Sureesh Mehta served as Chief of the Indian Navy from 31 October 2006 to 31 August 2009. He is the first service chief from India's armed forces to be born post-Indian Independence.

[ad] Dr. W. Lawrence S. Prabhakar is an Associate Professor of Strategic Studies and International Relations in the department of Political Science at Madras Christian College, India and Adjunct Research Fellow, S. Rajaratnam School of International Studies, Nanyang Technological University, Singapore.

gateway to the Indian Ocean where Sri Lanka is a clear geo-strategic hub. Recall the article published by Stratfor Global Intelligence: *"Despite its small size Sri Lanka holds substantial strategic value by virtue of its geographic position: it is at the centre of Asia's busiest maritime routes and has a wealth of natural deep harbours"*.[65] Since ancient times, Sri Lanka's attractive geographical location has been discussed by many historians and scholars. Sri Lanka, sitting at the centre of the new Maritime Silk Road as well as initiatives launched under OBOR, will play a pivotal role. In terms of connectivity and economic cooperation, Sri Lanka's geo-strategic hub location will be an essential factor in the Indo-Pacific, especially in the IOR.

Capitalising on Sri Lanka's physical location and its natural harbours, the country is better placed than any other nation in South Asia to pursue the agenda of being a *'trans-shipment hub'*. According to the American Association for Port Authorities, Colombo port is one of the leading ports in the world and is ranked 80th in terms of the total cargo volume and the 29th in terms of container traffic in 2011.[66] Colombo port handles around 49,615 metric tons of cargo volume per year and 3,651,963 TEUs of container traffic annually.[67] It is estimated that about 70% of the trans-shipment cargo in the container traffic in Colombo Port belongs to India.[68]

In Sri Lanka, international trade is a principal mode of market expansion, acquiring greater integration to the world economy. Therefore, Sri Lanka pursues this objective at different levels through three bilateral agreements — with India, Pakistan, and Iran — and three regional agreements: South Asian Free Trade Area (SAFTA) Agreement, the Asia-Pacific Trade Agreement (APTA), and the Bay of Bengal Initiative for Multi-Sectoral Technical and Economic Cooperation (BIMSTEC).

The India–Sri Lanka FTA,[69] which came into being in 2000, is the very first free trade agreement for both countries. It led to a new depth in economic relations for both countries by quadrupling the volume of bilateral trade. In the aftermath of the agreement, India emerged as Sri Lanka's third largest export destination and the largest import destination.

Recently, the World Economic Forum[70] identified Sri Lanka as one of the richest South Asian Nations in terms of per capita income and high literacy rate. Sri Lanka moved to Stage 2 efficiency-driven economy in its Global Competitiveness Index (GCI), the only South Asian nation to move to Stage 2 as most others still remain in Stage 1 — factor-driven economies. However, to achieve the best results from its geo-strategic location in the Indo-Pacific, Sri Lanka needs to address its internal political-economic challenges as a priority.

Sri Lanka has several challenges in this regard. The bi-partisan political model created by the President and the Prime Minister from two different political establishments is still at its infancy. Therefore, the model needs to mature to reap a benefit. This is the first challenge. Second is the poverty rate, which is at a headcount poverty rate of 4.6%[71] — but the actual rate is much higher, according to President Sirisena, which is why he declared 2017 the year to eradicate poverty.[72] Similarly, India and many other South Asian countries have high poverty rates which should be addressed. Regional and extra regional models should make poverty alleviation a priority. Without benefiting the public who are living in poverty, these discussions are merely unfruitful. Eradicating poverty, creating decent jobs, and ensuring health and education services are all essential in synergising integration and connectivity. Thus, Sri Lanka as a regional hub in the Indian Ocean has a huge role to offer the Indo-Pacific in terms of economic and trade cooperation but requires addressing its internal challenges to do so.

Recommendations: Sri Lanka's foreign policy according to President Sirisena is "Asia centric balanced". How best could we apply this to the Indo-Pacific for peaceful cooperation?

President Sirisena, who came to power two years ago,[ae] spelled out his foreign policy as '*Asia centric balanced*'. He has clearly re-calibrated and achieved a balance between the West and East during his short time in office.

Geopolitical tension between the existing powers of '*rising China*' and '*emerging India*' have clearly been felt in the island nation. Sri Lanka should maintain an equidistant foreign policy with all these powers. In applying its foreign policy to the Indo-Pacific region, Sri Lanka could develop peaceful cooperation with all nations, by practicing its balanced view.

[ae] Maithripala Sirisena is a Sri Lankan politician who is the 7th and current President of Sri Lanka, since 2015.

According to the late Lakshman Kadirgamar,[73] the Sri Lanka–India relationship runs deep and is often lost in the mist of time. The two nations have been through many challenges to strengthen their relationship. Speculative news has at times taken the two nations apart and antagonised this rich relationship. The recent CIA declassified information suggests that India had forcibly introduced the Indo–Lanka accord to the then President.[74] However, modern day India, with Modi's leadership, chose a brilliant initiative in establishing the *'Neighbourhood First Policy'*. This initiative gives priority to regional nations to spur their growth with India.

Resolving regional integration should be a top priority for India and India's neighbours in this regard. We could then look at extra-regional integration, as this is also vital. SAARC should be looked at from a positive angle in this context, despite bilateral disputes. Conflict management mechanisms should be built into the international system as many state disputes persist across time and extra-regional players could also assist in this process.

Japan is another nation and strategic partner who has helped Sri Lanka in many difficult times. The inception of this relationship was arguably the San Francisco Speech by then Sri Lankan President Jayewardene,[75] pleading the world to forgive Japan. Similarly, during the 2004 tsunami,[af] Japan was a stupendous donor in rebuilding the coastal belt of Sri Lanka, which is now an important geo-strategic environment in the Indo-Pacific. Japan regards Sri Lanka as a maritime security partner, whilst simultaneously promoting maritime security co-operation with India. A stronger Japan–Sri Lanka–India trilateral relationship will be an important factor in creating responsible behaviour and peaceful cooperation in the Indian Ocean. In maintaining its equidistant foreign policy, Sri Lanka will need to effectively counter aggression by any power. Trilateral

---

[af] The 2004 Indian Ocean earthquake occurred on 26 December with the epicentre off the west coast of Sumatra, Indonesia. The shock had a magnitude of 9.1–9.3. The earthquake occurred when the Indian Plate was subducted by the Burma Plate and triggered a series of devastating tsunamis along the coasts of most landmasses bordering the Indian Ocean, killing 230,000–280,000 people in 14 countries, and inundating coastal communities. It was one of the deadliest natural disasters in recorded history. Indonesia was the hardest-hit country, followed by Sri Lanka, India, and Thailand.

relationships such as Japan–Sri Lanka–India will help to counter such instances.

Dr. Satoru Nagao,[ag] in his latest paper, *Changing US-China Power Balance and the Role of Japan-Sri Lanka-India Co-operation*,[76] explains that for a long time bilateral alliances led by the United States (such as Japan–US, US–South Korea, US–Philippines, US–Australia) have endeavoured to maintain order in the Pacific. However, despite the many US alliances, a deep defence relationship is lacking. For example, both Japan and Australia are US allies, but they share no close interlinking security relations. Such security cooperatives would function effectively if the US had sufficient military resources to tackle all the looming difficulties in this region.

However, because US military resources have been declining, the '*old*' bilateral system is insufficient to maintain peace and order in this region. There is a need for an alternative system that can function better in these changed circumstances. Notably, a new system is gradually emerging. Several multinational security co-operation arrangements have been recently formed among Japan–India–US, Japan–US–Australia, Japan–India–US–Australia–Singapore, and other countries present in the IOR. In this context, Japan–Sri Lanka India relations can be further enhanced. Japan has a role to play as an important stabiliser for cordial Sri Lanka–India relations as well as the establishment of a Japan–Sri Lanka–India strategic dialogue.

Let me conclude with reference to an article I read in-flight to attend this important dialogue. According to P.K Balachandran, in *The New India Express*, "*some Indian projects sponsored by the State, such as the $7.5m ambulance service gifted to Sri Lanka, were seen as Trojan Horses of RAW (India's Research Analysis Wing). Lankan nationalists justified their stance, claiming that India should consider its aid to Sri Lanka not as charity but as reparation for the harm it did in promoting Tamil terror and then trying to divide the country*".[77] In light of such negativity, we must seek the best options to strengthen the Indo–Sri Lanka relationship, whilst thinking of the future of the IOR.

[ag] Senior Fellow at the Institute of National Security Studies Sri Lanka (INSSSL). See: http://www.insssl.lk/preview.php?id=34

Sri Lanka Facing the Geopolitical Game in the Indian Ocean[78]

"This land of such dear souls, this dear dear land, Dear for her reputation through the world, Is now leased out — I die pronouncing it — Like to a tenement or pelting farm... bound in with triumphant sea is now bound in with shame." — William Shakespeare[ah]

Abstract

The IOR has always played a significant role in the politics of international relations and the IOR will be where the '*great game*' unfolds in the future. In the geopolitical context, while the US as the global hegemon is strengthening its ties with the regional hegemon of India, other South Asian countries are strengthening ties with China to counterbalance the US/India sphere of influence in the region.

From the outset it is clear that geography ultimately determines history and your location determines what happens to you as a nation-state. Thus, to determine the changing geopolitical dynamics of the IOR, it is important to understand not only the great power's strategic aspirations in the Indian Ocean but also Sri Lanka's role as an island nation within this matrix.

Tensions on the lines of intersection are highest at geostrategic hotspots like Sri Lanka. Maintaining friendly ties with neighbouring countries and extra-regional powers is therefore vital for our nation's survival. The security interest vested in the strategic positioning of our nation in the IOR cannot be ignored when calibrating our foreign policy.

Hence, the structure of my talk will be one that ventures from the internal — by looking at Sri Lanka's own strategic posturing in the IOR — to the external — by looking at how great powers of our time are projecting themselves as maritime forces in the IOR. The underlying theme will be that of the geopolitical interplay between the internal and external that Sri Lanka must carefully tread.

[ah] Richard II 2.1.57-63, John of Gaunt, on his deathbed.

Geography of the Indian Ocean

Understanding the geography of the Indian Ocean is the key to understanding the regional and extra regional influences towards the Island of Sri Lanka.

The kingdom of Sri Lanka was flourishing in ancient times when most nations had not yet been discovered or mapped. In the ancient libraries of Alexandria, Sri Lanka was known as *Taprobana*, mapped in an oversized proportion by Ptolemy,[ai] the Greek-Egyptian cartographer (Map 1). Sri Lanka was known in this time due to its rich civilisation and trade relations with the rest of the world.

Recorded history speaks of emissaries between Sri Lanka and Rome in the 1st century A.D. According to the Roman author and philosopher

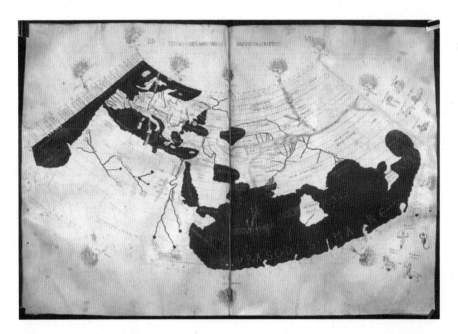

Map 1 Ptolemy's World Map. Credited to Francesco di Antonio del Chierico — *Ptolemy's Geography* (Harleian MS 7182, ff 58–59)

[ai] Claudius Ptolemy was a mathematician, astronomer, geographer, astrologer, and poet of a single epigram in the Greek Anthology.

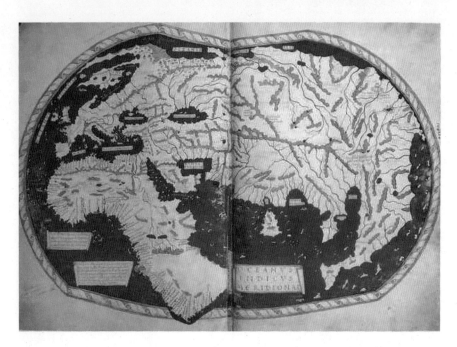

Map 2 The World Map of Henricus Martellus Germanus, Florence 1490–92. Credited to *Insularium Illustratum* (Account of the Islands of the Mediterranean)

Pliny the Elder,[aj] there were four members from Sri Lanka who visited (circa 50 A.D.) the Court of Emperor Claudius Caesar.[79] Another delegation from Sri Lanka arrived in Rome during the time of Emperor Julian (circa A.D. 375). This was during the reign of King Mahanama of Sri Lanka.[80] After the discovery and mapping of Cape of Good Hope and the subsequent discovery of the Indian Ocean, Henricus Martellus'[ak] world map (c.1489) also clearly depicts Sri Lanka (Map 2).

When it comes to the physical geography of the IOR, Sri Lanka is strategically positioned in the Indian Ocean, which covers approximately 20% of the water of the earth's surface — 70,560,000 square kilometres.[81]

[aj] Pliny the Elder was a Roman author, naturalist and natural philosopher, naval and army commander of the early Roman Empire, and friend of the emperor Vespasian.
[ak] Henricus Martellus Germanus was a geographer and cartographer from Nuremberg who lived and worked in Florence from 1480 to 1496.

The IOR is surrounded by the land masses of Asia, Africa, Australia, and Antarctica. The Indian Ocean is named after the Indian subcontinent and has several choke points such as the Bab-el-Mandeb, the Strait of Hormuz, the Lombok Strait, the Strait of Malacca, and the Palk Strait.[82]

The IOR is rich in living and non-living resources. About 11.3 million tonnes of fish, which is equivalent to 14.6 percent of the world's fish stock, is caught in this region, according to the FAO.[83] In terms of the latter, around 36 million barrels per day — equivalent to about 40 per cent of the world's oil supply and 64 per cent of oil trade[84] — travel through the entryways into and out of the Indian Ocean, including some of the aforementioned straits.

The land masses surrounding the region are densely populated with over two billion people (1/3 of the world's population). Yet from a cultural point of view, the region has yet to develop its own identity and its own maritime community. The only link for the region currently, barring trade and weak political links in combatting terrorism and transnational organized crime is an environmental one. Many of the countries in the IOR are threatened with rising sea-levels and submersion. The 2004 tsunami killed 228,000 people[85] in the region and cyclone Nargis, which hit Myanmar in 2008, took 138,300 lives.[86] Thus, the region is prone to deadly natural disasters and is most threatened by the incidence of climate change.

Sri Lanka's geo-strategic location

Having depicted the geographical landscape of the IOR, let us turn to Sri Lanka's strategic location in the region.

Sri Lanka could be defined as Sir Halford Mackinder's outer crescent touching the rim land. Two other nations which have similar geographical positioning are the islands of Britain and Japan, having access to the Atlantic and to the Pacific oceans respectively, close to the continent but separated by the ocean (Map 3). A century ago, the British geopolitical thinker, Mackinder,[87] argued that whoever controls the Eurasian heartland will control the world. Since Mackinder's land-based-pivot-area strategy in the 20th and now 21st century, the pivot area has veered towards having control of the oceans. In the same vein, Alfred Mahan's statement that

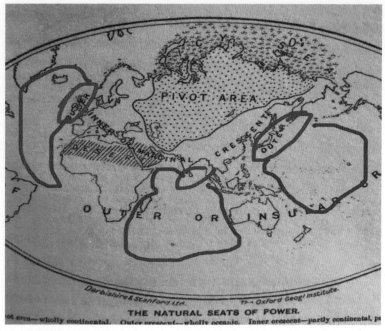

Map 3 Author's Markings of Sri Lanka, the Isle of Britain and Japan's Outer Crescents Touching the Rim Land. Credited to Halford J. Mackinder — "*The Geographical Pivot of History*", Geographical Journal 23, no. 4 (April 1904): 435

"whoever controls the Indian Ocean will dominate Asia, the destiny of the world will be decided on its waters"[88] has never been more apparent.

Sri Lanka's future development is intrinsically linked to the Indian Ocean. In this regard, maintaining the freedom of navigation is important for Sri Lanka as it aspires to become a hub in the IOR. External actors such as '*rising China*' and would-be-hegemons such as India will use Sri Lanka's strategic location for their own political and economic leverage. This is especially true with respect to the demand and transportation of hydrocarbons for energy. In light of the recent petrol crisis in Sri Lanka, it can be argued that our energy dependency on India has made our energy security position tenuous. Therefore, we must utilise other countries' strategic interests in the IOR to our own advantage. One such example is China's search for alternative maritime routes to protect its global trade, as a manufacturing hub can be provided via the sea-line of communication with Sri Lanka.

Importance of Indian Ocean Region (IOR) to China–Sino–Lankan relations

The Sino-Lankan relationship is one that dates back to the Chinese mariner Zheng He's visit to Sri Lanka in 1405,[89] an entire century prior to Vasco da Gama's[al] visit, the first Portuguese explorer who reached Sri Lanka in 1498. This confirms the vested Chinese interest in the IOR and in Sri Lanka in particular before the colonial period. The Sino-Lankan relationship is being revived today with the resurrection of the Maritime Silk Road and the One Belt, One Road initiative.

Today, China is Sri Lanka's second largest trading partner, surpassing the US and just behind India. Sino-Lankan trade remains at more than US$3 billion.[90] Our economic partnership will only grow with the Chinese economic zone and Hambantota Port in full operation. By 2025, China will become Sri Lanka's largest trading partner due to the significant investments in the island as well as in the region — including when CPEC is in operation.[91]

According to Robert Kaplan, Sri Lanka is a geo-strategic hub. He considers *"Sri Lanka part of the new [maritime] geography"*.[92] He also explains the geopolitical symbolism of Sri Lanka's location. *"It's part of China's plan to construct a string of pearls — ports that they don't own, but which they can use for their warships all across the Indian Ocean"*.[93] In this regard, Hambantota Port is centre-stage due to its geographical position and its Chinese-led development. Situated at the southern tip of Sri Lanka, Hambanthota is adjacent to the busiest shipping lanes of the world.

Kaplan speaks to the fact that beyond Sri Lanka's strategic relationship with China, the latter power has a broader presence in the IOR. This is in order to protect its Sea Lines of Communication (SLOCs) which is the most essential component needed to keep China's economy at its present level of growth as well as for future growth aspirations. China's dependency on the maritime lanes is due to its need for tons of

---

[al]Vasco da Gama, 1st Count of Vidigueira, was a Portuguese explorer and the first European to reach both India and Sri Lanka by sea. His initial voyage to India (1497–1499) was the first to link Europe and Asia by an ocean route, connecting the Atlantic and Indian oceans and, therefore, the West and the Orient.

hydrocarbons that are transported across the two choke points — the Strait of Hormuz[am] and the Strait of Malacca[an] — which are disputed geographically.

Kaplan and most Western scholars alike see military strategic reasons for China's posturing in the IOR. However, Sri Lanka and China continue to emphasise the fact that the Sino-Lankan partnership is for *"economic reasons and not for military reasons"*.[94] Currently, not many ships dock at Hambantota and it is not as busy a harbour as the Colombo Port. Yet this position will change with the development of the Gwadar port and CPEC in full operation. The Maritime Silk Road (MSR) is also a long term strategic project which Sri Lanka will benefit from if it plays to its strategic advantage.

Nevertheless, caution is being touted that *"Sri Lanka will not have the negotiation capacity and the economic strength to deter China when it wants a military base in the future"*.[ao] The foreign policy of the Sri Lankan government is explicitly clear in the face of such conjectures: *"The Sri Lankan government does not make its bases available to foreign forces"*.[95]

It's also important to consider China's geo-strategic disadvantages in the Indian Ocean when examining this point. According to Dr. David Brewster, *"China's strategic vulnerability is reinforced by the scarcity of overland transport connections between Chinese territory and the Indian Ocean."*[96] He further states that China currently has no ability to exert control over the chokepoints nor has it any regular naval presence in any of the IOR ports.

Chinese submarines in Sri Lanka

The cautious atmosphere has been trumped up by the recent Chinese submarine encounters in the IOR that have arguably created a few ripples

---

[am] The Strait of Hormuz is a strait between the Persian Gulf and the Gulf of Oman. It provides the only sea passage from the Persian Gulf to the open ocean and is one of the world's most strategically important choke points.

[an] The Strait of Malacca or Straits of Malacca is a narrow stretch of water between the Malay Peninsula and the Indonesian island of Sumatra. It is named after the Malacca Sultanate that ruled over the archipelago between 1400 and 1511.

[ao] Author's personal conversation with a Japanese scholar.

in the geopolitical context. According to Professor Shen Dingli at Fudan University, *"it is wrong for us to believe that we have no right to set up bases abroad"*.[97] He argues that China needs not only a blue-water navy but also overseas military bases to cut the supply cost.[98] This is a fair argument, as the US is seen implementing the same strategy by proposing to cut the budget of the United States Indo-Pacific Command (USPACOM) in 2018 and relying on its Asian bases to protect its maritime interests in the IOR.

One Belt, One Road (OBOR)

The Belt and Road Initiative (known commonly as OBOR) was a construct of the scholar Wang Jisi's[99] strategy to have a significant Chinese footprint in Eurasia, especially to recalibrate the existing world order. The OBOR is the *"project of the century"*,[100] according to President Xi Jinping (Map 4). This trillion-dollar initiative aims to integrate Eurasia through the development of infrastructure. It is unquestionably the most ambitious project ever launched in recent times, which seeks to revisit and resurrect the global legacy of the Ming Dynasty's Admiral Zheng He. Thus, the

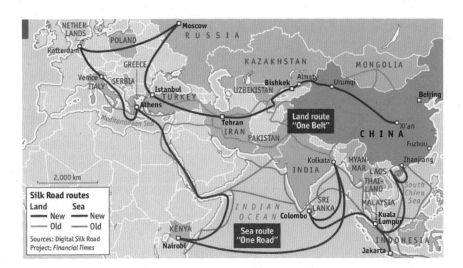

Map 4   Silk Road Routes for OBOR. Credited to Digital Silk Road Project — Financial Times

OBOR, when it comes to fruition, will symbolize what I have been talking about in this section — the twin powers of China's economic and military strength in the IOR.

As mentioned earlier, according to the World Economic Forum,[101] by 2030 the US will no longer be the only superpower and China will be well placed among the many countries to become one of the great powers. The OBOR is the medium through which China envisions this new world order. Sri Lanka, with its geostrategic position at the centre of the Maritime Silk Road, is a '*super-connector*' linking the east-west sea lanes. Therefore, as a nation we have a choice in how we calibrate our foreign policy based on this strategic advantage. It is my opinion that rather than following a process of leasing land and ports, Sri Lanka should instead chart a path that capitalises on our strategic advantage.

Not all nations support China's OBOR; India recently was absent from the OBOR summit (2017). According to Lee Kuan Yew School of Public Policy (LKYSPP) Professor Kanti Bajpai[ap] the real reasons for India's absence from the OBOR are quite different and it's not the CPEC. It is galling to New Delhi that the entire world is lining up to do business with a rampant China and no one is paying India much attention. Envy aside, there is the strategic worry that China will 'encircle' India. That China, with an economy five times the size of India, needs the BRI and an encirclement of India to deal with its weak neighbour is unlikely, but clearly this assumption motivates Indian strategic thinking.

US pivot to Asia

The presidency of Barack Obama brought with it the term "*pivot to Asia*" and the Obama administration asserted itself as America's first "*Pacific President*".[102] However, the trajectory of the US since 2009 has been one of "*strategic partnerships [that] have generally expanded in the region, as they did from 2001 to 2008*".[103] Rather than a "*pivot*",

---

[ap] Kanti Bajpai is an Indian academic-analyst. He is known to be an expert on Indo-China relations. He is currently a professor at National University of Singapore and was the Vice-Dean for Research of the Lee Kuan Yew School of Public Policy.

Obama can be seen as giving credence to the development of a strategic relationship with Asia.

The US-Sri Lanka relationship was at its strongest during President Jayawardene's[aq] time. Back then, India opposed that relationship and posed many challenges to Sri Lanka. *Voice of America* (a U.S. government-funded international radio broadcast) was a threat at that time, but all that has changed in the present due to India's close relationship with US. Now India sees Sri Lanka's close strategic relationship with China as a threat.

Notably, former Secretary of State John Kerry's report to the Senate Foreign Relations Committee in 2009 urges the US Government to forge closer ties with Sri Lanka to prevent it from drifting into the *"Chinese orbit"*.[104] Fast forward to September 2017, a visit by Acting Assistant Secretary of State for South and Central Asian Affairs, Ms. Alice Wells, to Sri Lanka saw her tout the Trump foreign policy that the US was seriously concerned over the *"unsustainable debt burden on Sri Lanka due to non-concessional loans from China"*.[105]

This illustrates the US's soft-power projections to influence not only the Sino-Lankan relationship but the maritime dynamics of the entire IOR. There is no hope for a geopolitical triad for Sri Lanka in this respect. Rather, our nation will have to face the US sphere of influence as well as the Chinese sphere of influence and find intersections that are to our strategic advantage.

India's Strategic Aspiration in the Indian Ocean Region (IOR)

India's SAGAR vision

In 2015, Indian Prime Minister Modi launched the concept of *SAGAR* — *'Security and Growth for All in the Region'*.[106] According to India's External Affairs Minister, Sushma Swaraj, *"this is a clear, high-level*

[aq] J.R. Jayewardene was the leader of Sri Lanka from 1977 to 1989, serving as Prime Minister from 1977 to 1978 and as the second President of Sri Lanka from 1978 till 1989. A long-time member of the United National Party, he led it to a crushing victory in 1977 and served as Prime Minister for half a year before becoming the country's first executive President under an amended constitution.

articulation of India's vision for the Indian Ocean. SAGAR has distinct but inter-related elements and underscores India's engagement in the Indian Ocean".[107] The vision entails enhancing India's capacity to safeguard land and maritime territories and interests; deepening economic and security cooperation in the littoral; promoting collective action to deal with natural disasters and maritime threats like piracy, terrorism, and emergent non-state actors; working towards sustainable regional development through enhanced collaboration; and engaging with countries beyond Indian shores with the aim of building greater trust and promoting respect for maritime rules, norms, and the peaceful resolution of disputes.

According to Ms. Swaraj, *"the principles enshrined in SAGAR provide us with a coherent framework to address some of the challenges relating to economic revival, connectivity, security, culture and identity, and India's own evolving approach to these issues. The challenge before us is to ensure intra-ocean trade and investment, and the sustainable harnessing of the wealth of the seas, including food, medicines and clean energy"*.[108]

The SAGAR vision has also laid out the objective of integrated maritime security coordination between India, Sri Lanka, the Maldives, the Seychelles, and Mauritius; building on the 2011 trilateral India-Sri Lanka-Maldives arrangement.[109] While India's efforts to foster collaboration with regional countries is a positive sign, its policy of keeping extra-regional powers at bay in the IOR will only be to its own detriment. If one studies the works of Jawaharlal Nehru,[ar] one can see that India is following model similar to the Monroe Doctrine,[as] by excluding extra-regional powers from the vicinity (in this case) of India and the Indian Ocean.

[ar] Jawaharlal Nehru was the first Prime Minister of India and a central figure in Indian politics before and after independence. He emerged as the paramount leader of the Indian independence movement under the tutelage of Mahatma Gandhi and ruled India from its establishment as an independent nation in 1947 until his death in 1964. He is considered to be the architect of the modern Indian nation-state: a sovereign, socialist, secular, and democratic republic.

[as] The Monroe Doctrine was a United States policy of opposing European colonialism in the Americas beginning in 1823. It stated that further efforts by European nations to take control of any independent state in North or South America would be viewed as *"the*

This illustrates the strategic thinking of modern India, in its determination to rid the subcontinent of residual colonial influence and exclude other powers from the entire South Asian region. It is further explained by the Indian scholar Bhabani Sen Gupta[110] that this is an underlying theme in Indian strategic thinking, where the presence of outside powers in India's neighbourhood is considered illegitimate. Thus, India's aspiration is for its neighbours to solely rely upon it as a regional hegemon and security provider. Furthermore, the scholar K. Subrahmanyam stated that leadership in the Indian Ocean is part of India's *"manifest destiny"*.[111]

The SAGAR vision also includes trilateral relationships for India with Iran and Afghanistan in developing ports. This is to geopolitically challenge India's arch rival of Pakistan in its partnership with China in the creation of the Gwadar port and the CPEC corridor as well as to entice neighbouring Afghanistan into maritime collaboration initiatives.

Sri Lankan scholar Dr. Vernon Mendis brings the geopolitical context into perspective for our island nation when he states that: *"the short-sighted policy pursued by successive Indian Governments to make India the sole dominant power in South Asia has created suspicions in the minds of smaller States like Sri Lanka"*.[112] However, perhaps to quell such suspicions, India has engaged in a joint military exercise '*Mitra Shakti 2017*' with Sri Lanka in October. According to the *Indian Express*,[113] the joint military exercise is India's response to China's growing influence in South Asia and the IOR. I believe this article is speculative, since the military exercise clearly falls short of limiting China's growing power in the region. In this vein, many speculative media-stories will raise similar tensions with regard to Sri Lanka's relationship with its overarching neighbour India.

Indo-Lanka relations

Let us now examine the historical, political, and geographical relationship that is the crux of Indo-Lanka relations. Historic entries in the Ramayana[at]

---

manifestation of an unfriendly disposition toward the United States." The Doctrine was issued on 2 December 1823.

[at] The Ramayana is an ancient Indian epic poem which narrates the struggle of the divine prince Rama to rescue his wife Sita from the demon king Ravana. Along with the Mahabharata, it forms the Sanskrit Itihasa.

that refer to the religious and cultural ties Sri Lanka has shared with India since ancient times have strengthened the cultural diplomacy between the two countries. India and Sri Lanka also share a common colonial past, post-colonial institutions, and political culture, all of which have ensured mutual confidence between the two strong democracies.

Arguably, elements of this relationship have persisted till the present day. Today, Prime Minister Modi's *'Look East Policy'*[au] has been extended to accommodate regional and cultural integration as well as the *'Neighbourhood First Policy'*.[av] The latter policy has to be valued in the context of India giving first priority to its neighbouring nations. I have clearly stated the importance of this in the book *Modi Doctrine*.[114] However, Indo-Lankan political anxieties persist due to the volatile geopolitics of the IOR and therefore understanding this is key to resolving such tensions.

India, naturally, has an interest in the outcome of elections in Sri Lanka due to our geographical proximity. Thus, geography and politics are intrinsically linked for our two nations. This has unfolded from Government to Government, and at its peak, New Delhi was especially concerned about the growing friendship between Rajapaksa's[aw] Government and those in charge in Beijing. *"The trigger, according to Reuters, was Rajapaksa's decision [in 2014] to allow two Chinese submarines to dock in Sri Lanka without informing New Delhi first"*,[115] as required by the maritime security pact between India and Sri Lanka. The geopolitical strain culminated in President Rajapaksa stating in an interview that *"it was very open, the Americans, the Norwegians, the Europeans were openly working against me. And RAW (India's Research Analysis Wing)"*.[116]

[au] India's Look East policy is an effort to cultivate extensive economic and strategic relations with the nations of Southeast Asia in order to bolster its standing as a regional power and counterweight to the strategic influence of the People's Republic of China.

[av] Even before becoming the Prime Minister Narendra Modi hinted that his foreign policy would actively focus on improving ties with India's immediate neighbours, which the media has termed the *'Neighbourhood First Policy'*. PM Modi started off well by inviting all heads of state of South Asian countries to his inauguration; then, on his second day in office, he held bilateral talks with all of them individually.

[aw] Mahinda Rajapaksa is a Sri Lankan politician who served as the sixth President of Sri Lanka from 19 November 2005 to 9 January 2015.

Today, the geopolitical context is such that one cannot understand the Indo-Lanka relationship without simultaneously considering the Sino-Lanka relationship. India and China are two players with different strengths and weaknesses on the chessboard of the Indian Ocean. The relationship that Sri Lanka shares with India is historical and socio-cultural. Moreover, Sri Lanka's proximity to India means that they share a bond that cannot be compared to any other relationship. However, today this bond is frail and therefore should be further strengthened at all levels political, economic, social, and cultural, and especially at the scholarly level between think tanks. The IOR presents an opportunity for the Indo-Lankan relationship to thrive. Yet, to strengthen any relationship, nations need to understand the limitations that have plagued their past, in order to orchestrate a better future.

India's hegemonic influence towards its neighbouring nations will only deteriorate this relationship. This was evident during Chinese submarine port calls to Sri Lanka. India and Sri Lanka should maintain a proactive long term defence stance on such important matters rather than a reactive position. Sri Lanka has received more than 200 warships since 2010.[117] The latest was a US Nimitz Class air craft carrier. The previous aircraft carrier was of Indian origin in 2016. While Sri Lanka receives warships from all these nations, there should not be a question about Chinese submarines. Sri Lankan security policy makers have carefully made these decisions; they are not kneejerk policies.

Meanwhile, India[118] is building 48 warships, including one aircraft carrier, one nuclear submarine, six conventional submarines, and a variety of destroyers, frigates, and corvettes. By 2027,[119] capacity will be expanded to accommodate 198 warships. What warships are Sri Lanka building? Sri Lanka as a sovereign nation has the power to build its own fleet or purchase ships from abroad, yet it has not done so. Thus, the region remains in the status quo. Other countries in the region, such as Bangladesh and Pakistan, have their own submarines. Therefore, if in the future Sri Lanka chooses to build our underwater anti-submarine capacity, India should not see this as a threat. At the regional level, India has resisted inviting Pakistan to join the Indian Ocean Rim Association (IORA)[120] or allow China to become a full member of the Indian Ocean Naval Symposium (IONS).[121] India is building its massive naval fleet, thereby constituting a silent yet aggressive naval build-up in Sri Lanka's neighbourhood. Colombo should be ready to proactively face any future challenges as Indian Ocean security is expected to remain complex.

Eelam war — the Tamil Nadu factor

A clear challenge in the Indo-Lankan relationship is the Tamil Nadu[ax] factor. A plethora of opportunities were missed by Sri Lanka to enhance its strategic relationships in the IOR due to the prolonged conflict with the Tamil Tigers[ay] that lasted nearly three decades.

India manifested an arguably adversarial relationship in dealing with the almost 30-year civil war in Sri Lanka. South India occupies 19% of India's land mass and Tamil Nadu is 130,060 km^2, with close to 72 million in population.[122] The South Indian geographical influence in the North of Sri Lanka is clearly evident when you look at the history; this influence fuelled much of the political turmoil in the island nation. For instance, India entered Sri Lankan air space on the pretext of food aid while LTTE terrorist fighters were being trained on Indian soil. *"The Third Agency of RAW, a supra-intelligence outfit, was entrusted with the task. Within a year, the number of Sri Lankan Tamil training camps in Tamil Nadu mushroomed to 32. By mid-1987, over 20,000 Sri Lankan Tamil insurgents had been provided sanctuary, finance, training and weapons either by the central Government or the state Government of Tamil Nadu or by the insurgent groups themselves"*.[123] According to Professor Rohan Gunaratna, *"the LTTE-India nexus did not secure the geopolitical security New Delhi needed from Sri Lanka. It weakened Indian as well as Sri Lankan domestic security"*.[124]

Given the geographical factor of Tamil Nadu and its direct impact on Northern Sri Lanka, power devolution is not the most desirable option as it would create further instability in Sri Lanka. Constitution-making has to

---

[ax] Tamil Nadu is one of the 29 states of India. Its capital and largest city is Chennai. Tamil Nadu lies in the southernmost part of the Indian Peninsular. The state shares a maritime border with the nation of Sri Lanka.

[ay] The Liberation Tigers of Tamil Eelam was a Tamil militant organization that was based in northeastern Sri Lanka.

consider geographical factors and its effects. Without a federal system, India would be impossible to manage with its vast geography and numerous ethnic groups and religions. Thus, it has in this respect considered the intrinsic link between politics and geography. Muhammad Ali Jinnah,[az] the founder of Pakistan observed, *"India is not a nation, nor a country. It is a subcontinent of nationalities."*

Therefore, the Federalist model may not apply to Sri Lanka due to its geographical scale and close proximity to South India. This is primarily because of the state of Tamil Nadu which affects both the politics of the Federal State of India as well as Colombo. Ambassador Shivshankar Menon's[ba] latest book, *Choices*,[125] clearly explains the limitations of foreign policy decisions made by India towards Sri Lanka.[126] The same limitation was echoed at a Delhi conference organized by ICWA[bb] a few years ago, on the same day India voted against Sri Lanka at the Human Rights Council in Geneva. Salman Kurshid[bc] explained how a regional Government could dictate terms to the central Government at the conference. This was a clear example of how strong the Tamil Nadu factor was and still is in the Indo-Lanka relationship.

In today's context, it is noteworthy that after 30 years, an Indian Prime Minister made an official visit to Sri Lanka in March 2015.[127] This was mainly due to the leadership of President Maithripala Sirisena. During Prime Minister Modi's last visit, President Sirisena spoke about the devolution of power and the need to go beyond the 13th Amendment to the Constitution.[128] This was the same promise made by President Rajapaksa during his term in office.

[az] Muhammad Ali Jinnah was a lawyer, a politician, and the founder of Pakistan. Jinnah served as the leader of the All-India Muslim League from 1913 until Pakistan's independence on 14 August 1947, and then as Pakistan's first Governor-General until his death.

[ba] Shivshankar Menon is an Indian diplomat, who served as National Security Adviser of India under Prime Minister of India Manmohan Singh. He had previously served as the Foreign Secretary, the top diplomat in India. Prior to that he was Indian High Commissioner to Pakistan, and Sri Lanka and ambassador to China and Israel.

[bb] Indian Council of World Affairs. See: http://www.icwa.in/

[bc] Salman Khurshid is an Indian politician. He was the Cabinet Minister of the Ministry of External Affairs. He belongs to the Indian National Congress.

Furthermore, the Indo-Sri Lanka Peace Accord, which was forcefully introduced according to the latest CIA declassified report,[129] is a clear example of a weak and watered-down policy advocated due to the pressure of certain political groups in India and Sri Lanka. In this regard, the Sri Lankan government also failed to have public consultations with the general public of the country prior to introducing this important political milestone. This created further tension between the two countries and within Sri Lanka's domestic political establishment and its détente toward India. On a visit to Sri Lanka, Dr. S. Jaishankar,[bd] India's Foreign Secretary, met with members of the Tamil National Alliance (TNA) and the Tamil Progressive Alliance (TPA). In doing so, he was perhaps emphasising the unity that Tamil political leadership needed in order to fulfil Tamil political aspirations. All these examples serve to illustrate the fact that Tamil Nadu still has political clout in Sri Lanka in the geopolitical context.

Conclusion

Geopolitics has elements of geo-economics to achieve economic goals and geo-strategy to achieve strategic goals, with the only limitation being that of natural geography itself. The Indian Ocean Region is a pivotal area in this century and to understand the geopolitical game, one must assess the on-going and future risk to Sri Lanka. You may lease out Tricomalee Port[be] (East of Sri Lanka) to India and Japan, Hambanthota Port (South Sri Lanka) to China, or the Western shore to another country, but doing so without the proper foresight analysis and understanding of strategic risk is a grave mistake.

Sri Lanka, from its independence, has failed to produce in-house capabilities as a nation to develop its economy. Innovation is at the lowest

---

[bd] S. Jaishankar is an Indian diplomat who has been Foreign Secretary of India since January 2015. He joined Indian Foreign Service in 1977.

[be] Trincomalee Harbour is a seaport in Trincomalee Bay or Koddiyar Bay, a large natural harbour situated on the north-east coast of Sri Lanka. Located by Trincomalee, Sri Lanka is in the heart of the Indian Ocean, and its strategic importance has shaped its recent history. There have been many sea battles to control the harbour. The Portuguese, Dutch, French, and the English have each held it in turn. In 1942 the Japanese Imperial Navy attacked Trincomalee harbour and sunk three British warship anchored there.

and investment in research is very poor. The Sri Lankan economy has become weaker due to massive debt and less revenue generated. This year Sri Lanka dropped 14 places in the World Economic Forum Global Competitiveness Index[130] (GCI) Report. Becoming less competitive means less productivity; thus it is pivotal that Sri Lanka strengthens its economy with the right policy prescription to face its geopolitical challenges. In this regard, Sri Lanka could benefit immensely from tourism in posturing itself to the rest of the world.

With regards to geopolitics and foreign policy, balancing New Delhi, Washington, and Beijing will be a priority for Sri Lanka, which President Sirisena has rightly spelled out as a *"balanced Asia centric"* foreign policy. Clearly an equidistant foreign policy is what Sri Lanka should have with global powers. The late Lakshman Kadirgamar is the best example in this regard, as he established relationships with the West and the rest, while achieving his objective to dismantle the LTTE[bf] from the foreign theatre. Today, engagement of Tamil diaspora with an effective foreign policy and re-engagement plan is essential and should be presented by the current Government.

In addition, a consistent foreign and defence policy should be clearly spelled out to the Sri Lankan public and Sri Lanka could thereby cooperate in security dialogues in the IOR. This could be done through maritime conferences and defence agreements to build trust among regional and extra regional powers. Sri Lanka could potentially take a lead role in establishing a movement that demilitarises and de-securitises the Indian Ocean by building a regime for peaceful cooperation.[131] In this manner, we could construct a peaceful region which will benefit all and, most importantly, secure and engage our nation in the game played in the Indian Ocean Region (IOR). Sri Lanka's strategic geography should be understood by our policy makers, diplomats, business community, and the civil society in this context.

What we can witness today in Sri Lanka is the Indian sphere of influence centred on South India, the Chinese Sphere of influence centred

---

[bf] Liberation Tigers of Tamil Eelam (LTTE), commonly known as the Tamil Tigers, was a militant organization that had been waging a violent secessionist campaign against the Sri Lankan government since the 1970s in order to create a separate Tamil state in the north and east of Sri Lanka.

on OBOR, and the US Sphere of influence centred on a US pivot to Asia and the IOR. Yet what is apparent is that *"Colombo matters because the Indian Ocean matters"*.[132] We started our examination into the IOR in the context of the 'Great Game' and it is how we shall end it. *"The 'Great Game of this Century' will be played on the waters of the Indian Ocean. Though India's location gives it great operational advantages in the IOR, it is by no means certain that New Delhi is in a position to hold on to its geographical advantages. China is rapidly catching up and its ties with Sri Lanka are aimed at expanding its profile in this crucial part of the world. Indian policymakers realize that unless they are more proactive they might end up losing this 'game' for good"*.[133]

Chapter 2

Political Landscape

"We both alike know that into the discussion of human affairs the question of justice only enters where the pressure of necessity is equal, and that the powerful exact what they can, and the weak grant what they must."

Thucydides

Changing Political Horizons in Sri Lanka?[1]

"Yet you don't have any democratic machinery — voting, and so on?"
"Oh, no. Our people would be completely shocked by having to declare that one policy was completely right and another completely wrong."[2]
— James Hilton, Lost Horizon

The circumstances were right in 1933 for James Hilton[a] to craft the image of '*Shangri-La*' in his novel *Lost Horizon*.[3] It appeared as food for thought to many thinkers in the West who were disillusioned with the direction of world events and keen to entertain notions of a fantastical Oriental utopia. The effects of the First World War prevailed at the time, and against the backdrop of economic insecurity, many sought a '*Shangri-La*' such as that in the picture painted by Hilton.

With China at its helm, the rise of the East — once better known as the Orient — is clear. According to the European Union Institute for Security Studies (EUISS) 2030 report,[4] the largest economies in terms of global GDP in 2030 will be China (23.8 per cent), the US (17.3 per cent), and the EU (14.3 per cent), followed by India. The Indian Ocean port city of Colombo is among the most recent to welcome the luxury hotel chain, Shangri-La. The palatial space at the very heart of the city was declared open by President Sirisena weeks ago.[5] His predecessor, President Rajapaksa, initiated the development and provided 10 acres of prime land previously occupied by the Ministry of Defence. This new landmark will add value to the tourism industry of the island. But in an unfavourable economic environment with high debts of approximately US$ 64 billion, and 95 per cent of Government revenue going towards debt repayment,[6] the Sri Lankan economy has become weaker due to low revenue generation. Sri Lanka dropped 14 places in the 2017 World Economic Forum Global Competitiveness Index (GCI) Report.[7] In a few months, another vision of utopia will be contrived in the next election campaign for public consumption.

Polarising events challenge world leaders daily to find solutions to complex problems. The capacity, capability, and courage to find solutions are best demonstrated after assuming power, if the aim is achievable. In Sri Lanka, several leaders who have had the vision to work toward a

---

[a] James Hilton was an English novelist best remembered for several best-sellers, including *Lost Horizon*.

prosperous nation were cut off by prevailing circumstances. Globally esteemed statesmen from Sri Lanka include the late Lalith Athulathmudali,[b] SWRD Bandaranaike,[c] and Lakshman Kadirgamar. This fact is no more apparent than in the Oxford Union, where portraits of these three visionary Sri Lankan statesmen serve as a reminder of their prolific work cut short by their untimely demise. All three were transformational leaders who played a significant role in Sri Lankan society and the nation's political life. Yet common to the three leaders was also their untimely end due to political assassination. The trifecta of tragedy is but another of many reflections of Sri Lanka's brutal political culture.

Lalith Athulathmudali was even offered a high-level position by Singapore's Prime Minister Lee Kuan Yew,[d] which he declined. Sri Lanka, however, failed to reap the benefits of this visionary leader. Today the question stands whether new leaders will emerge and transform Sri Lankan society for the better; whether politicians and practitioners have the capacity and aptitude to deliver. One could point to challenges presented by the Constitution or from elsewhere, but even if the Constitution is redrafted, the right personnel must be in place to turn legislation into policy.

Venerable Sobitha Thero,[e] the influential Buddhist monk who pursued a non-violent path towards a *'silent revolution'* in the hope of creating a better political culture, was commemorated a few weeks ago on the anniversary of his death. The political elite — the executioners of the promises and pledges of the Sri Lankan people — should reflect on

---

[b] Lalith Athulathmudali, was a prominent Sri Lankan politician of the United National Party and former Cabinet Minister of Trade, National Security, Agriculture, Education and deputy minister of defence.

[c] S.W.R.D. Bandaranaike was the fourth Prime Minister of Ceylon (later Sri Lanka) and founder of the left wing and Sinhala nationalist Sri Lanka Freedom Party, serving as Prime Minister from 1956 until his assassination by a man posing as a Buddhist monk in 1959.

[d] Lee Kuan Yew was the first Prime Minister of Singapore, governing for three decades. Lee is recognised as the nation's founding father, with the country described as transitioning from the *"third world to first world in a single generation"* under his leadership.

[e] Maduluwawe Sobitha Thero was an influential Sinhalese Buddhist monk regarded for his nonviolent revolutionary leadership in Sri Lanka. The chief incumbent of the Kotte Naga Vihara, he was a prominent social-political activist and an independent thinker who endured to improve the positive and constructive aspects of Sri Lankan Politics.

the great prelate's words and ask themselves if the silent revolution has delivered during the past three years.

President Sirisena has provided an answer and at the same time justified his Government's attempts to investigate a bond scam at the Central Bank: "*If Venerable Sobitha Thero was alive he would have approved of what I did. Why did we come here? Why did we change the previous Government? What is our objective? Did we come here to fill our pockets? Did we come to rob? I did not appoint [the Commission on Central Bank Bond investigation] targeting anyone.*"[8] Yet those appointed to stamp out corruption have become embroiled in controversy due to revelations linked to this investigation, which has led to the Prime Minister providing testimony. A daily newspaper revealed that the leading suspect in the corruption probe made multiple phone calls to high-level investigating officers. Upon further inquiry it was revealed that the communications concerned plans to publish a book about the infamous bond fiasco. Whatever the content, it is certain to be a bestseller in the run-up to local elections.

This scenario recalls a parable in Orwell's *Animal Farm*[9] that was also relevant prior to Sirisena's electoral victory in January 2015: replacement of the farm owner and a name change from Manor Farm to Animal Farm was futile; the expected political transformation did not materialise since the animals soon behaved the same as, and transformed into, the human lot from the past. The nation will be in election mode in a few months.[10] Leaders will emerge from the provincial and local levels to fulfil election targets and promises of prosperity. Whatever the result, there is indeed one essence distilled through the ages and preserved in time: democracy.

Monuments Over Mortality?[11]

"The true work of art is but a shadow of the divine perfection." — Michelangelo Buonarroti

At the time of the Renaissance, a not-so-tall statue of a brave young underdog warrior David,[f] standing just over five metres tall and weighing

---

[f] David is a masterpiece of Renaissance sculpture created in marble between 1501 and 1504 by Michelangelo. David is a 5.17-metre marble statue of a standing male nude. The statue represents the Biblical hero David, a favoured subject in the art of Florence.

six tons, mesmerised the world. This masterpiece was set into stone with a hammer and chisel by Michelangelo. On 8 September 1504, when Michelangelo unveiled his masterpiece in the city square in Florence, Italy, the crowd looked on in amazement since they had never seen anything of that nature before. The takeaway from this anecdote is that sometimes it does not have to be the tallest piece of work to be the grandest.

In Sri Lanka, this is evident in the fact that the Lotus Tower[g] stands at 350 m against the Colombo skyline; it is the tallest structure in South Asia with a cost of US$ 100 million. According to Professor Patrick Mendis, *"For defense analysts, this elaborate complex is an electronic surveillance facility funded by the Chinese Export-Import Bank (EXIM), constructed by the China National Electronics Import and Export Corporation (CEIEC) and the Chinese Aerospace Long–March International Trade (CALMIT), which are subsidiaries of the People's Liberation Army of China."*[12] The tower is already an area of concern for Sri Lanka's neighbour, similar to the past concern about Sri Lanka's *Voice of America*[h] transmission station.

Highlighting a crisis in Sri Lankan society, former Auditor General S.C. Mayadunne stated, *"from among forty-five who exceeded one hundred thousand preferential votes, a considerable amount of individuals elected had a history of being corrupt. If the people favour corruption whichever Government that comes into power will honour the aspirations of people. Therefore, the public must have a sincere feeling that they wish to defeat corrupt candidates."*[13] In the past two months, the Foreign Minister of Sri Lanka, the former President's secretary, and the former chairman of Telecommunication Regulatory Commission have been accused of corruption. The foreign minister resigned[14] and the other two were imprisoned.

---

[g] The Lotus Tower (Colombo Lotus Tower) is a tower under construction but architecturally topped out at 350 m (1,150 ft), located in Colombo, Sri Lanka. When completed, the tower will be the tallest structure in South Asia. The lotus-shaped tower will be used for communication, observation, and other leisure facilities, with construction costing $104.3 million, funded by EXIM Bank of Peoples' Republic of China.

[h] *Voice of America* is a U.S. Government-funded international news source that serves as the United States Federal Government's official institution for non-military, external broadcasting.

Corruption has poisoned many nations with weak government institutions and weak political cultures. As William Shakespeare aptly puts it in *Hamlet*, "*It will but skin and film the ulcerous place/Whilst rank corruption, mining all within/Infects unseen.*"[15] In present day Sri Lanka, the former Auditor General attempted an explanation in an interview for the Sri Lankan newspaper *Daily Mirror*[16] by stating that the audit bill will assist this Government in their central theme of fighting corruption and establishing rule of law.

In September 2017, a Symposium of Economic Crime was held at Cambridge University,[17] with 700 senior legal experts, public officials, and scholars. The author spoke at the symposium[18] on the importance of strengthening Sri Lanka's regulatory body, including the Auditor General's office. Professor Tim Morris of Oxford University explains in this regard that "*to lead change in society, education and participation are key.*"[19] Today, education and social consciousness have dramatically reduced the numbers of smokers when compared to smoking in the previous generations. In the same way, education on fighting economic crime and the involvement of all stakeholders are essential to root out corruption from society. The fight against corruption was at the heart of the Arab Spring and other large-scale protests in many countries, including Pakistan. Similarly, the Panama Papers[i] are still to be investigated in Sri Lanka. Due to the amazing work of whistle-blowers and a free media, global citizens are demanding greater transparency and accountability. A culture of impunity need not be the norm — greater social awareness can drive out corruption.

The general population is often uninformed about the extent to which corruption can impact communities. Civic education, activism, an investigative media, technology, and social media campaigns can generate interest and engagement in national dialogues on corruption and how it affects the everyday lives of citizens. When people are better educated on how corruption burdens their society's development and exacerbates

---

[i] The Panama Papers are 11.5 million leaked documents that detail financial and attorney-client information for more than 214,488 offshore entities. The documents, some dating back to the 1970s, were created by, and taken from, Panamanian law firm and corporate service provider Mossack Fonseca and were leaked in 2015 by an anonymous source.

inequality, poverty, and conflict, they can mobilise to fight it. Education and awareness are tools for change, allowing for vocalisation of grievances and an amplification of public pressure on governments to call for greater accountability.

There is a lot that Sri Lankan policy-makers need to do before focusing on beautification projects such as the Lotus Tower. In particular, projects to improve the quality of life in urban and rural areas of the country deserve immediate attention. While corruption is seen as the primary problem, there are many other issues that need to be addressed, such as the high suicide rate in the country. According to the World Health Organisation (WHO), Sri Lanka has the highest suicide mortality rate in South Asia, with 35.3 suicides per 100,000 of the population.[20]

The Lotus Tower, albeit monumentally, in essence symbolises *'enlightenment'* and *'purity'*. The lotus flower grows in muddy water and lives to rise above the murk to bloom. It is the ones who set the rules (and hold the luxury permits) who need to emulate the words of Buddha in practicing impermanence in physical structures and political thought.

Sri Lanka: National Interests in a Globalized World[21]

The first 100 days of the US President Donald Trump's administration revealed the complexity of a head of state's task. One of his predecessors, former US President John F Kennedy,[j] during his first 100 days, had learned a costly lesson with the failure of the Bay of Pigs[k] invasion. His reaction to the event was to *"splinter the CIA into a thousand pieces and scatter it into the wind."*[22] Thus, most Presidents realize the gravity of decision-making during the first 100 days; and this applies to Sri Lanka as well.

In this new emerging global order, Sri Lanka, a nation in transition from the third world to the second, with a GDP per capita of around US$ 3800[23] in 2016, will need to craft itself into a developed country. Even in

---

[j] John Kennedy, was an American politician who served as the 35th President of the United States from January 1961 until his assassination in November 1963.
[k] The Bay of Pigs invasion was a failed military invasion of Cuba undertaken by the Central Intelligence Agency-sponsored paramilitary group Brigade 2506 on 17 April 1961.

its current economic state, with a headcount poverty index of 4.1%,[24,1] a small section of the Sri Lankan society remains extremely wealthy. In a recent article,[25] Malinda Seneviratne argued that *"beggars can't be choosers"*. Sri Lanka will beg more from the international community given the relative weakness of its domestic industries. The Central Bank projection of achieving a GDP per capita of over US$ 5500 by 2020[26] will be unachievable with the current state of the economy.

In March 2017,[27] Sri Lankan President Maithripala Sirisena became the first Sri Lankan Head of State to visit Russia in several decades. President Sirisena's official visit will strengthen Sri Lanka's relations with a geo-strategically important country. This was Sirisena exercising his own foreign policy, carefully calibrated in the right direction. No previous Sri Lankan President held the values and teachings of Vladimir Lenin and Karl Marx in such high esteem as President Sirisena; their portraits even adorn the main boardroom of the current President's residence. This is a clear indication of the deep socialist values that President Sirisena holds. These values probably echo to remind the President not to sell any state resources. If the United National Party (UNP) is the pro-Western business-oriented party that advocates joint ventures, Sirisena is the inward looking farmer attempting to advocate the importance of an indigenous economy. Russia, with its gilded chambers suffering from the imperial hangover, is a reminder of deep nationalistic values. Russian President Vladimir Putin's symbolic gesture[28] of handing a 19th century sword belonging to Sri Lanka in the past to President Sirisena was a reminder of the need to preserve the Sri Lankan values and historical treasures smuggled or taken out of the island nation.

Having looked at Sri Lanka's national economy and its foreign policy with regards to socialism, we now pivot to strategic construction in the country. There have been some recent developments regarding the future of two strategic projects in Sri Lanka, one undertaken by India in Trincomalee and the other by China in Hambantota. According to Sri Lankan Prime Minister Ranil Wickremesinghe,[29] he has saved the nation from a joint

---

[1] This figure is the official figure given by the department of Census and Statistics. However, this figure does not account for overall poverty in the country which is estimated to be much higher.

venture with the Chinese. He claimed that he was able to negotiate a better, less harmful deal with China as compared to the one agreed to by former Sri Lankan President Mahinda Rajapaksa.

With regards to these strategic long-term projects, it is unclear how public input has been taken. Elected representatives are appointed for a period of six years for the Executive and five years for Members of Parliament. If such representatives enter into a deal that will conclude beyond their tenure, it is important to include public observations. If a certain project is awarded for a 99-year lease agreement, most of the policymakers who decide today will not live to see its conclusion. In China, a large-scale strategic foreign project will not be approved if there is no national security clearance. Sri Lanka should also think of national security clearance when deciding on large-scale strategic foreign projects. The clearance or the study report could be preserved for the next generation as a point of reference. Furthermore, the report should also assess if these projects add strategic value to Sri Lanka's economy. It is important to remember that given the volatile global order, what may be the best strategic option today may not be the same in a few years' time. A model should be designed to deeply understand future events and scenarios.

Foresight analysis is a methodology that Sri Lanka could adopt to predict the best future scenarios in this context. Has Sri Lanka assessed the strategic and economic significance of the Hambantota and Trincomalee port projects in 2030, 2050, and beyond? Sri Lankan policymakers should take these questions into consideration while making strategic decisions. If they do not have the necessary data sets to decide, they should defer the decision. Due to Sri Lanka's geographically strategic position, it cannot ignore regional and extra-regional entities' interests in it. However, what is paramount is that the Sri Lankan government should view its national interest as the first point of reference.

Securing Sri Lanka's National Interests[30]

"My golden island, my birth place, my victories land, my great motherland, Our patriots are like gems in the treasures of our land…" — *Mahagama Sekara ,"Rathna Deepa Janma Bhumi"; sung by maestro Dr. Amaradeva*[31]

One set of rules for Mosul and another for Aleppo; there are double standards when it comes to Syria. The international community justifies one bombing while condemning the other. Russia's operations in Aleppo against extremist groups are denounced by some Western officials and media as *"war crimes"*. In contrast, the civilian casualties as a consequence of the US-led operation to recapture Mosul in October this year (2016) are defined as unavoidable collateral damage.

While innocent children and civilians in Iraq and Syria fight for survival, double standards seem to prevail everywhere. Case in point, the furore over the email scandal involving Hillary Clinton smacks of such double standards. If a male US Government official were caught in the same scandal, he would have been treated in a different way.

Meanwhile, in Sri Lanka, a Committee on Public Enterprises report[32] on the Central Bank bond issue has been the topic of discussion. The well-known bond issue has created tremors in the political arena of the Prime Minister's party (UNP). The report, which was meant to be confidential, is now under strict public scrutiny. Hopefully, global double standards that rule to protect a few powerful people will not be used in this situation if the key people involved are found guilty. The trust deficit between the Government and public will widen if the corrupt are not punished, especially since battling corruption was a central electoral theme for the Government during the election campaign. According to Sri Lankan President Maithripala Sirisena, investigations into the Central Bank issue will be free of political interference, and he will initiate an impartial and independent judicial process.

Recently, President Sirisena presented gallantry awards to war heroes.[33] At the award ceremony, many recipients were young children who had lost their fathers at a very early age due to the war. This event was a clear reminder of the sacrifices made by Sri Lankans in securing the national interest for the next generation. In this regard, the State should give top priority to assist these young victims and ensure they receive a proper education so that they may go on to ensure that the double standard is not reflected in Sri Lanka's political future.

With regards to this future, major domestic developments and an ever-challenging economic situation looms ahead. This will be further highlighted on 10 November,[34] when the national budget is announced, marked by a rise of debt stock with high levels of fiscal sustainability risk.

Moreover, developments in Sri Lanka's neighbourhood should also be a matter of concern. India is building the *INS Arihant*,^m a nuclear submarine propelled by an 83 MW pressurized light water reactor at its core. The 6000-tonne nuclear submarine with nuclear-tipped long-range ballistic missiles in its four silos, capable of lurking underwater for months without being detected, is a most effective and deadly platform for a retaliatory nuclear strike. In addition, India has already begun to utilise the space arena for military purposes, evident from the launch of the first Synthetic Aperture Radar (SAR) reconnaissance satellite in 2009.[35] In 2013 and 2015, India launched two military communications satellites.[36] According to some experts, the Indian Regional Navigation Satellite System launched in 2013 is also meant for military use.[37] Japan will also launch in 2016 and 2017 two next generation X-band communications satellites,[38] owned by the Ministry of Defence and Self-Defense Force (SDF), which will enhance its capabilities in space.

With such military capabilities developed in close geographical proximity to Sri Lanka, it is important for the Sri Lankan government to invest its time and encourage youth participation in innovative and productive domestic sectors. The fourth industrial revolution has arrived with self-driving cars already on the roads as well as the advancements in artificial intelligence. Sri Lanka has a role to play in this hi-tech arena, and this can only happen with a strong vision and by collaborating and working as a community focused on achieving targets to secure the national interest in this new age; not by political rhetoric.

The Role of Independence in an Interchanging World Order

"Geographic facts do not change, but their meaning for foreign policy will."[39] — *Nicholas J. Spykman*

A new world order has begun with interchanging roles. The US as the leader of the free world and the architect of globalisation is advocating

---

^m INS Arihant is the lead ship of India's Arihant class of nuclear-powered ballistic missile submarines. The 6,000 tonne vessel was built under the Advanced Technology Vessel (ATV) project at the Ship Building Centre in the port city of Visakhapatnam.

nationalism and closing its borders while China, having espoused nationalist values, is now embracing globalisation. President Xi, during his visit to Davos, clearly gave his support for the case of globalisation. According to President Xi: *"there was a time when China also had doubts about economic globalisation and was not sure whether it should join the World Trade Organization. But we came to the conclusion that integration into the global economy is a historical trend. To grow its economy, China must have the courage to swim in the vast ocean of the global market. If one is always afraid of bracing the storm and exploring the new world, he will sooner or later get drowned in the ocean. Therefore, China took a brave step to embrace the global market. We have had our fair share of choking in the water and encountered whirlpools and choppy waves, but we have learned how to swim in this process. It has proved to be a right strategic choice"*.[40]

Back in the 1960s, the US position on boundaries was explained clearly by President Kennedy, in his remarkable oration *"ich bin ein berliner"*.[41] President Kennedy was alluding to the fact that there should be one Berlin; the Iron Curtain[n] which divided nations will fall one day and it did fall in 1989. It took only 30 years for the US to change its position and propose building a wall and confine itself to its border. In the same vein, in the ancient past, China exercised its power and developed a *'Great Wall'* to secure itself from outside invaders. Today, the US is revisiting what China did several thousand years ago, thereby showing the evolution of China and the regression of the US. Thus, in geopolitics it is vital to understand the politics of borders and frontiers. According to Robert Kaplan, *"the ability of states to control events will be diluted, in some cases destroyed. Artificial borders will crumble and become more fissiparous, leaving only rivers, deserts, mountains, and other enduring facts of geography. Indeed, the physical features of the landscape may be the only reliable guides left to understanding the shape of future conflict"*.[42]

Yale Professor Nicholas Spykman explained in his *'Rim Land'* theory[43] that the arc surrounding the heartland,[44] described by Halford J.

---

[n] The Iron Curtain was the name for the boundary dividing Europe into two separate areas from the end of World War II in 1945 until the end of the Cold War in 1991. The term symbolises the efforts of the Soviet Union to block itself and its satellite states from open contact with the West and non-Soviet-controlled areas.

Mackinder, is where tectonics shifts will occur and that nations will use their military power in this important crescent. In the 20th century, most wars, including the Korean war, Vietnam war, India-Pakistan, Iraq, Iran, Syria, and Balkan wars, were fought on this *'Rim Land'*. The next war could be triggered in the South China Sea, which comprises an area of the *'Rim Land'*. China, which is seeking a historical claim of the South China Sea to unlock its power in the Indian Ocean, has revived in its past via OBOR to do so.

Thus, the political landscape of the international arena is such that the North Atlantic power axis is clearly turning towards the East. This is evidenced by the fact that the newly elected President Trump stated that *"NATO is obsolete"*[45] and challenged its values. China will gain better control and win more allies in the East. Liberal democracy will be seen by Asians as a model that does not deliver efficient results. Asia could see itself drift towards a technocracy: a model operated by technical experts and expert Government servants who deliver quick results. China has clearly proven, far more than the 100 liberal democracies around the world, that 500 million people[46] can be taken out of poverty using this technocratic model. Similarly, Singapore has proven itself as an East Asian miracle, performing through a meritocracy at its highest value and delivering results to the public. The Corruption Perception Index[47] for 2016–2017 ranks Singapore at 7th place while Sri Lanka is ranked at 95th place in comparison. The concept of a technocracy is therefore paramount for Sri Lanka to develop as a nation. In this regard, Senior Research Fellow Parag Khanna from the LKYSPP states that *"increasingly, Asians favour pragmatic, outcome-oriented governance, and prefer to be ruled by civil servants rather than politicians"*,[48] predicting that Asia could turn to technocrats and depart from Western democracy.

Duality in the form of double standards was a significant factor in interrupting the course of glory of the Western empire. The notable double standards in human rights, democratic values, and politics between the West and the East are clear indicators of the erosion of the former's ideals. For example, Trump has stated that *"waterboarding is not torture, it's one step below torture"*.[49] Yet, at the same time, a nation like Sri Lanka is accused by the International Truth and Justice Project (ITJP) for crimes of abduction and torture.[50] Another juxtaposition is the

UK's *Sir John Chilcot report*,[51] which made a lot of noise about British soldiers committing war crimes in Iraq, even laying allegations against the Prime Minister at the time, but which hasn't had any repercussions on the UK's world standing. In comparison, the West has sought to interfere in Sri Lanka's post-war reconciliation, suggesting the establishment of a hybrid court with foreign judges to adjudicate on an internal civil war.[52]

Strat for Global Intelligence, one of the leading US security think tanks in the world, published an article about Sri Lanka which explained the fact that *"despite its small size Sri Lanka holds substantial strategic value by virtue of its geographic position: it is at the centre of Asia's busiest maritime routes and has a wealth of natural deep harbours"*.[53] It further points out that the Sri Lankan government owes Beijing $8 billion, more than 12% of its $64.9 billion national debt.[54]

Upon celebrating Sri Lanka's 69th year of independence,[55] it is important to clearly identify our internal and external geopolitical threats as a nation, with the hope of charting our path towards a developed and independent sovereign nation in this interchanging world order.

Politics of Promise: Between Sirisena and Rajapaksa[56]

"Those that are most slow in making a promise are the most faithful in the performance of it."[57] — Jean-Jacques Rousseau

On Easter Day, a day of rejoicing and celebration for Christians, shrapnel and ball bearings pierced through innocent civilians in a children's park in Lahore, where a majority of the victims were children. This disgraceful suicide attack,[58] which killed 69 and injured nearly 400, was a sad day for Pakistan and the region. Days before, another terrorist attack in Brussels[59] targeted innocent civilians. The world has become unstable due to terrorism and the highest priority on the global agenda should be towards combatting it. Without a safe environment it is difficult to talk about economic prosperity, a lesson Sri Lanka has learned from its brutal three-decade war. The physical and mental scars from terrorism are deep; as victims, they are not easy to forget.

In order to combat terrorism, consensus at the highest political level is necessary. In Sri Lanka, the daunting task of bringing together two different political parties with different values — the United National Party (UNP) and the Sri Lanka Freedom Party (SLFP) — was established a year ago. Recent developments within the political party of the current President Sirisena have not been very positive; thus, the advantage has moved to the former President Rajapaksa. Frustrations with the current Government have also led to an uptick in Sri Lankan civilian engagement on social media to air their grievances or general political sentiments, the consensus being: "we have given you the power, so fix it."

High expectations and promises were set at the beginning of the Sirisena Presidency and the delivery has been slow but steady. From 8 January 2015, beginning with the 100-day reforms,[60] until the present day, it has been 16 months of the new Government. The Right to Information (RTI) Act° was tabled in Parliament last week — a considerable achievement in this regard — but which needs further amendment, as it prevents access to some important areas that defeat the main purpose of the Act. Yet notably, such an Act would have been impossible under the former regime with its control and censorship of the media, not to mention its attacks on both media outfits and individuals.

Nevertheless, political stirrings in the country are now looking at change that could bring back the former regime. These political entrepreneurs tend to forget the situation in the past, where power revolved around a single individual who took over the independent commissions, including the bribery commission,[61] further extending his political term by more than two terms. The former regime practiced family politics in that Mahinda Rajapaksa's once-powerful family member would bestow a political rite of passage onto SLFP members; that was the politics of practice at the time. One senior Minister and a party leader, who currently has a small Ministry office and a nominal budget, showed his displeasure during the Rajapaksa period, but is now a front runner in the campaign to bring Rajapaksa back to power. Another senior politician from SLFP, who got many more votes than several other candidates elected from the

---

°With the establishment of republic states, a concept which denotes that the ownership of the state lies with people was evolved. State and the public institutions are maintained by the tax monies of people. Thus, the fundamental principle being established is that the people have the right to know information of which the functions of the state are accomplished using public funds. See: https://www.rti.gov.lk/

National List[p] spoke to the author of his displeasure at the handing of positions, based not on the consensus of the people but on party and power politics in the country.

Despite all obstacles, the triple power centres of the Government — President Sirisena, Prime Minister Wickremesinghe, and former President Kumaratunga — have found a working order on crucial subjects, despite their differences. International consensus is that there has been much praise for the Government's efforts to move towards introducing good governance, minimising massive spending, and working towards a more citizen-centric government. The colossal spending, including expenditure for State events, foreign visits with over-sized delegations, overseas missions in places that have no direct benefit for Sri Lanka, and other such characteristics of the Rajapaksa regime have now seen restructuring under the new Government. Presently, the Rajapaksa connection for reclaiming power seems weak and has not yielded much support, especially from the youth who believe in creating a society with less corruption. If the delivery of the central promise — anti-corruption — is equal to or worse than its delivery in the past regime, the tide could turn against the Sirisena Government. Yet, in the current context, there is much positivity in the political landscape, with attempts to correct the economic downturn created by the former regime in the form of excessive loans and financial misappropriation at all levels. Thus, under President Sirisena, there is much hope for the *'politics of promise'* to reign in Sri Lanka.

Sri Lanka: Moving Towards a Higher Collective Outcome[62]

"Don't think the enemies are weak as there are pro-Eelam forces on one hand while forces belonging to the last regime are also waiting to

---

[p] A National List Member of Parliament (National List MP) is an unelected Member of Parliament who is appointed by a political party or an independent group to the Parliament of Sri Lanka. The number of national list MPs allocated to a contending party or an independent group depends on the proportion to their share of the national vote. A total of 29 national list MPs are appointed alongside 196 elected MPs (elected from 22 multi-member electoral districts), making a total of 225 members in the Parliament.

sabotage the destiny of the national Government." — Sri Lankan President Maithripala Sirisena[63]

One of the largest catastrophes in modern human history is unfolding in Syria, due to the meteoric rise of the Islamic State (IS), which now has control over more than half of the Syrian territory. According to UN Secretary General Ban Ki-moon, the country has lost the equivalent of four decades of human development.[64] The suffering of the Syrians, especially a picture of a lifeless Syrian boy on the beach,[65] has caught the attention of the entire world. According to the UN Secretary General, four out of every five Syrians live in poverty.[66] The Syrian nation is in chaos, leaving citizens with no choice but to flee. It is time the international community collaborates in crushing the root cause: the IS. With the joint political will of the West and the Middle East, the IS infrastructure can be dismantled; by building international partnerships, global harmony can be restored.

Meanwhile, Sri Lanka is going through its own political transition. After the January 2015 Presidential election, which overthrew the Rajapaksa regime, Sri Lankans reaffirmed their verdict in the recent August 2015 Parliamentary election,[67] defeating Rajapaksa yet again. This secured a clear victory for the United National Front for Good Governance (UNFGG[q]) which took 106 seats while the opposition could secure only 95 seats.[68] The new Government, with the leadership of Prime Minister Ranil Wickremesinghe will be ready to introduce good governance and fight corruption to bring economic prosperity. It is time for this Government to execute the promises it made while electioneering, with the right calibre of cabinet ministers. From an international perspective Sri Lanka is now seen as a shining example of democratic, peaceful elections and political transition. We must therefore strive to ensure that the democratic values in our society are not beholden to the will of individual politicians.

R. Sampanthan,[r] a minority party leader, was appointed opposition leader. 48 Cabinet Ministers were elected from the two main parties,[69] the

---

[q] The United National Front for Good Governance is a political alliance in Sri Lanka which is led by professionals and activists. The front contested the 2015 Sri Lankan elections under United National Party symbol and name, and was elected the 1st party to form a Government.

[r] R. Sampanthan is a Sri Lankan Tamil politician and lawyer who has led the Tamil National Alliance since 2001.

UNFGG and United People's Freedom Alliance (UPFA). For the first time, Sri Lanka's opposition leader, who should have been a UPFA member given the people's mandate of more than four million voters,[70] came from a minority regional party due to the Memorandum of Understanding (MOU[71]) to create a national Government. This move garnered both positive and negative reactions but at this critical juncture, with the upcoming decision on Sri Lanka at the UNHCR[72] and the absence of a clear majority Government, this was the best possible option.

However, the Sri Lankan government, under UNSC Resolution 1373,[73] proscribed 15 Liberation Tigers of the Tamil Eelam fronts with effect from 1 April 2014.[74] The order enabled funds, assets, and economic resources belonging to the listed persons and entities to remain frozen until the removal of their names from the designated list. It is important to continue the ban and to not review it at this point because these fronts still could be a threat to our national security.

In the next few days, some members of the Tamil National Alliance (TNA[s]) will leave for Geneva to pressure for an international investigation. Sustaining the national government model will be the next challenge as we understand the capabilities of some of our politicians and how quickly they move from one party to another. For a country that has gone through a peaceful political transition, it is now important to move towards the nation-building process to double our per capita income by 2020. To this end, two important factors need to be considered. Firstly, we need to move as a nation to a higher collective outcome. The four-time Prime Minister Ranil Wickremesinghe will have to learn the art of moving away from playing Prisoner's Dilemma[t] as he needs to get both parties to cooperate and move

---

[s] The Tamil National Alliance is a political alliance in Sri Lanka that represents the country's Sri Lankan Tamil minority. It was formed in October 2001 by a group of moderate Tamil nationalist parties and former militant groups. The alliance originally supported determination in an autonomous state (Tamil Eelam) for the island's Tamils. It supported negotiations with the rebel Liberation Tigers of Tamil Eelam (LTTE) to resolve the civil war in Sri Lanka.

[t] The Prisoner's Dilemma is a standard example of a game analysed in game theory that shows why two completely '*rational*' individuals might not cooperate, even if it appears that it is in their best interests to do so. It was originally framed by Merrill Flood and Melvin Dresher working at RAND in 1950.

forward instead of stagnating. *"If you and I were to change our ways together, we could both get to a better place. However, if I was to change and you were not, I'd be much worse off. And because I can't be sure that you will move, I won't make the move either"*.[75] These words demonstrate a classic Prisoner's Dilemma, where groups of people settle for a sub-optimal outcome because they cannot ensure coordinated action that could take them all to a better outcome. Great leadership, especially in the context of national leadership is about orchestrating coordinated movement away from the Prisoner's Dilemma to a higher collective outcome.

Secondly, we need to introduce meritocracy into our system, which essentially means appointing suitable and qualified individuals for the job and ensuring strong government appointments to strengthen our institutions. All appointments should go through a recommendation committee appointed jointly by the President and Prime Minister, to screen the most appropriate person for the job, in the absence of which ad hoc appointments by some ministers could be established. Similarly, chairpersons, directors, and all executives who are political appointments need to be carefully vetted as they are the key individuals who will work in the ministries and develop national institutions.

As a nation, we have undergone the scourge of conflict, first during the struggle for independence, then during the fight against terrorism for nearly three decades, not to mention two youth insurrections and the many political transitions over the past several decades. It is important to develop a national plan with the contributions of all political parties for the next several decades to take our nation towards a higher collective outcome in the form of prosperity.

The Importance of Electing the Best to Our Nation's Parliament[76]

"People who live in Sri Lanka are first and foremost Sri Lankans, then we have our race and religion, which is something given to us at birth." — *Lakshman Kadirgamar*[77]

On 17 August 2015,[78] Sri Lankans will elect their new parliamentarians for the next five years. It is important to elect the best candidates to steer this nation towards prosperity. The current situation in the country thrives on fundamental blunders made by some of the nation's politicians. Today, most parliamentary proceedings have little or no bearing on the direction and development of the country. The discipline and intellect displayed by some of its members are heinous. The use of inappropriate language and the conduct of politicians illustrate the standard of politics in the country today. It has become a vicious circle of uneducated people elected to lead. Out of 225 parliament members, 192 members have failed their higher education studies.[79]

This has resulted in poor policy decisions and contributed towards the country's staggering unemployment rate, the rise in drug peddlers and barons with powerful connections, the depreciating economy, the brain drain, and the spiralling socio-economic status of the country.[80] Today, the people are deceived by beautification projects, cityscape development, and the construction of major infrastructure like highways and buildings. However, in the midst of all of these developments, poverty-stricken villagers still suffer. Some rural areas are still not equipped with basic facilities like roads and drinking water. Some children walk for miles over dangerously neglected bridges to receive a basic education. Nearly 50 per cent of students failed higher education mathematics in 2014.[81] This has resulted in mothers, sisters, and wives working under inhumane circumstances as housemaids in the Middle East to support their households financially. According to recent news, a Sri Lankan maid was advertised in Saudi Arabia for sale at the price of 25,000 riyals.[82] Exporting domestic help to the Middle East has become an industry within Sri Lanka and, for most families, the only option for income, through the repatriation of foreign exchange.

We need to change the present system of governance and introduce a meritocracy to our government institutes in order to combat these societal challenges. If you appoint the most suitable person with due respect to their intellectual expertise to govern, it will be a step forward in increasing the efficiency of government institutions. One cannot dream of a developed nation without strengthening government institutes. The vision for Sri Lanka needs to be followed up with the development of a national strategic plan, one that doesn't change with the ushering in of a new government.

According to Singapore's Lee Kuan Yew: *"we have got to live with the consequences of our actions and we are responsible for our own people... When I went to Colombo for the first time in 1956 it was a better city than Singapore*".[83] The Sri Lanka of today needs to live up to Lee Kuan Yew's words and focus on moving towards the position Singapore and other such developed nations occupy in the world. It is important to improve investment in education and research in this regard. As we move to achieve a knowledge-based economy, we should develop our most precious resource: our human capital. We under-invest in these important areas and rely on quick fixes. STEM (science, technology, engineering, and mathematics) needs to be the primary focus to achieve the technological heights we wish to achieve by 2020 and beyond. The development of STEM is a priority in countries such as Singapore, which have already developed a world-class education system. Singaporean universities are listed in the top 75 slots of the *'world's best'* rankings.[84]

Sri Lanka too needs to facilitate the education of its youth, who will be the country's next generation of leaders. Yet the reality is that many Sri Lankan youth are sent to foreign countries to study and most are encouraged to stay on and serve those countries. In the end it is a losing battle. Our country is deprived of talent that could truly make a difference. We need to create an ecosystem for our educated youth to return to their country and include these young professionals in our workforce for the betterment of the country. According to US President Barack Obama, it is important for us to pave the way for the next generation. He says in this regard: "*I don't understand this phenomenon of leaders who refuse to step aside when their terms end... No one is above the law, not even the President*".[85] Similar to any other occupation, it is important to provide an opportunity for the youth to lead in the political arena whilst the establishment willingly and peacefully leaves office when their terms end. Unfortunately, politicians do not retire in Sri Lanka to pave way for our young leaders.

Sri Lanka is slowly but surely rising from the ashes and developing in the post-war era. In order to truly reap the benefits and move towards development, the political arena needs to be cleansed. We need to refrain from pointing fingers at each other and focus on rebuilding the country. We need to gain the strength of the next generation to be the force of change. Developing the education system and educating the youth, rebuilding villages and rural areas, and creating an innovative culture to sustain development are all factors that will contribute to this change. Furthermore, there needs to be a focus on creating different channels to bring in foreign investments as well as creating employment within the country, which will also discourage the option of exporting our rich human resources as domestic help. This will result in the development and enrichment of Sri Lanka.

We need to follow the examples of great visionaries such as Lakshman Kadirgamar, who once spearheaded the direction of the country. We all should remember this remarkable politician who was committed to creating a better nation for all of us. He won the hearts of everyone around the world and was the best foreign minister we ever had. We need dedicated leaders like him for our country; we need to vote as one nation for politicians with suitable values and intellect to navigate our country to prosperity.

Sri Lanka: Brain Drain, 'Connection Culture', and National Development[86]

"Always vote for principle, though you may vote alone, and you may cherish the sweetest reflection that your vote is never lost." — John Quincy Adams[87]

Many people avert their eyes from the extent of inequality in the present world. Poverty and uneven patterns of growth are among the top causes for this inequality. Yet the world we live in has not changed much. The 30 richest nations and the 30 poorest nations have remained the same for the past 20 or, in some cases, 50 years.[88] Some nations grow rapidly and experience rapid collapse. Of the 30 poorest nations in sub-Saharan Africa, South America, South Asia, and East Asia, some nations still struggle with a per capita income below $2500; meanwhile, the richest nations' per capita incomes have been between $20,000 and $50,000.[89]

Analysis is required as to why, barring a few nations, nations have failed to or are struggling to achieve purchasing power similar to that of the US and Western Europe. Populations from poorer countries choose migration as the most preferable option as their political and economic institutions consistently fail to deliver a better standard of living and/or employment. 150–200 Rohingya migrants fleeing their own country due to persecution were rescued from a boat off the coast of Myanmar and are now in refugee camps crammed into warehouses by the Myanmar police.[90] The situation is the same for many other nationalities, including Sri Lankan migrants in labour camps in many foreign countries. During the author's recent visit to Slovenia, it was established that the biggest issue for the country was unemployment and brain drain culture. Similarly, Serbia, Bosnia, and Croatia are nations with high levels of migrant workers without jobs who seek employment in the more prosperous Western Europe. Thus, these countries lose the best of their labour force's talent due to economic migration.

This is a recurrent theme in Sri Lanka as well: Many of its youth leave the country, both legally and illegally, for better economic prospects abroad. A recent conversation with a politician in Sri Lanka produced a shocking response regarding the brain drain issue. He explained in this context: *"brain drain is good [.] When they go it's good for us [because] we don't need to look after them [and] those countries will do our job"*.[91] Yet the only way a nation can reverse this situation is by strengthening the internal political and economic institutions that are currently weak. If politicians create hope for the youth, the chances that they would remain in their own nation and contribute to economic development are perhaps higher. Existing institutions in a poor nation probably support a political culture where everyone has to have political support to climb the ladder of prosperity. It could well be the reason why individuals such as Thomas Edison[u] with over 1000 patents or Steve Jobs[v] who started Apple at 21 or Bill Gates[w] who started Microsoft at 22 never emerged in our part of the world. Innovation and financial support was readily available for these individuals' prosperity, without political connections.

---

[u] Thomas Edison was an American inventor and businessman. He developed many devices that greatly influenced life around the world, including the phonograph, the motion picture camera, and the long-lasting, practical electric light bulb.

[v] Steven Jobs was an American entrepreneur, business magnate, inventor, and industrial designer. He was the chairman, chief executive officer (CEO), and co-founder of Apple Inc.

[w] William Gates is an American business magnate, investor, author, philanthropist, humanitarian, and co-founder of the Microsoft Corporation along with Paul Allen. In 1975, Gates and Allen launched Microsoft, which became the world's largest PC software company.

An intellectual of global repute, whom this author met, made a comment about the political environment in Sri Lanka. When he asked another Sri Lankan as to how he could contribute to the country, the answer was: *"Don't worry, anything can be done because I know the establishment and a lot of politicians"*.[92] This culture of connection needs to change. Individuals without any political connections should be able to achieve in life. One should not need a letter from a politician to get an employer to extend terms of employment. Qualifications and achievements should be the sole criteria to earn a position. A key factor that helped countries such as Singapore transform from poor countries to well-performing nations was that they ensured that a minimum standard of education was necessary to achieve political status or to represent the citizenry in the Parliament. The highest-paid salaries in the world are also accorded to Singaporean politicians,[93] thereby ensuring that they don't steal from any tender or project. The crux of the issue is changing the political culture — a difficult task due to the level of entrenchment of this problem.

Nevertheless, the people's power still exists to bring about this change. An example of such change was the 2015 Sri Lankan presidential election. The upcoming general election will also be a crucial moment for our island nation to make our society a better place. Electing the best to our nation's Parliament will ensure that boat people[x] are not generated, and that the country's youth don't have to leave our nation just for want of a better life.

---

[x] Boat people refer to refugees who have fled a country by boat, usually without sufficient provisions, navigational aids, or a set destination, especially those who left Indochina by sea as a result of the fall of South Vietnam in 1975.

Chapter 3

Foreign Relations

"China, in short, has the potential to be considerably more powerful than even the United States."

John J. Mearsheimer[a]

---

[a] John J. Mearsheimer (2003). *"The Tragedy of Great Power Politics (Updated Edition)"*, p. 415, W. W. Norton & Company.

Sri Lankan Foreign Policy: Diaspora and Lobbying[1]

"No foreign policy — no matter how ingenious — has any chance of success if it is born in the minds of a few and carried in the hearts of none." — *Henry A Kissinger*[2]

7 December 2016 marks the 75th anniversary of the Pearl Harbour[b] attack — a reminder of a history of imperialism and fascism, and how the world order moved toward bipolarity with the onset of the Cold War. Today, China and many other countries, some with nuclear weapons capabilities, are emerging as the new powers in a multi-polar world. According to Professor Amitav Acharya,[3] *"a multi-polar world includes many powerful individual groups apart from Governments."*[4] The US, however, remains a superpower. Yet its foreign policy could undergo dramatic adjustments with the induction of President-elect Donald Trump's administration. The President's recent phone call[5] to the Taiwanese leader Tsai Ing-wen[c] — not a standard practice since 1979 — has hinted at this change.

In a threatened neo-liberal world order, Sri Lanka should craft its foreign policy to suit the international environment of the day. Sri Lanka was a founding member[6] of the Non-Aligned Movement (NAM).[d] During the period when smaller nations had to commit allegiance to either the US or the Soviet Union, Sri Lanka's first female Prime Minister, Sirimavo Bandaranaike, showed courageous leadership to the world, and her foreign policy was guided by a combination of interests, values, and power.

Today too, President Sirisena's Government has balanced the country's relations with the West and the East. The '*Asia-centric balanced*'[7] foreign policy spelled out by the President clearly prioritises relations with Asia while balancing the rest. Sri Lanka has a policy of equidistance with global powers including India, China, and the US. While gaining support

---

[b] The attack on Pearl Harbor was a surprise military strike by the Imperial Japanese Navy Air Service against the United States naval base at Pearl Harbour, Hawaii Territory, on the morning of 7 December 1941. The attack led to the United States' entry into World War II.
[c] Tsai Ing-wen is a Taiwanese politician and the President of the Republic of China, commonly known as Taiwan. Tsai is the second president from the Democratic Progressive Party (DPP), and the first woman elected to the office.
[d] The Non-Aligned Movement is a group of states that are not formally aligned with or against any major power bloc. As of 2012, the movement has 120 members.

from foreign governments, the Sri Lankan government should also reach out to the three million-strong[8] Sri Lankan diaspora, which includes Sinhalese, Tamils, and other ethnic groups who live overseas.

The term *'lobby'* in this case implies a loose coalition of individuals and organisations who actively work to achieve a positive outcome for their nation of birth. A lobby might not be a unified movement with a central leadership, and individuals within the coalition might also disagree on certain issues. Certain sections of the Sri Lankan Tamil diaspora are still engaged in lobbying for a separate homeland, *'Eelam'*.[e] A diaspora has the ability to manoeuvre the nation's policy so that it advances their interests. Voting for candidates, writing and commenting, making financial contributions, and supporting individuals who could contribute to achieve their goals are among the diasporas' key functionalities.

Sri Lanka's diaspora is pivotal for three reasons. First, a Sri Lankan diaspora that is re-aligned with the county helps to project the country's positive image. What is therefore required is a re-alignment strategy that opens strong communication channels for whoever is disconnected from Sri Lanka for various reasons. Second, the diaspora could act as a powerful lobby, hitherto an untapped asset. Third, the diaspora could contribute to economic prosperity if Sri Lanka opens its doors to expatriates with professional expertise to join the ailing Government enterprises, assist other sectors of the economy, and bring in investment.

In benefitting from the support and strength of the diaspora, Sri Lanka stands to learn a lot from Israel. The Israeli diaspora is a much larger and more powerful group that receives huge donations and assistance from the US. This diaspora also acts as a lobby group and exerts influence on US foreign policy. The scholars John Mearsheimer and Stephen M Walt explain this factor in their book *The Israel Lobby and US Foreign Policy*.[9] They assert that *"Israel receives about $3 billion in direct foreign assistance each year, which is roughly one fifth of America's foreign aid budget. In per capita terms, the United States gives each Israeli a direct subsidy worth about $500 per year. This largesse is especially striking when one realizes that Israel is now a wealthy industrial state with a per capita income roughly equal to South Korea or Spain."*[10]

---

[e] Eelam is the native Tamil name for the South Asian island state of Sri Lanka. Eelam means *'homeland'*.

The overseas Indian diaspora is yet another example of a group that contributes immensely to the Indian economy, especially through the Information Communications Technology (ICT) sector. Indians account for the second largest student population in the US,[11] after the Chinese. In a similar vein, the Sri Lankan diaspora can become a positive force. The communal riots in Sri Lanka's history led to a brain drain. Even today, many youngsters are leaving the country because of political uncertainty and weak economic conditions. The emigrating population is in fact a loss in wealth and resources for the nation. The diaspora should be transformed into a valuable lobby group instead of spending millions on lobby firms. It is important for Sri Lanka to take strategic steps in readjusting its foreign policy in a multi-polar world, and these steps should include an important role for the Sri Lankan diaspora.

The Island and the Mainland: Impact of Fisheries on Indo-Lanka Relations[12]

"India will walk side by side with Sri Lanka as it charts its own path to progress and prosperity for all of its citizens." — PM Modi[13]

At the southern tip of India, in a narrow stretch of water where the seascape begins, is one of the region's geopolitical hot spots. The waters between India and Sri Lanka are rich in history and mythology. According to Valmiki's *Ramayana*,[f] there is only one point of connection between the two nations: the man-made bridge that Rama and Hanuman used to reach Sri Lanka to rescue Rama's wife Sita from the demon King Ravana of Lanka.[14] This bridge was renamed the Adams Bridge by British cartographers at the beginning of the 20th century.[15] The geographical stretch of water here, called the Palk Strait, has served as a rich fishing ground for fishermen.

From a historical perspective, the thirty-year war that devastated Sri Lanka has had many implications for the state of Tamil Nadu in southern India. Central government policy in India heavily influences

---

[f] Ramayana is an ancient Indian epic poem which narrates the struggle of the divine prince Rama to rescue his wife Sita from the demon king Ravana. Along with the Mahabharata, it forms the Sanskrit Itihasa.

popular Tamil Nadu party politics and vice versa, which has threatened Indo-Sri Lanka relations on many occasions. Post-war Indo-Sri Lanka relations have been challenging and have sometimes even threatened the sovereignty of Sri Lanka. For example, the recent announcement[16] by (then) Tamil Nadu Chief Minister Jayalalitha claiming Katchatheevu island,[g] as well as the idea of a separate State, '*Eelam*', pose a direct national security threat to Sri Lanka.

Thus, the most pressing issue for Sri Lanka remains protecting state sovereignty and resolving the fishermen dispute between India and Sri Lanka. Chief Minister Jayalalitha plays a pivotal role as a sympathiser of Tamil Nadu fishermen who encroach on Sri Lankan fishing grounds, and also as a protector of the fisheries' business owners who own and operate mechanised industrial bottom trawlers.[17] Indian fisherman ripped out the rich seabed using bottom trawlers, a practice now banned globally.[18] There is also evidence of a few Sri Lankan fishing boats being converted with this method,[19] the justification being, if India can do it in Sri Lankan waters, why can't Sri Lankans themselves? The authorities should take strict measures to confiscate these trawlers as they destroy the rich biodiversity of the ocean.

The fishermen claim they are ignorant of the existence of the International Maritime Boundary Line (IMBL).[20] There are reports that more than 3,000 Indian fishing boats engaged in illegal, unregulated, and unreported (IUU) fishing in Sri Lankan waters.[21] Both the Sri Lankan and Indian Governments have met many times to resolve this dispute with arrests of fishermen from both sides. During Sri Lankan President Sirisena's recent visit to India, Prime Minister Modi stated the need to find a permanent solution to the issue of fishermen straying into each other's waters.[22] As a solution, the issuing of licenses to a few Indian fishing trawlers with limited catch — to minimize mass scale fisheries and resource depletion — is on the anvil.[23] However, this is not a new effort. In 1976,[24] the maritime boundary agreement between the two countries endeavoured

---

[g] Katchatheevu is an uninhabited island administered by Sri Lanka and was a disputed territory claimed by India until 1976. The island is located between Neduntheevu, Sri Lanka and Rameswaram, India and has been traditionally used by both Sri Lankan Tamil and Tamil Nadu fishermen.

to issue up to six permits to Sri Lankan vessels with 2,000 tons per year for three years at Wadge Bank, south of Kanyakumari. A recent newspaper reports the Sri Lankan Minister of Fisheries and Aquatic Resources Development as having said: *"At present 5000 Indian trawlers fish in our waters. The aim is to reduce it to 250 and to issue licenses to them."*[25]

If these licenses are issued to the Indian mechanised bottom trawlers, there will be objections from Sri Lankan fishermen. If the licenses are for ordinary fishing vessels, templates such as New Zealand's Quota Management System (QMS)[26] could be looked at. In the past, when fisheries' resources in New Zealand were depleting, the authorities set up a QMS to allocate fishing vessels to demarcated zones inside the Exclusive Economic Zone (EEZ),[h] with an annual quota that could be traded in an electronic trading market. If a fisherman had stocks left, he could trade with another.

The Sri Lankan fisheries association and its Indian counterpart could study a system like the QMS to resolve the issue, as the former has reservations about granting licenses to Indian trawlers to fish in Sri Lankan waters. A customized QMS and the creation of a joint fisheries association with a registered database of fishing vessels is an option. As it stands, the existing GPS devices used by Indian fishermen, which indicates proximity to the IMBL with a beep, is of no use if the transponders are switched off to engage in illegal fishing. Any effort to resolve the issue will fail if certain standards are not met and rule-breakers are not punished. In Malaysia, for example, if the transponders are switched off, the authorities automatically fine the fishermen.[27]

There is still no legislation in Sri Lanka banning bottom trawling,[i] and this should be taken up immediately to preserve the rich ocean ecology. The department of fisheries has currently stopped issuing licenses, but this is not sufficient — introducing the right law is essential. In fact, this situation involving bottom trawlers has worsened this year in comparison to the last, with a serious increase in the number of boats. More than 50,000 Sri Lankan fishing families in the north have been affected and

---

[h] An exclusive economic zone is a sea zone prescribed by the United Nations Convention on the Law of the Sea over which a state has special rights regarding the exploration and use of marine resources, including energy production from water and wind.

[i] Since the publication of this article, bottom trawling has been banned in Sri Lanka (July 2017).

huge revenue losses are incurred everyday due to illegal fishing by Indian trawlers.[28] The Governments of India and Sri Lanka should come together to find a comprehensive and sustainable solution that takes into account both the challenging geographical space and the rich biodiversity in this area. If left alone in its present state, the issue could create a serious strain on the India-Sri Lanka bilateral relationship.

New Delhi-Tamil Nadu Relations and India's Sri Lanka Policy[29]

"Could a provincial State take hostage of a central Government's decision, especially affecting its foreign policy towards another nation? A State cannot put pressure on the central Government's decisions. I am tired and like Muhammed Ali I will allow them to punch me continuously but wait for the right moment to strike,"[30] said Salman Khurshid, the then Indian external affairs minister. He said this the same day India voted for the UN Human Rights Council resolution against its neighbour Sri Lanka due to much pressure from South India.[31] It is worth remembering the incident and the statement to forecast how much pressure the southern Indian state of Tamil Nadu has and could lay on New Delhi in the future, regarding relations between the two countries. India's Sri Lanka policy has thus long been hostage to the Tamil Nadu political parties' stance on the Sri Lankan Tamils issue.

During the election campaign, the (then) recently re-elected Chief Minister of Tamil Nadu, Jayalalitha,[32] had promised that her party would pressure the Centre to provide dual citizenship to Sri Lankan Tamils in Tamil Nadu and to create a separate *'Eelam'* in Sri Lanka. This would fulfil the dream of the defeated terrorist leader of the LTTE, Prabhakaran.[j] With Jayalalitha's victory in the State elections, the Sri Lanka-South India relationship is back to square one. Sri Lankan President Maithripala Sirisena will have to navigate his New Delhi-Colombo relationship with respect to all these external political pressures.

---

[j] Velupillai Prabhakaran was the founder and leader of the Liberation Tigers of Tamil Eelam (LTTE), a militant organisation that sought to create an independent Tamil state in the north and east of Sri Lanka.

During her election campaign in 2009, Jayalalitha had said, *"We will fight to attain that independent, separate Eelam. Till today, I have never said that separate Eelam is the only solution. I have spoken about political solution, this and that. But, now I emphatically say, a separate Eelam is the only permanent solution to the Lankan conflict."*[33] This demonstrates a clear indication of repetition in each election of a promised land, thereby extending hope to the Tamils. Katchatheevu Island is also played up during the election time. Meanwhile, in Sri Lanka, Chief Minister of the Northern Province, V. Vigneswaran,[k] congratulated and admired Jayalalitha's statement. Given such rhetoric, it is likely that both chief ministers will meet in the near future, most probably without the consent of their central Governments.

Seeking external assistance from Jayalalitha for Sri Lankan Tamils is, in the author's opinion, a trivial move, given the amount of assistance past and present Governments of Sri Lanka have given to the northern Tamilians. The recent request by Chief Minister Vigneswaran[34] to evacuate the Army from Sri Lanka's northern peninsula could antagonise the national security of the entire country. Sri Lanka has recently come out of a three-decade war with deep scars and security should therefore still be a top priority in the country. Strengthening the intelligence and security components of the island nation should not be compromised for any political gains of individuals or groups. On another dimension, we have also seen another threat slowly emerging, with around 40 Sri Lankans having joined the terrorist group ISIS.[35]

With regards to the current India-Sri Lanka relationship, when asked as to what India's position will be if Sri Lanka gets another Chinese submarine port call, the Indian defence minister said it will be looked at on a case by case basis.[36] Yet it is necessary to have a proactive defence strategy among the two nations in such situations. On 20 June 2016, the Nuclear Suppliers Group[37] meeting will take place in Seoul, South Korea. India is supposed to accede to membership of this group with the assistance of the US, which China has already resisted. If given

---

[k] Justice C.V. Vigneswaran is a Sri Lankan Tamil lawyer, judge, and politician. He is the current Chief Minister of the Northern Province. He is also the head of the Tamil People's Council.

membership, the regional geopolitical tension on the Indo-Pakistan and Indo-China fronts will be exacerbated.

President Sirisena has clearly mastered his decisions on foreign policy during his short time in office. He has endeavoured to strengthen the India-Sri Lanka relationship in a positive way, far more than his predecessor. The success of the G7 and his last visit to China show clear indications of perfect balance of foreign policy. These events could only predict a scenario where a positive sum game will be played by President Sirisena with regards to Sri Lanka's India policy.

Remembering Tagore in Turbulent Times[38]

"I have become my own version of an optimist. If I can't make it through one door, I'll go through another door — or I'll make a door. Something terrific will come no matter how dark the present."— Rabindranath Tagore[39]

One hundred and fifty five years ago, the greatest and most illustrious son of Asia, Gurudev Rabindranath Tagore,[1] was born. Tagore's work inspired many individuals around the world including many Sri Lankan scholars and musicians. Tagore believed in creating an environment of multiculturalism and tolerance. He spoke of the importance of world peace, dialogue, and non-violence. This vision remains unfulfilled. The value of Tagore's vision — the restoration of human values — is more relevant than ever today.

Had the essence of Tagore's philosophy been practiced, Bangladesh, one of the countries he wrote the national anthem for, would not be going through its present crisis. There have been more than fifty terrorist attacks in the last few years and out of these, IS was responsible for 13 of the attacks,[40] including the recent killing of a Sufi Muslim spiritual leader. The IS has clearly stated that the *"soldiers"* of its declared caliphate have also been murdering targets in Bangladesh, and that it would expand further in South Asia and would *"continue to terrorise the crusaders [Westerners] and their allies until the rule of Allah is established on the earth."*[41]

---

[1] Rabindranath Tagore was a Bengali polymath who reshaped Bengali literature and music. In 1913, he became the first non-European to win the Nobel Prize in Literature.

The South Asian region has been devastated by terrorist attacks in Afghanistan, Pakistan, and now Bangladesh. Providing security to civilians has become the top priority for many countries around the world. From Sri Lanka, more than forty individuals have joined the IS, according to experts.[42] The Government must invest in focused strategic and security initiatives to keep track of such activities and work closely with Muslim organisations, particularly Muslim youth, to prevent them from joining the ISIS.

Thus, the region indicates clear variables for a geopolitical nightmare as states surrounding India have shown much instability. All South Asian countries face similar and, in some cases, common economic challenges. Weak institutions, weak political culture, unemployment, and inequality are potent triggers for youth unrest. From Naxalism[m] in India to other domiciled terrorist entities, it can be predicted that they will take the advantage provided by weak states. Weak states surrounding India are also a direct threat to Indian security. It is important to strengthen smaller and larger states in South Asia through economic and social revival and through regional cooperation and global integration to address problems of commonality, particularly those of poverty and deprivation.

President Sirisena of Sri Lanka recently delivered the Lalith Athulathmudali memorial lecture.[43] The legacy of the Oxford and Harvard scholar-turned-politician, who was brutally gunned down in 1993, thus remains. The President addressed the importance of intellectuals such as Lalith in today's politics. Lalith was ethical and the yeoman service he rendered to Sri Lanka was immense. He initiated *'Mahapola'*, a scholarship scheme to inspire many young minds from rural villages by giving them access to university education. Speaking at the event, Lalith's only brother said, "*Lalith was offered an important place by Prime Minister Lee Kuan Yew to serve Singapore but he declined [in order] to serve his own country.*"[44] Had he accepted this offer, his life would have not ended with an assassin's bullets — a clear example of Sri Lankan political culture.

President Sirisena was elected to change this culture. Fighting corruption and introducing transparent methods of governance remain a

---

[m] A Naxal or Naxalite is a member of Communist Party of India (Maoist). Naxalites are considered far-left radical communists, supportive of Maoist political sentiment and ideology.

top priority. This week in London, world leaders including the Sri Lankan President and many economists will meet at the Anti-Corruption Summit to discuss measures to tackle corruption.[45] This coincides with the revelations made by the Panama Papers, in which many global leaders including British Prime Minister David Cameron, the host of the landmark summit, feature. While large-scale initiatives are important, citizen-centric stakeholder movements have created better results in quantifying corruption data and educating the public. All South Asian countries, except Bhutan, rank below the score of 50 on the corruption scale — qualifying as *'highly corrupt'* — according to the Corruption Perception Index (CPI) by Transparency International.[46] Corruption increases the cost of doing business up by 10 per cent globally, says the World Bank.[47] With corruption and the absence of transparency, market growth and sustainability cannot be attained.

Addressing another social issue, Prime Minister Wickremesinghe initiated a high level dialogue on *'Ragging'*[n] and sexual and gender-based violence (SGBV) in Sri Lankan universities. This is a very important step in teaching dignity at the school level and at universities. With all these social implications, the much forgotten words of Tagore could help reinvigorate efforts to change society as it is now. No matter how dark the present, optimism is crucial.

Trumpism and the Diplomatic Dragon: Balancing Interests in the New Year[48]

"I'm gonna do what's right, I want to be unpredictable, The voters want unpredictability." — Donald J. Trump

Trumpism thrives. It influences decisions with a sense of unpredictability and the effects of Trumpism on policy has affected the

---

[n] Ragging is the term used for the so-called *'initiation ritual'* practiced in higher education institutions in South Asian countries, including India, Pakistan, Bangladesh, and Sri Lanka. The practice is similar to hazing in North America, bizutage in France, praxe in Portugal, and other similar practices in educational institutions across the world. Ragging involves abuse, humiliation, or harassment of new entrants or junior students by their seniors. It often takes a malignant form wherein the newcomers may be subjected to psychological or physical torture.

entire world. The release of the National Security Strategy articulates and reaffirms his policy of America First. Trump's National Security Advisor H. R. Macmaster[o] explained to BBC that all decisions are carefully calibrated and security risks considered.

At the centre of the Strategy's decisions is the recognition of Jerusalem, the City of David, as the capital of Israel. The city sits on a plateau in the Judaean Mountains between the Mediterranean and the Dead Sea. Through history, the city has been destroyed, besieged, attacked, captured, and recaptured so many times. The city is important for strategic reasons. Geopolitically, it sits in the middle of Middle East. Control of the city has been a constant struggle through time. From 2400 BC, it remains the cradle of the three Abrahamic faiths: Judaism, Christianity, and Islam. The walls around the Old City dividing the city into different quarters were set into place by the Ottoman emperor Suleiman the Magnificent.

Moving into 2018, Trumpism spills deeper through the city walls. The unpredictability threatens and challenges the entire Middle East. US hegemony was seen by its vetoing the UN Security Council resolution calling for the withdrawal of Trump's recognition of Jerusalem as Israel's capital. It was a move backed by every other council member.

As promised during his election campaign, Trump's promise was delivered. This has affected several nations, including Sri Lanka. Sri Lankan resistance to this decision came in the form of a Palestine Parliamentary association and Sri Lanka committee for solidarity with Palestine holding joint protests and signing a declaration against Trump's decision.

The US President warns that he will cut off aid to countries that vote against the US resolution. These unfolding events signal the height of geopolitical tensions unfolding at the dawn of the year. Perhaps, as an indirect consequence and a New Year's gift, Sri Lanka will lose the GSP[p] for their largest export market, the USA.

---

[o] H. R. Macmaster is a retired United States Army officer. In 2017, he became the 26th National Security Advisor, serving under President Donald J. Trump.

[p] The Generalized System of Preferences or GSP is a preferential tariff system which provides for a formal system of exemption from the more general rules of the World Trade Organization.

From the politics of the geography of city walls in the Middle East, I now shift my focus to the politics of geology along ocean scapes.

Along the Indian Ocean geopolitical hotspot, Rama Setu,[q] geologists have found stones along the surface that are older than the sand below it. It indicates avenues to perhaps demystifying the ancient mythological tale of the Ramayan. The bridge may have been human-engineered, built and not natural. If this reveals that the bridge was indeed manmade, the civilisations of Indo-Lanka will be one of the most ancient. The rocks have been dated back 7,000 years. Despite the antiquity of Indo-Lanka relations, the Chinese sphere of influence is undeniable due to the strong strategic relationship built over time. China has already become Sri Lanka's largest trading partner, beating out India. Ripple effects are already being felt even prior to the full functioning of the grand OBOR project.[r] China has acquired 15,000 acres, the largest portion of land ever leased out to a foreign investor for an Economic Zone in recent times. The Economic Zone closer to Hambantota Port, the strategic harbour built by Chinese money, is another pearl in the string of pearls theory that will supposedly surround India. What China has given to nations like Sri Lanka is connectivity to outside world.

Geopolitically, China has made a significant presence with ports and other infrastructure projects in the Indian Ocean region, including investment in Gwadar Port, the *'crown jewel'* of the CPEC corridor,[s] with another $230m grant for a new international airport. Geostrategically, the Chinese have already carved out their access to warm Indian Ocean waters.

Several of these projects are funded by Chinese commercial loans. US Secretary of State Rex Tillerson at a recent lecture at CSIS explained that as these are predatory loans given by China to developing nations, it is important for the US to strengthen its relationship with India to ensure *"it does not become a region of disorder, conflict, and predatory economics."*

---

[q] Ram Setu or Rama's Bridge is a causeway that connects Pamban Island in Tamil Nadu to Mannar Island in Sri Lanka over the sea.
[r] One Belt, One Road (OBOR), also known as the Belt and Road Initiative (BRI), is a project initiated by the Chinese President Xi Jinping.
[s] China Pakistan Economic Corridor is collection of infrastructure projects that are currently under construction throughout Pakistan. The massive bilateral project should improve infrastructure within Pakistan for better trade with China.

Speaking at the monthly Security Salon of the INSS, the security studies think tank, Professor Patrick Mendis described how there is no stopping China from having its military base in Sri Lanka. The present Government and the ones that follow will not have the muscle to stop it. Prime Minister of Sri Lanka denies that he will allow a Chinese base and further pledges to the Indians to lease them the new Chinese-built airport known as the Ghost Airport for US$300m for 40 years. India is set to take over the airport in Mattala to minimise the Chinese influence.

Chinese tourists have constituted about 13% of two million tourist arrivals, denoting a significant yearly increase. Events such as the recent marriage ceremony of 50 Chinese couples shows Sri Lanka has already become a popular destination for Chinese tourists, adding to OBOR cultural relations between the two nations. The Chinese ambassador in Colombo had his farewell bid from a traditional Kung Fu show at the Mahinda Rajapaksa Theatre, which also commemorated 60 years of diplomatic relations and the 65th anniversary of the historic 1952 Rubber-Rice Pact.[t]

The Chinese Ambassador Yi Xianliang played crucial role in Sino-Lankan relations as he had to face the newly appointed Sri Lankan government in 2015. One month after starting his tenure with anti-Chinese sentiment, due to large-scale corruption in Chinese projects initiated during Rajapaksa's tenure, the new administration found themselves in a minefield, having to reverse decisions and rhetoric a presidential election campaign was based upon. The dragon cannot be investigated. Its economic might resonates through the island in a deeply interwoven web of infrastructural support. The speculative argument begs the question: will the transfer to predatory loans become military bases? The Pentagon report released in June that China will establish military bases in Indian Ocean echoes this view.

A view from the Chinese-built Lotus Tower presents a deepening of the above mentioned interconnected global issues. An aerial view of the island surrounded by the Indian Ocean presents a scene of Chinese soft

---

[t] The historic Rubber-Rice Pact was signed by the Minister of Commerce, the late R.G Senanayake, and his Chinese counterpart in the presence of then Prime Minister of China, Zhou En Lai in Beijing. This was five years before establishing diplomatic relations. It was the first trade agreement signed by China with a non-communist country.

power and diplomacy sweeping through the island, while global forces contend over the waters that have connected the island through time — the waters of the Indian Ocean.

Sri Lanka: The New Regime and the Revolution[49]

"The most perilous moment for a bad government is one when it seeks to mend its ways." — Alexis de Tocqueville, *L'Ancien Régime et la Révolution (1856)*

At a meeting in Davos in 2017, Chinese President Xi Jinping made a speech supporting the agenda on globalisation. Even Trump said to Davos, "America only does not mean America alone," even as, back in the US, he was highlighting the importance of the US confining its national boundaries. The president received a standing ovation for a speech that resonated the importance of collective action to build a better world. However, the global reality, with its increasing political fractures, tells a different story.

Sri Lanka too is witness to political bipolarity at a critical moment in the island's political narrative. For a closer examination of the developments underway in Sri Lanka, a study of the '*Silent Revolution*' of 2015 against the monumental French Revolution provides illuminating points for analysis. Alexis de Tocqueville's[u] ideas on the French Revolution state that the "*chief permanent achievement of the French revolution was the suppression of those political institutions, commonly described as feudal, which for many centuries had held unquestioned sway in most European countries. The revolution set out to replace them with a new social and political order, at once simple and more uniform, based on the concept of equality of all men.*"

In comparison, what did the Sri Lanka's Silent Revolution achieve? Did the present government take precautions to make sure that nothing from the past would be imported into the new regime? What kind of process did the new regime follow? And what restrictions were set to differentiate themselves in every possible way? Was the word "*revolution*" used simply to fulfil a political aspiration?

---

[u] Alexis de Tocqueville was a French philosopher and statesman.

Messages from the leadership are loud but inconsistent. Sufficiently exposed to bipolar political promises, public absorption of rhetoric has reached exhaustion. This is a poor note to send the electorate after they have cast their vote at the local elections in Sri Lanka. Looking at this bipolarity from the top, one could design a *'political bipolar index'* (PBI) to assess local leaders' (lack of) responsibility.

For politicians, political power remains the raison d'être. The struggle toward electoral victory, subsequent power struggles, and influence over public policy is visible across societies. In certain dignified societies, persuasion remains an acceptable choice over coercion. However, in some societies, politicians prefer the baton, tear gas, and machine guns. In an orderly society, coercion and conflict are transferred from the battleground to councils of law.

Some regimes have the muscle to ward off a revolution while others fail. Sri Lanka's Rajapaksa regime failed to ward off the Silent Revolution in 2015. It was a peaceful revolution by ballot. To apply Tocqueville's words, *"The regime which is destroyed by a revolution is almost always an improvement on its immediate predecessor, and experience teaches that the most critical moment for bad governments is the one which witnesses their first steps toward reform."* Today, the Sri Lankan government is experiencing what Tocqueville wrote in 1856 on the French Revolution.

The result of local government elections revealed the mood of the polity. Local elections remain a perfect barometer to identify political cyclones on the horizon. Then one could also name the next revolution *'Silent Revolution 2.0'* in 2020. An actual revolutionary scenario will offer new faces and fresh voices. However, such a reality remains doubtful.

Sri Lanka celebrated 70 years of independence on 4 February this year (2018). The country displayed its achievements since independence in the print and electronic media. Alongside its achievements, the country has also faced a nearly thirty-year war with two youth insurrections in 1971 and 1989. The revolt was against the political system of that time, which failed to create better economic conditions, particularly in the field of employment. The situation has not improved. The economic condition worsens with high borrowing and debt. This was clearly indicated by the latest Moody's Asia Pacific rating. Sri Lanka did not rank favourably, especially when compared with 24 Asia Pacific countries. Earlier, the World Economic Forum's Global Competitiveness Index report reflected the same dismal ratings.

Since independence, successive governments have failed to make Sri Lanka a developed nation. A toxic mix of high-level corruption and bad governance remain at the heart of the problem. According to senior journalist Malinda Senevirathne,[v] *"a system of government run by the worst, least qualified or most unscrupulous citizens"* and an absence of technocrats with the right skill set to deliver could be the cause of this situation.

President Sirisena's findings from the Central Bank Bond Commission and the revelation of malpractice to the public should be appreciated. His actions reflected transparency at the highest level. In a country like Sri Lanka where the appearance of civil power is little more than a wispy gauze veiling the reality of political power, disclosures from the Bond Commission are grist for the mill of politics-as-usual and not a force disrupting the status quo. Only if appropriate action is taken report and the funds recovered to the public can progress be measured in terms of restoring civil power over political power.

In this revolutionary political moment that began in 2015, revolutions within revolutions are needed to harness the scattered and disgruntled polity. The ballot in hand has proven that the results will be a clear epiphany.

Maritime Security in the Indian Ocean — A Geopolitical Perspective from Sri Lanka and the Role of the EU in the Indian Ocean Region (IOR)[50]

Sri Lanka's geostrategic position in the Indian Ocean

As Napoleon once said, *"to know a nation's geography is to know its foreign policy"*.[51] In terms of '*geopolitical manometers*',[52] Sri Lanka's geographical position in the Indian Ocean has been the most significant driver of its foreign policy and arguably other countries' foreign policy

---

[v] Malinda Seneviratne is a Sri Lankan poet, critic, journalist, translator, political commentator, and activist.

towards it since ancient times. The Greeks, Arabs, Portuguese, Chinese, Dutch, French, and the English have all seen the importance of the island's geographical position. Today, Sri Lanka's foreign policy, delineated by President Sirisena, is an *"Asia-centric middle-path foreign policy"*,[53] stemming from the island's geography and its relationship with regional and extra-regional countries.

With regard to the relevance of Sri Lanka in terms of geopolitics, analyst Robert Kaplan explains, *"It's a great age in history to be a Chinese civil engineer; they are really building things the way the US built infrastructure in the 1930s and 50s. The opening up of Chinese built Hambantota Port in Sri Lanka has real geopolitical significance"*.[54] In fact, a century ago, Admiral Mahan saw the strategic importance of the Indian Ocean, followed by many other geopolitical scholars throughout history. In the present day, Harsh V. Pant further elaborates, *"The 'Great Game' of this century will be played on the waters of the Indian Ocean."*[55]

Furthermore, Sri Lanka is geographically at the centre of sea lines of communication (SLOC), geo-strategically at the heart of Indian Ocean and therefore a *'super-connector'*. At one of the initial Belt and Road conferences in Hong Kong a few years ago, I referred to Sri Lanka as a *'super-connector'* in the Indian Ocean (in a similar context to a trading hub) in comparison to the island of Hong Kong located next to the massive geographical land mass of China. Notably, Sri Lanka has been mapped as an elongated island even by ancient cartographers, stemming from Ptolemy of Alexandria,[56] due to its rich trade with the West and the East. From a historical perspective, the east of Sri Lanka, specifically the strategic port of Trincomalee,[w] was of great interest to the French. On 22 March 1672, the great French fleet arrived in Trincomalee with more than 2,250 men on board with 251 guns, under the command of Jacob Blaquet de la Haye.[57] In hindsight, this was a strategic move to position French military power in the Indian Ocean. However, this manoeuvre was cut short by the Dutch presence and the interest in the island.

Nevertheless, in the present day, Sri Lanka has managed to navigate its critical geographical location at the crossroads of the important sea lines of communication (SLOCs). The island has thus displayed its

---

[w] Trincomalee is a port city on the northeast coast of Sri Lanka.

catalytic ability in balancing three powerful spheres of influence: the regional hegemon in South Asia that is India, the US, and China. As such, Sri Lanka is playing a larger role in the South Asian Indian Ocean littorals, in order to protect the proximate SLOCs and its own maritime domain.

In terms of international relations, there is a marked geopolitical power shift from the Atlantic Ocean to the Indo-Pacific. Analysing geopolitical manometers, Sri Lanka faces the complex geography of the Indian subcontinent intertwined with India's past Monroe Doctrine mentality and Prime Minister Modi's new vision for the region.[58] I have discussed this aspect in detail, in a chapter I contributed to the book *The Modi Doctrine*.[59] Additionally, with regards to international relations, one of the biggest setbacks in the region is the absence of the SAARC summit due to India-Pakistan tensions subverting regional forums such as these. Nevertheless, policy-makers around the world including in the European Union (EU) ought to pay closer attention to the vast developments in the IOR. There is an increasing naval presence with military capabilities built up in various strategic positions along the IOR rim. Nations like Sri Lanka, sitting at the heart of SLOCs with large amounts of cargo and transshipment capacity, will be significantly important for the existing and the emerging powers in this geopolitical backdrop.

Triple spheres of influence

The teardrop-shaped island hanging off the southern tip of Indian subcontinent is faced with triple spheres of influence from China, India, and the US. The Sri Lankan port of Hambantota was leased out to China for operations last year, just like Kyaukpyu[x] Port in Myanmar.[60] India views these strategic indents in its territorial waters as an encirclement strategy by the Chinese, speculatively calling it a '*String of Pearls*'.[61] While India is faced with the fear of encirclement, the country is also investing to actively counter the Chinese sphere of influence in the region. Indian interest

---

[x] Kyaukpyu is a major town in Rakhine State, in western Myanmar. It is located on the north western corner of Yanbye Island on Combermere Bay, and is 250 miles north-west of Yangon.

towards the Eastern port of Trincomalee and the Chinese-built Mattala airport[y] closer to the Hambantota Port are clear examples of such an investment in the Sri Lankan context.

The Sri Lankan maritime forum *Galle Dialogue*, introduced by former Secretary of Defence Gotabaya Rajapaksa, has become another popular venue for discussion about the topics from '*strategic maritime partnerships*' to '*collaborative approaches in the Indian Ocean*' and thereby showcases Sri Lanka's interest and role in the Indian Ocean.

In the Sri Lankan context, the last time a People's Liberation Army Navy (PLAN) submarine was docked in Colombo,[62] tensions arose with New Delhi and intense speculation was rampant in strategic circles. New Delhi officially expressed their concern, reminding Sri Lanka that it should inform India first of such submarine dockings as it has a direct bearing on India's national security. In response, Sri Lanka informed its neighbour that the PLAN submarine visit was not a knee jerk reaction to a Chinese request but a carefully calibrated action by the Government of Sri Lanka. The increased investment by Beijing in Sri Lankan infrastructure is a clear sign of the Chinese sphere of influence in the island and Sri Lanka's receipt of such influence.

The opening of the tallest tower in South Asia — the '*Lotus Tower*', built by the Chinese in Colombo — set off another widely discussed topic in India. This was over the concern that the antenna at the top of the tower could be used for monitoring and surveillance by the Chinese Government. Thus, the growing Indo-China tension is felt clearly across the region. The Sir Lankan Government position has been to find equilibrium between these two powers. But to give equal space in the maritime domain will be a challenging task. Last year, China surpassed India in becoming the largest trading partner for Sri Lanka, thereby signalling a strategic shift. However, it can be contented that India, being the closer neighbour to Sri Lanka, has had a stronger historical and cultural relationship with the island, especially with reference to the '*Kaveri Delta*'[z] sphere of influence

---

[y] Mattala Rajapaksha International Airport is an international airport serving southeast Sri Lanka. It is located in the town of Mattala.

[z] Kaveri delta, also referred as Ponni, is an Indian river following through the states of Karnataka and Tamil Nadu.

from South India towards the north of Sri Lanka as well as the political influence from Tamil Nadu[aa] towards Sri Lankan politics.

Let us return to the point about India's Monroe Doctrine mentality, referring to Jawaharlal Nehru's selected works.[63] It can be argued from this frame of reference that India followed a similar model to the Monroe Doctrine which is to exclude extra regional powers from the vicinity of India and the IOR. This would constitute strategic thinking on the part of modern India's determination to rid the subcontinent of residual colonial influence and exclude other powers from the entire South Asian region.[64] This is further explained by Bhabani Sen Gupta as an underlying theme in Indian strategic thinking, where the presence of outside powers in India's neighbourhood is illegitimate and therefore India's neighbours must solely rely upon India as a regional manager and security provider.[65] Furthermore, the scholar K. Subrahmanyam expounds the fact that leadership in the Indian Ocean is part of India's *'manifest destiny'*.[66]

On a regional level, India has resisted inviting Pakistan to join the Indian Ocean Rim Association (IORA) or allowing China to become a full member of the Indian Ocean Naval Symposium (IONS). On the other hand, India is building up its massive naval fleet with 48 warships under construction, including one aircraft carrier, one nuclear submarine and six conventional submarines as well as a variety of destroyers, frigates and corvettes.[67] By 2027 the Indian naval capacity is projected to expand to 198 warships.[68]

When looking at the US sphere of influence, according to USPACOM Commander Harry Harris, "*the Indian Ocean matters to the United States, Sri Lanka matters to the United States, and the United States matters to Sri Lanka*".[69] US interest in Sri Lanka and the surrounding South Asian maritime security architecture is felt with the growing Chinese influence in the South China Sea and the spill-over influence on the IOR. Presently, Sri Lanka is considered by the US as a contributor to the rules-based order in the Indian Ocean system, and a good example of a like-minded partner in the Indian Ocean Region.

[aa] Tamil Nadu, a South Indian state, is famed for its Dravidian-style Hindu temple.

Maritime security and the role of the EU in IOR

Instability in some of the littorals of the IOR and the rise of new naval powers within the geopolitical power game are the key drivers for insecurity in the Indian Ocean. The maritime rivalry between India and China is visible across the Indian Ocean and felt clearly by nations like Sri Lanka. The modernisation and expansion of China's and India's maritime capabilities to advance their military presence in the IOR make the region vulnerable in terms of security and power-rivalries. The absence of a comprehensive multilateral agreement on maritime security in the Indian Ocean is a highly problematic issue in this context. Arguably, the Indian Ocean Rim Association for Regional Cooperation (IOR-ARC) is for economic cooperation and not for security cooperation. Nevertheless, the Galle dialogue and the IONS (an Indian initiative) bring together the naval chiefs of a large number of littoral countries for discussions on security challenges in the IOR. However, forums such as the ASEAN Regional Forum (ARF) aimed at South-East Asia, with ministerial level representation explicitly addressing maritime security issues that involve both regional countries and extra-regional major powers are, in comparison, clearly lacking in the IOR. The Indian Ocean Conference (IOC), which was begun in 2016 by the India Foundation[70] with its inaugural meeting in Singapore and followed last year in Colombo, is arguably the only conference to address important issues of the IOR at both a ministerial and an academic level; but it has its limitations due to the degree of extra regional representation. At the Indian Ocean conference in 2017 in Colombo, Prime Minister Ranil Wickremesinghe emphasised that *"we remain convinced that a code of conduct that ensures the freedom of navigation in our Ocean will be an essential component of this vision"*.[71]

Now let us examine how the EU could play a role in the Indian Ocean Region.

Fighting piracy, counter-terrorism, and providing safe passage for the large amount of trade between the EU and IOR littorals is a high priority. Thus, the EU could assist IOR countries to establish and maintain a code of conduct — the essential component of the vision for a peaceful IOR.

In 1971, an ad-hoc committee was established with seven European members in the UN General Assembly's Declaration of the Indian Ocean as a Zone of Peace.[72] This Declaration called for Great Powers to curb further escalation and expansion of their military presence in the Indian Ocean.[73] Establishment of a system of universal collective security is also embedded in the Declaration. Sri Lankan Prime Minister Sirimavo Bandaranaike[ab] played an important role in this endeavour and today we should revisit this Declaration due to the geopolitical tension among Great Powers in the IOR, which has made the region unstable.

In this context, the EU should play an active and long-term role as a contributor to maritime security in the IOR, especially given the risk of emerging Great Power rivalries, which pose a fundamental threat to security in the IOR and its littoral states. To establish a rules-based ocean system of governance and a framework of multilateral maritime security, the EU could develop a strategic plan, like an initiative to work with the Indian Ocean's littoral states to establish a track-II platform comparable to the Council for Security Cooperation in the Asia Pacific (CSCAP)[74] for dialogue on maritime security in the IOR. Such a platform could provide the groundwork for preparing frameworks and mechanisms for cooperation amongst all IOR littorals.

The EU should coordinate closely with existing multilateral security initiatives such as the UN Ad-Hoc Committee on the Indian Ocean and IOR-ARC as well as IONS and SAARC.

By taking such an active role in these areas, the EU could enhance security cooperation and strengthen security dialogue. An island nation like Sri Lanka, which has a role to play in balancing the triple spheres of influence, fighting maritime piracy, and ensuring a rules-based order in the Indian Ocean, could stand to benefit by a more active role played by the EU in the IOR. This would further reduce mistrust and threat perception among actors in the IOR and its waters.

[ab] Sirimavo Bandaranaike was a Sri Lankan stateswoman. She became the world's first female head of government.

Chapter 4

Peace Building and Reconciliation

"He felt unwanted because he wasn't allowed to come home."

Sithie Tiruchelvam[a]

---

[a] Ms. Tiruchelvam speaking about her husband Dr. Neelan Tiruchelvam, the internationally respected academic and peace maker who was assassinated by Tamil Tigers. New York Times on 24 August 1999. "Sri Lanka Peacemaker's High-Risk Life, and Death" by Celia Dugger.

Racism, Riots, and the Sri Lankan State[1]

"One's life has value so long as one attributes value to the life of others, by means of love, friendship, indignation, and compassion." — Simone de Beauvoir

Only when fear and hatred is spread by extremists does serious reflection haunt a community. The teardrop-shaped island of Sri Lanka, a seeming paradise hanging off the Indian subcontinent, has been provoked yet again. Within a few hours arose an ugly incident of violence, the hill country's vibrant colours serving as a backdrop to death and destruction — a systematic breakdown of lives, religious spaces, and personal property.

The July 1983 riots, insurrections quashed in 1971 and 1989, and 2014 Aluthgama[b] riots were among these unexpected bursts of violence. In all cases, the unprepared state reacted slowly before resorting to brute force to restore order. How could Sri Lanka become riven by hostility and terror in a short time? Recent events suggest that this question deserves further attention and study to better inform the work of policymakers.

The present situation in Sri Lanka is that of a nation plunged into a state of emergency with a heavily state-influenced media. Terrorism exercised blatantly in the streets by violent, extremist nationalists to harm other religious or ethnic groups should not be met with silence, especially in a town that treasures Buddha's Temple of the Sacred Tooth Relic, which symbolises the purity of the words of non-violence uttered by Buddha. Extremists should be punished to restore the rule of law in society, regardless of the religious or political affiliations of the perpetrators.

Violence was sparked by the death of a Sinhalese Buddhist man on 4 March, who was allegedly attacked by three Muslim men due to a traffic accident in Teldeniya.[c] Following this, a state of emergency was declared by the Government. The last time a state of emergency was in place was during the country's 26-year civil war with the Tamil Tigers. During the

---

[b] Aluthgama is a coastal town in Kalutara District in the Western Province of Sri Lanka.
[c] Teldeniya is a village in Sri Lanka. It is located within Central Province. It was the epicenter of racially motivated attacks on the Sri Lanka Muslim minority by mobs led by Buddhist monks in 2018.

quarter century-long war, one of the most significant incidents that triggered communal violence among the Sinhala Buddhist majority and the Tamil minority was the 1983 riots. Yet neither the majority of Sinhalese Buddhists nor Tamils were part of the riots. It was terrorists, extremist nationalists — mainly Sinhalese Buddhists — who set off anti-Tamil pogroms in the south. The government at that time was silent and so were prominent members of the majority religious community, including the preachers of Buddha's words of *'Ahimsa'* (*'do no harm'*), just like the present.

The recent racially and communally-minded riots targeting the Muslim minority by certain segments of the majority Sinhalese Buddhist community was a warning of the deteriorating threads holding together Sri Lankan society. Yet it was several days later that the Government tightened its control over the ugly situation by blocking social media platforms through which *'fake news'* was disseminated to create more tension. Stories of exploding Muslim population growth and surreptitious administering of sterilization pills to Sinhalese were attempts to escalate the situation by pandering to extremist elements promoting hatred and fear. The vulnerability to social distress and division caused by *'fake news'* in Sri Lanka is high in the persisting shadow of ethnic tensions. The central aim of a nation on the path to reconciliation should be to ensure zero tolerance for hate speech and violent nationalism.

On a recent visit among fellow South Asian and East Asian researchers at a programme on *'Digitization in Asia and Germany'* with a special focus of tackling fake news, this author was present at the Berlin Ministry of Information and Foreign Affairs on the day the Ministry's website was hacked. Not limited to smaller nations like Sri Lanka, cybercrime prevails. Tackling fake news is a costly and serious challenge. Sri Lanka could learn from Germany, which has taken rigorous steps to tackle fake news deemed dangerous to public peace and discourse. The 2018 Network Enforcement Act (NEA) aimed at major social networks without much radical alteration to existing German law is only a restatement to German panel code. Social media companies are now setting up legal compliance offices specifically for the NEA. Facebook in Germany has hired over one thousand content moderators to comply with NEA.

Fake news aside, President Maithripala Sirisena's[d] Government has taken measures to curb the tension. However, it should not allow violent nationalists to routinely and easily spread their message, as this runs counter to the Government's wishes to achieve sincere reconciliation in the country. A Sedition Act to prevent hate speech and swift action could ease the situation and assist the process of seeking ethnic harmony.

The perpetrators of these vicious attacks should be punished. If unpunished, extremists working towards different agendas will take advantage of the opportunity to dominate the narrative and shape the national agenda. *'Fake news'* and misinformation could construct a powerful narrative that would gain traction and detrimentally influence society. This would be a dangerous path, perpetuating and exacerbating instability across the nation. Examples of this phenomenon have played out globally in recent years, from the US and Europe to the far corners of Asia. Yet Sri Lanka cannot become another Myanmar and it is the role of majority Buddhists and clergy to ensure this is not the case, to defeat the ideologies of extremism.

To make sense of and exist safely in the midst of rising extremism and violent nationalism, it is vital to promote the true essence of various religions. An attempt to address fear and hatred spread by extremism can be made by placing an emphasis on the ethic of non-violence. This task will require a sturdy and responsible government safeguarding justice and the rule of law. But as the past reflects, it could also choose to do little while leaving the innocent to burn.

Re-building Sri Lanka: An Island at a Crossroads[2]

In 1908, Mahatma Gandhi[e] said, *"[the] English have not taken India, we have given it to them."*[3] This expression is applicable to Sri Lanka as well when one observes how some elites handed the island nation over to Britain with the optimism of better rule. Before the Indian subcontinent

---

[d] Maithripala Yapa Sirisena is a Sri Lankan politician and the 7th and current President of Sri Lanka, in office since January 2015.
[e] Mahātmā Gandhi was an Indian activist who led the Indian independence movement against British rule.

won back its independence, Britain ruled the region with the support of fewer than 100,000 troops and managed to control 400 million people via draconian policies and supporting local allies who worked to secure the British interests.[4] Irrespective of the upper hand they enjoyed due to advanced military technology, this was possible largely due to their capacity to divide targeted populations and co-opt locals into becoming British allies. This *'divide and rule strategy'*[f] was employed in Sri Lanka too; and the communal discrimination and differences between different ethnic groups fuelled by the colonial British rulers at that time continues to overshadow the Sri Lankan nation even today.

Sri Lankan President Mathripala Sirisena's dissolution of the gazette notification[5] issued by the British rulers, which declared 82 rebels as traitors during the 1818 rebellion, is remarkable in this regard. Some of the Sri Lankans who had fought in the rebellion had been assassinated in cruel ways., while others were exiled and imprisoned outside the country. Several decades on, a Sri Lankan President was bold enough to remember the country's national heroes who had sacrificed their lives for an independent Sri Lanka.[6] Many countries still remember the gross human rights violations and plunder of national wealth during the British colonial period. To date, the resultant scars run deep in post-colonial societies.

In another positive development, President Sirisena's *'Asia-centric balanced'* foreign policy has delivered results, winning support and trust from several world leaders. The levels of external pressure witnessed during the past are no longer visible and have drastically diminished, owing to the commitment to rectify the situation. However, at the UNHRC, the Sri Lankan foreign minister assured the Commission that *"the Constitution drafting process is for us both central and essential not only for democratization, but also for ensuring non-recurrence of conflict...The Parliamentary process and referendum are, for us, imperative."*[7] This was in response to the criticism levied by the UN of the Sri Lankan mechanism being *"worryingly slow,"*[8] accusing the latter's leadership of neglecting the widespread torture and abuse that are still a reality in the country.

---

[f] *'Divide and Rule'* — the policy of maintaining control over one's subordinates or opponents by encouraging dissent between them, thereby preventing them from uniting in opposition.

In Sri Lanka, different members of the Government have also voiced different opinions on the Constitutional process. Thus, the practice of sending mixed signals has not helped the Government much. Therefore, an internal consensus has to be reached on the Constitutional process and the possibility of a referendum.

Neville Ladduwahetty, in his recent article The Referendum Trap,[9] clearly explains that it is also vital to consider how "unintended consequences would be exploited by the Tamil leadership both nationally and internationally to make claims for the right of self-determination followed by other claims that go far beyond what was intended through Constitutional Reforms"[10] and argues that this "is the end game the Tamil leadership is striving for by pushing for a referendum."[11] What if the referendum has dual outcomes such as a huge loss in the South and a victory in the North? It will clearly send a message of further division in the polity.

Similarly, President Sirisena's stance regarding the UNHRC appeal for a hybrid court has been clear, in that he will not allow foreign judges into the process and has explained that the local judicial process is dependable and capable.[12] At a recent event, President Sirisena reiterated his position by saying, *"I am not going to allow non-Governmental organizations to dictate how to run my Government. I will not listen to their calls to prosecute my troops."*[13] Having foreign judges in Sri Lanka will definitely aggravate political tensions.

Thus, it is apparent that Sri Lanka still suffers from an imperial hangover, as the West (albeit different countries than in the past) is still interfering in the post-war reconciliation process. There are three essential elements that can be easily introduced to bring credibility and results to the local reconciliation process. First, the Government could consider international engagement with institutions such as *Interpeace*,[14] a reputed body which could be used to provide technical assistance for the reconciliation process with terms of reference from the Government. In January 2016, the Director General of Sri Lanka's Reconciliation taskforce met the Director General of *Interpeace*.[15] Unfortunately, there has been no forward movement since then. Second, certain recommendations of the eight national reconciliation conferences conducted during 2011–2015 could be implemented.[16] Civil society contributed significant recommendations vis-a-vis the outcome reports of the eight conferences. Third, top priority must be given to fostering Tamil Nadu-Sri Lanka relations and Sri Lankan diaspora re-engagement strategies.

There is much to be done to heal the hearts and minds in the deeply divided Sri Lankan community. It is hoped that one of these options succeeds in becoming a lasting policy. As a wise *Wazir*[g] in 9th century Baghdad once said: *"the basis of Government is jugglery. If it works, and lasts, it becomes policy."*[17]

Understanding Our 'Blind Spot' to Make Peace Building Comprehensive[18]

"The sailor cannot see the North —but knows the needle can." — Emily Dickinson[19]

The young soldiers and Tamilians who sacrificed their lives for a cause created by a previous generation perhaps did not know the underlying politics of why they had to fight. The younger generation has taken up a burden passed to them by certain political leaders that they have neither seen nor heard. On the other hand, at the Apartheid Museum[20] in Johannesburg, South Africa, one can study the apartheid period and understand what has gone wrong. Photographs of racial discrimination (such as separate walkways for transport) and even the most horrific portrayals of apartheid are exhibited at the museum. What if Sri Lanka had a museum to educate our younger generations of our past mistakes, such as the burning of the Jaffna Library[h] and the bombing of the Central Bank[i] by the LTTE, among other atrocities?

---

[g] A Wazir is a high-ranking official, such as the Chief Minister of Muslim regimes starting with the Abbasid Caliphate.

[h] The burning of the Jaffna Public Library was an important event in the Sri Lankan civil war. An organised mob went on a rampage on the night of 1 June 1981, burning the library. At the time of its destruction, the library was one of the biggest in Asia, containing over 97,000 books and manuscripts.

[i] The Central Bank bombing was one of the deadliest terrorist attacks carried out by the LTTE. The attack took place on 31 January 1996. A truck containing about 440 pounds of high explosives crashed through the main gate of the Central Bank of Sri Lanka. As gunmen traded fire with security guards, the suicide bomber in the lorry detonated the massive bomb. The lorry was followed by a three-wheeler, carrying two LTTE cadres armed with automatic rifles and an RPG launcher.

The recent *'Eluga Tamil'*[21] (*Let Tamils Rise!*) demonstrations will serve neither the younger generation nor the Sri Lankan nation at large. The aforementioned slogan was used and given much hype by the Chief Minister of the Northern Province, C.V. Wigneswaran. How does a rising of one ethnic group help another, at a time when the nation is going through reconciliation to attain ethnic harmony?

If we look at the international arena, we can see that the modern world is in the Fourth Industrial Revolution.[j] Our lives, however, still revolve around the slogans of old ideas of the yesteryears. White officers shooting African Americans and many other incidents around the world are still racially fuelled because most of us are wired in that way due to the environment we live in.

The Race Implicit Association Test (IAT[22]) is a good test to examine how biased we are towards our own race and how we see others. As a nation, we Sri Lankans have been living with these biases for a long time. According to Mahzarine Banaji and Anthony Greenwald,[23] we all have hidden biases, and the phenomenon is called our *'blindspot'*. *'Blindspot'* is a metaphor for the section of the mind that houses hidden biases. *"The authors use it to ask about the extent to which social groups — without our awareness or conscious control — shape our likes and dislikes, our judgments about people's character, abilities, and potential"*.[24]

A progressive society would not associate words and deeds with ethnicity and/or religion. Good people are those of us who strive to align our behaviour with our intentions. Well intentioned people should not speak of a rise of one ethnic group but the rise of a common identity, a Sri Lankan identity. This is the new identity President Maithripala Sirisena wishes to establish in the country with his new vision.

Stereotyping — i.e. associating a group with an attribute — is another area where prejudice manifests. Assuming that all Tamils want *'Eelam'* is such a stereotype. The first scientific research on stereotypes was published in 1933 by Princeton psychologists Daniel Katz and Kenneth Braly.[25] They found that one could identify a group with an attribute that

---

[j] The Fourth Industrial Revolution is described as a range of new technologies that are fusing the physical, digital, and biological worlds, and impacting all disciplines, economies, and industries.

could evolve over time into a different attribute. The 1933 stereotype study of African Americans did not include an association with the word *'athletic'*;[26] but modern studies would likely show such an association. *'Scientific'* and *'technical'* were not part of the 1930s stereotype study[27] of people of Chinese origin but almost certainly appear in modern day stereotypes. Thus, a race with one set of attributes could evolve to have different attributes with societal changes over time. Certain issues of the world tied to racism and prejudice have unfortunately remained static and have not evolved in a positive direction, even after violence has manifested in response to such issues. For instance, India and Pakistan are still lost in the past trying to demarcate borders and frontiers.

Indian columnist Dr. Miniya Chatterji[28] rightly points out that in assessing the situation after recent military attacks in India and Pakistan that *"the reality is that we have placed ourselves in a conundrum of our own making. Political institutions were made by us to grant us order in society so that we can busy ourselves with more instinctual activities."*[29] It is important all South Asian leaders refer to this statement and combat the trend of ethnic and religious manipulation to consolidate power.

The Darkest Day in the City of Lights

"A man without ethics is a wild beast loosed upon this world." — Albert Camus[30]

The *Charlie Hebdo*[k] massacre in January 2015, which took the lives of 12 people,[31] was the second terror attack in Paris this year. Another series of attacks resulted in the loss of 129 innocent civilians on the evening of 13 November 2015.[32] This was a carefully planned and coordinated attack in six different locations by eight gunmen. Out of the eight killers, seven committed suicide. The worst of these multiple attacks

---

[k] Charlie Hebdo is a French satirical weekly magazine, featuring cartoons, reports, polemics, and jokes. The publication describes itself as above all secular, skeptic, and atheist, far-left-wing, and anti-racist positions, publishing articles about the extreme right, religion, politics, and culture. The magazine has been the target of two terrorist attacks, in 2011 and 2015. Both were presumed to be in response to a number of controversial Muhammad cartoons it published. In the second of these attacks, 12 people were killed, including the publishing director.

was at a live concert at Bataclan Theatre, which killed more than 80.[33] It was a painful day which will be remembered by the entire world — a particular hit to human values. ISIS, who claim responsibility, have declared a war beyond their geographical area to the entire world.

In another incident of terror, the Russian flight carrying passengers from *Sharm el-Sheik* was bombed,[34] according to Western intelligence agency reports. In addition, another suicide attack in Beirut killed 43 innocent civilians within days of the Paris attacks.[35] These terror acts by the ISIS militant group is a clear message to the Western world. It is perhaps a manifestation of Samuel Huntington's *'Clash of Civilizations'*[36] unfolding between the West and ISIS. We live at a point in history where the height of terrorism has led the world to be desensitised to terror, from 9/11[l] to the Mumbai attacks,[m] not to mention the terror witnessed in our own nation of Sri Lanka.

The French philosopher André Glucksmann's[n] recent passing reminds us that the characteristic form of modern terrorism is nihilism. *"What do extremist ideologies like the Communism or Nazism of yesteryear and the Islamism of today have in common? After all, they support ostensibly very different ideals — mankind united in Socialism, the superior race, the community of Muslim believers (the Umma). Tomorrow, it could be altogether different ideals: some theological, some scientific, others racist. But the common characteristic is nihilism."*[37] Whatever the cause, ISIS killing innocent people is most certainly not a representation of Islam.

World leaders meeting at the G20 conference in Antalya in November 2015[38] could use the summit as an opportunity to adopt a counter-strategy against ISIS. With a coordinated effort from global powers, ISIS could be defeated. Beyond this, every nation should be encouraged to support the fight against ISIS and its extremist ideology; in particular,

---

[l] The September 11 attacks were a series of four coordinated terrorist attacks by the Islamic terrorist group Al-Qaeda on the United States on the morning of Tuesday, September 11, 2001.

[m] The 2008 Mumbai attacks were a group of terrorist attacks that took place in November 2008, when 10 members of Lashkar-e-Taiba, an Islamic terrorist organisation based in Pakistan, carried out a series of 12 coordinated shooting and bombing attacks lasting four days across Mumbai.

[n] André Glucksmann was a French philosopher, activist and writer. He was a member of the French new philosophers.

the Eastern powers of China and India should add their weight to this cause. A political and military solution to ISIS should be ranked as a top priority on the global agenda.

ISIS use of social media[39] for propaganda and their online radicalisation tools are more evident than ever, evidenced by the aforementioned attacks perpetuated by the group, more than any other terrorist group in history. ISIS has also managed to galvanise a mass number of foreign fighters, many of whom are from the US and Europe and who receive training, motivation, and skills in Syria in order to perpetrate attacks on Western soil. The ISIS threat is not only endemic to the West but also includes two dozen threat groups in Asia,[40] which have either pledged support to ISIS or taken an oath of allegiance to Abu Bakr al Baghdadi.º Over 1,000 recruits from Central Asia, South Asia, Southeast Asia, China, Australia, and New Zealand have travelled to Syria and Iraq as foreign terrorist fighters.[41]

The above incidents and statistics give cause for all sectors of society to combat the threat of ISIS head on. Several months ago, at the annual Strategic Studies Summit held in Antalya,[42] on the topic of '*Counter-radicalism policies and strategies: lessons learned and future steps*', this author highlighted the importance of focusing on de-radicalisation and counter-radicalisation programs. In this context, those subject to radicalisation should engage in rehabilitation programs with the assistance of civil society. Furthermore, civil society and governments can work in partnership to prevent radicalisation by tackling economic, social, and political drivers of such radicalisation. When governments set policy frameworks in countering terrorism, they should do so by providing funding and addressing the structural causes of radicalisation, which is a central factor leading to terrorism. However, communities also need to play their part for the overall approach to be successful. Civil society has a role to play to counter messages of radicalisation and often it will be more effective when counter-radicalisation initiatives come from communities rather than governments. Another focus area is the enhancement of the intelligence apparatus, as Paris and a few other attacks demonstrated a

---

º Abū Bakr al-Baghdadi is the leader of the Salafi jihadist militant terrorist organisation known as the Islamic State of Iraq and the Levant, which controls territory in several countries.

failure in the intelligence capabilities of states. A nation like Sri Lanka, which has battled terrorism for nearly three decades, could provide expertise to fight terrorism. Our military and intelligence services have shown that any terrorist outfit can be destroyed with the right strategy and skill. All nations including Sri Lanka should invest in national security and strategic defence studies, an important area that is underinvested in by many nations.

As President Obama rightly stated at the G20 meeting in 2015: "The killing of innocent people based on a twisted ideology is an attack not just on France, not just on Turkey, it is an attack on the civilized world".[43] The world needs a secure order and we should not underestimate the threat from terrorists in destabilising this order. Today, a nation may mourn the victims of a terrorist attack and the ripple effects of such acts may shock the world. Yet the nature of terror is capricious; tomorrow, it may affect another nation altogether. On the darkest day in the city of lights, we all should stand together to defeat terrorism.

Sri Lanka and the World: Terrorism and Effective Reconciliation[44]

"There is no other solution to the Syrian crisis than strengthening the effective government structures and rendering them help in fighting terrorism." — Vladimir Putin[45]

With the on-going Russian bombing campaign in Syria, for the first time, Syrian President Bashar al-Assad[p] has shown confidence in defeating ISIS. The sustained destruction caused by ISIS in Syria is nothing short of a human tragedy. According to the *Syrian Observatory for Human Rights,* over 200,000 Syrians have been killed since the start of the country's civil war in 2011.[46] Millions of refugees fleeing Syria have become one of the biggest issues in terms of uncontrolled mass migration for Europe. ISIS' brutality has drastically affected important

---

[p] Bashar al-Assad is the 19th and current President of Syria, holding the office since 17 July 2000. He is also commander-in-chief of the Syrian Armed Forces, General Secretary of the ruling Arab Socialist Ba'ath Party, and Regional Secretary of the party's branch in Syria.

infrastructure and has also caused the destruction of historical sites in Syria, such as the Arch of Triumph[q] in Palmyra.

Survival is more important to the Syrian population's interests than the power play between the global actors engaged in the country. The Syrians and neighbouring nations want a safe and better life. Unfortunately, global actors have miserably failed to address this crisis so far. A grand alliance to defeat the brutal terrorist group could create a measure of hope. However, dismantling the supply of weaponry to the terrorist outfit and weakening the group will be key to the defeat of ISIS.

A Sri Lankan lesson is relevant here. Valiant armed soldiers of the Sri Lankan military and intelligence community defeated the LTTE, cutting off all weapons supplies to precision. Sri Lanka proved to the entire world that any terrorist outfit can be destroyed with political will and with the bravery of a dedicated military. In his recent remarks at the UN,[47] incumbent Sri Lankan President Maithripala Sirisena clearly stated that his country's experience could be studied by other developing countries affected by terrorism. He further stated that Sri Lanka was prepared to engage in an active dialogue with those affected countries and would continue to campaign against terrorism.

Recently, the Office of the United Nations High Commission for Human Rights (OHCHR[48]) released its report[49] containing disturbing revelations on Sri Lanka. Several groups in the country have voiced their opinions on the matter. Some opposed the investigation report, citing it as a threat to the country's sovereignty and viewing it as undermining the Sri Lankan judicial system. On the other hand, the TNA and the Tamil diaspora organizations such as the Global Tamil Forum (GTF)[r] have praised the report and pressed for its recommendations to be implemented in the country.

GTF spokesperson Suren Surendiran urged the 47 members of UNHRC to implement recommendations to set up the special court for criminal prosecution. Surendiran added that the GTF wouldn't compromise

---

[q] The Monumental Arch was a Roman ornamental archway in Palmyra, Syria. Its ruins later became one of the main attractions of Palmyra until it was officially destroyed by ISIS in 2015.

[r] Global Tamil Forum is an International Tamil organisation meant to further Tamil causes in Tamil areas of Sri Lanka.

under any circumstances. Meanwhile, the Sri Lankan Minister of Foreign Affairs Mangala Samaraweera has assured the international community of a domestic mechanism to probe the issue within eighteen months.[50] According to Samaraweera, the Government is ready to accept international support.

It is also evident that the previous regime, with its more hard line nationalistic stance, illiberal political decisions, such as the 18th amendment[51] to extend Presidential powers and include independent commissions under the President as well as the removal of the Chief Justice of Sri Lanka's Supreme Court,[52] are a direct cause of the state of our nation today. Thus, a clear stumbling block of the previous political regime was their lack of engagement with the Tamil diaspora and under-investing in the reconciliation process. Reconciliation requires engagement to progress.

The challenge for Sri Lanka, with regards to the OHCHR report, is the recommendation to implement a hybrid court to prosecute against alleged war crimes.[53] The author's opinion on the matter is that it is important to involve and obtain international technical assistance from globally reputed agencies in addressing reconciliation. Assistance in reconciliation should come with a Terms of Reference (TOR) on the way the Sri Lankan government wants to engage with international partners on reconciliation. Taking lessons from the past, we should engage with the international community while also always protecting our sovereignty as a nation. Any truth and reconciliation model requires time and patience to find sustainable solutions — whether it be in Syria or in Sri Lanka.

Sri Lanka: Toward a Diaspora Re-Engagement Plan[54]

"There is an unofficial leader of the opposition. What we have is confusion; there are MPs of the same party in Government as well as in the opposition."— Anura Kumara Dissanayaka, JVP Leader[55]

With the Parliament of Sri Lanka in a state of dissolution and elections looming ahead, the costs confronting the nation remain high. Three billion rupees was spent on the last election and four billion on the upcoming election, according to the election commissioner.[56] It is hoped that the return on investment of the people's money will be worth the exorbitant spending. Colossal expenditure in the name of statecraft should help reap rich benefits, and the country awaits the promised gains. Now, the priority is to elect the best representatives for the next few years to the Parliament.

In the name of regime change and developmental politics, the country faced a large-scale reshuffling of roles in the public service with strategic positions in the nation's administration being vacated overnight. Will August see a repeat of January's changes? If so, the year 2015 will be marked as a year wasted. It is hoped that the same old actors do not emerge in the political arena: small nations such as Sri Lanka cannot afford years wasted to this kind of politics.

To fulfil the recommendations of the Commission of Inquiry on the Lessons Learnt and Reconciliation (LLRC[s]), the Foreign Minister held discussions with the GTF in London.[57] Direct engagement with these groups (some of whom are former sympathisers of the LTTE) ensures multi-faceted debate. While some see engagement with the GTF as a positive step, others brand it illegal. GTF and many other diaspora organisations supported the ideology of LTTE and were therefore deemed terrorist fronts by the previous Government through a gazette notification.[58] Under UN Security Council Resolution 1373,[59] 15 LTTE fronts were proscribed with effect from 1 April 2014. Recently, Suren Surendran and GTF requested a review of the list of organisations and individuals proscribed in the gazette notification.[60] If the Government takes them off the list, this would have a serious impact on the re-engagement process with the diaspora. It may open the door towards greater reconciliation. On the other hand, it may also risk strengthening the LTTE network and cause its re-emergence. How does the Government decide whom to talk to and whom not to? Are the listed organizations willing to drop the LTTE ideology of a separate state?

Local Parliamentary opposition to the Government's actions, raised the all-important question as to how the Foreign Minster could engage in such

---

[s] The Lessons Learnt and Reconciliation Commission was a commission of inquiry appointed by Sri Lankan President Mahinda Rajapaksa in May 2010 after the 26-year-long civil war in Sri Lanka. See: http://slembassyusa.org/downloads/LLRC-REPORT.pdf

talks without prior approval from the cabinet, President, or without informing Parliament. It was further noted that it is illegal to engage in discussions with an organisation listed as a *'terrorist'* organization. MP Vasudeva Nanayakkara said with regards to this: *"They should first give up the Eelam objective and declare that they are not aligned to the LTTE anymore."*[61] Similarly, MP Prof. GL Peiris said that post war stability was at stake due to the Government's failure to take tangible measures to counter the threat posed by the LTTE rump.[62] However, according to Venerable Sobitha Thero, this is a positive step to re-engage with GTF. Given the opposition's scattered response, it is important to reach consensus to introduce solutions that bridge the gap between the Sri Lankan diaspora and those residing in Sri Lanka.

One may ask what the way forward should be. First, the *Eelam* ideology should be fully given up without any further support to the LTTE cause. Following this, the reconciliation process should involve genuine intentions on both sides. Finally, a review of the aforementioned gazetted list could be considered. Notably, it was Suren Surendran who defended the LTTE recruitment of child soldiers and accused the Sri Lankan military of using cluster bombs in his interview with Al Jazeera in 2009.[63] The process of engaging with a person who previously defended the LTTE's position will take time, and therefore, a step-by-step method rather than a one-off process should be looked at. A process that includes the engagement of all stakeholders — not only the Government but also civil society and NGOs — is required. Furthermore, it is important to learn from countries that have worked on reconciliation such as South Africa and Rwanda. Yet Sri Lanka should also develop its own process and model fit for its reconciliation action.

Thus, a comprehensive diaspora re-engagement plan should be prepared by the Foreign Ministry and presented to the Parliament. Rather than taking ad hoc measures, a systematic approach to engaging with these groups is necessary. The engagement plan could include assigning diaspora officers to Sri Lankan embassies to engage with the disconnected diaspora, gather information, and attend to their requests. Most importantly, the re-engagement plan should include input from the opposition members of Parliament, all political parties, and the general public, in order to bring about a truly sustainable method of reconciliation.

Countering Youth Radicalisation in South Asia: A Sri Lankan Perspective[64]

President Sirisena is a great example of someone (one of the only leaders in the world) who has forgiven his own attempted killer — a suicide bomber named Sivaraja Jenivan, who attempted to assassinate him in 2005.The following is a quote from Jenivan: *"if there were a leader such as President Sirisena 50 years ago, the national issue in the country and destruction caused to the country would have never taken place. You are the only leader in the country accepted by all communities and love all communities in an equal manner. I pray to God that you become the real Father of the Nation by resolving the national issue and the issues of political prisoners"*.[65]

Thus, Sri Lanka is a very good example to the entire world for study and reflection, especially concerning radicalisation, as we have experienced the radicalisation of LTTE youth as well as the radicalisation of Southern JVP extremist youth. During his university days, this author established the *Sri Lanka Youth Peace Movement* with a few Sri Lankan university students in Australia, with the objective of raising funds to assist wounded Sri Lankan soldiers. As the author is a victim himself of the LTTE, this action could perhaps be construed as an attempt at revenge for a personal loss. However, with time and listening to different perspectives, the only wise option is to forgive; such was the process that broadened this author's perspective. In Sri Lanka, most of the LTTE suicide attackers were youths with personal grievances that led them to become radicalised. Today's radicalised terrorist was yesterday's youth, most of whom were in a helpless search for acceptance, identity, and opportunity; and with whom, had the Government approached them positively, we could have built a counter narrative.

Youth radicalisation is not a new phenomenon to Sri Lanka. With a prolonged ethnic conflict for nearly three decades, the country has experienced religious as well as political radicalisation in all its manifestations. It was the radicalisation of Tamil youth that rewrote the history of Sri Lanka, adding a crucial chapter to the global history of terrorism. A significant aspect of the LTTE was the introduction of youth to suicide bombing culture. Radicalised Tamil youth were not driven by religious belief but directly by a political cause. The dream of a separate geographical homeland called *Eelam* was created by LTTE leader Velupillai Prabhakaran and every single fighter, especially young children, was ready to die for this cause by means of a cyanide capsule.⁶⁶

This paper will examine youth radicalisation and how to counter it from a Sri Lankan perspective by studying the LTTE Black Tigers, JVP, and subsequent youth radicalisation; the Sri Lankan rehabilitation program for de-radicalisation; the role of civil society in counter radicalisation and de-radicalisation; and the importance of global dignity for youth.

The LTTE Black Tigers

According to M.R. Narayan Swamy, "The members do what the leadership says. Theirs is not to ask why, theirs is to do and die. Matters little what the directive from the leadership is; the leader is always right, he is god, he alone knows what is good for the Tamil community. If the leader orders to kill, it will be carried out — without any question".⁶⁷ On 5 July 1987 the first suicide attack was launched by Vallipuram Vasanthan᛫ (also known as 'Captain Miller') by ramming a truck packed with explosives into a military camp in the north of Sri Lanka. Captain Miller was born in 1966. The son of a bank manager, this 21 year old became the first LTTE Black Tiger Suicide Bomber.

The Black Tiger Brigade operated directly under the command of the LTTE leader Prabhakaran and the Intelligence Chief Pottu Amman. Past evidence has shown that Black Tiger cadres were handpicked by Velupillai Prabakaran. Most carders were youth from families who had been severely affected by the military operations of the Government or opposition groups. Thenmozhi Rajaratnam (also known as *'Dhanu'*) — the garland carrying woman suicide bomber who killed former Indian Prime Minister Rajiv Gandhi — is the prime example. Her family was subjected to severe harassment by the Indian Peace Keeping Force (IPKF) in Sri Lanka.

᛫Vallipuram Vasanthan was a Sri Lankan Tamil rebel and member of the Liberation Tigers of Tamil Eelam, a separatist Tamil militant organisation in Sri Lanka. He was the LTTE's first Black Tiger.

Dhanu was born in 1974 and was 17 years old when she died, exemplifying the kind of youth radicalised by the LTTE cause.

It is said that the LTTE had implemented compulsory military training for all people over the age of 15 in areas under LTTE control in the Vanni region. They had also established a Leopard Brigade[68] ('*Sirasu Puli*') made up of children. By early 1984, the nucleus of the LTTE Baby Brigade was formed.[69] The feature that attracted young minds to the LTTE was the glamour and the perceived respect it was paid by society. These Baby Brigades were used as '*body guards*' and not for suicide missions. In 1998, Sri Lanka's Directorate of Military Intelligence estimated that 60 per cent of LTTE fighters were below the age of 18 and that a third of all LTTE recruits were women.[70] The LTTE leadership mastered the indoctrination of masses, especially the youth. LTTE leaders groomed and motivated their members to sacrifice themselves in suicide attacks and to sacrifice the wellbeing of one's own kith and kin in the pursuit of a violent radical ideology. Radicalisation was the tool used to engage and sustain the LTTE's membership. Therefore, a multifaceted rehabilitation program was necessary to engage the surrendered and apprehended detainees' hearts and minds to facilitate de-radicalisation.

JVP and youth radicalisation

The Janatha Vimukthi Peramuna (JVP), a Communist and Marxist — Leninist party in Sri Lanka, was founded in 1965 with the aim of providing a leading force for a Socialist revolution in the country.[71] Radicalisation of the Sri Lankan youth in the early 1970s was not limited to the northern Tamils. The majority of southern Sinhalese youth, too, were radicalised by Marxist ideologies and took up arms against the Government in an unsuccessful countrywide armed resistance.[72] Like the LTTE, the JVP flourished among the underprivileged and marginalised youth, managing to establish a strong support base at the grassroots level and in universities.

The Sri Lankan rehabilitation program for de-radicalisation

The country's rehabilitation of radicalised youth dates back to the post-insurrection period in the south in 1971, 1987, and 1989. After the Civil

War ended in 2009, the rehabilitation process was aimed at reintegrating the former LTTE leaders, members, and collaborators into the community. During the process, beneficiaries within the *Protective Accommodation and Rehabilitation Centres*[73] (PARCS) were supported to engage in a range of activities and through these activities reconnect to all aspects of individual and communal life, including familial, social, cultural, and religious. The beneficiaries were supported to shift their thinking away from the narrow hate-filled ideology targeted towards the Sinhalese, Muslims, national, and international figures that opposed the LTTE agenda. Upon reflection on their actions and experiences, the former terrorists and insurgents found new meaning in their lives. They were transformed into champions of peace with values of moderation, toleration, and co-existence replacing hate, anger, and the mono-ethnic single narrative.[74] It is therefore clear that rather than adopting a retributive justice model, Sri Lanka has always embraced a restorative justice model by drawing on the country's rich heritage of moderation, toleration, and coexistence.

Role of civil society in counter radicalisation and de-radicalisation

The threat of ISIS and Al-Qaeda directed attacks persists; the dominant threat is by self-radicalised, home-grown cells and individuals. The strategy is to create a multinational, multi-pronged, multiagency, and a multi-jurisdictional framework to fight using upstream counter radicalisation and downstream de-radicalisation. The role of civil society in counter-radicalisation and de-radicalisation is essential in this process. Civil society and governments can work in partnership to prevent radicalisation by tackling economic, social, and political drivers. When governments set the policy framework, provide funding, and address structural issues, communities also need to play their part for the overall approach to be successful.

Civil society has a role to play to counter messages of radicalisation; often it will be more effective when these messages come from communities rather than governments. It is important to create a space for dialogue and discussion among youth. This is part of the process of taking on divisive narratives and creating an inclusive society that listens and responds to the needs and concerns of the citizens. Civil society can spot the signs of vulnerability and work upstream to protect individuals from radicalisation, through improved parenting, neighbourhood support, and community resilience.[75] Civil society can play a role in the de-radicalisation process. Some community organisations and individuals could contribute immensely to this process. Thus, policies and strategies should include civil society and be given top priority.

Global dignity for youth

This author was invited by His Royal Highness, The Crown Prince of Norway to speak on the subject of Global Dignity for Youth at the Oslo Nobel Peace Centre last year. The author admires the Crown Prince's work on Global Dignity, a programme in 60 nations that instils values of dignity to school children. Understanding dignity and respecting different ethno-religious groups is essential learning from a very young age, especially at a time when the world order is threatened by multiple extremist ideologies. Unfortunately, the Sri Lankan education system has yet to introduce this important programme to the school curriculum. President Sirisena, recognising the importance of this global initiative, stated: *"My country is trying to recover from the three-decade long brutal conflict that left deep scars on our social fabric. In 2015 when I was elected President I promised my people to introduce genuine reconciliation. It is important to learn at school level to respect other ethnic and religious groups, especially at a time like this with the rise of violent non state actors disturbing the global order"*.[76]

At the Nobel Peace Centre, this author mentioned that individuals can also be radicalised to do good to society when injustice is evident. In Sri Lanka, the late leader Vijaya Kumaranathunga[u] was assassinated by radical southern extremists, even though he himself was also a radical. Therefore, it is apparent that sometimes the state itself causes the radicalisation of its citizens. South Asia has weak institutions with

---

[u] Vijaya Kumaranatunga was a Sri Lankan film actor and politician, married to former Sri Lankan president Chandrika Kumaranatunga from 1978 until his assassination in 1988.

serious corruption, political and otherwise. Weak states have a higher propensity to encourage and provide environments conducive to the youth radicalisation. Another serious issue is the youth frustration concerning the high poverty rates in South Asia and the way governments fail to provide basic necessary living conditions. Economic factors also should not be ignored. The root cause has to be understood and addressed by the state at an early stage. Sri Lanka has learned this fact from its bitter past and our policy makers seriously consider the subject of youth radicalisation.

Conclusion

In conclusion, finding collaborative approaches to counter youth radicalisation is essential. South Asian nations should work together as one community to find solutions to youth radicalisation in the region. The key to the issue at hand is in assisting our youth in identifying a moderate counter narrative, rather than merely managing the symptoms of this problem.

The Role of Youth in Reconciliation[v]

I believe this is the first time the two ministries — the Ministry of Defence[77] and the Ministry of National Integration and Reconciliation[78] — have got together to discuss a timely and important topic of the '*Role of Youth in Reconciliation*'.[79] Today, we have embarked on a very important initiative. I wish to recollect and remember the youth who did the initial conference on the same subject on 2 January 2013 at the Lakshman Kadirgamar Institute.[80] It was our researchers who organized this successful conference. We had speakers who shared their experiences from Cambodia as well as a child soldier from South Sudan.

Most of you who are here with us today were born during the period of the civil war. Therefore, you have been witness to the mass cruelty and

---

[v] Opening remarks by the author in his capacity as the Director General of the Institute of National Security Studies Sri Lanka (INSSSL) at the conference on '*The Role of Youth in Reconciliation*', held on 13 December 2017.

some of you are direct victims; perhaps having lost a friend or close family member. You did not start this war; it was the generation before you who passed this burden on. The youth here today are much more intelligent and can see the problem in a different way than perhaps the older generation — who do not accept your way of thinking. You perhaps believe in a different set of solutions and have a fresh approach in addressing the aftermath of the conflict.

During the weekend, I was reading Sidartha Mukarjee's *Gene: An intimate history*,[81] a fascinating book of human beings' genes. With regards to this, I remember mentioning in a 2013 speech on the *Genome Sequencing Project*[82] that human beings with three billion genomes are 99.9% identical and the difference is only 0.1%.[83] Thus, most of our time is wasted by fighting over this 0.1% difference rather than focusing our energy on what is common to all of us. The scientific community will soon prove that we are all united despite being from different parts of the world as well as the fact that some of our past generations' ways of thinking were wrong. Thus, Sri Lanka has a golden opportunity to work towards reconciliation by reintegrating the disconnected diaspora overseas.

Reconciliation begins by admitting and accepting that we have done wrong. It's a simple notion but very powerful. I have participated in a discussion in this vein in South Africa, where I learned about the different perspectives on the subject of reconciliation. One generation may choose to forgive and another generation may think that this is wrong. It is a process that should have genuine political leadership and support. When I met President Kagame of Rwanda, I discussed the amazing work he had done towards reconciliation and the examples he set for the younger generation of Rwandans. You need genuine strong political leadership to recognise the important recommendations and ideas coming out of these conferences. Our President, H.E. Maithripala Sirisena of the Democratic Socialist Republic of Sri Lanka, has clearly displayed this notion by forgiving his own suicide bomber.[84] This was indeed a great deed towards reconciliation. In this regard, policymakers need to hear more of the youth's voices and as such they need to lend an ear to hearing out these voices. Today's youth are tomorrow's policy makers — the leaders, the champions — who will make a meaningful difference!

Remembering General Denzil Kobbekaduwa[w]

When I look at the audience today, it is a clear sign that INSSSL has taken the right decision in honouring Gen. Kobbekaduwa[x] through this annual memorial lecture series, to invoke the memory of a great military strategist and discuss an important strategic topic for our nation. It has been 25 years since the loss of Gen. Kobbekaduwa, Brigadier Vijaya Wimalaratne,[y] along with other brave military officers. We have lost many valiant warriors in our history and as a proud nation with rich values, we should remember these patriots who gave their last full measure of devotion for this country that they loved. The values that drive men like Gen. Kobbekaduwa and many other brave men and women in uniform are honour, selflessness, and courage.

Any nation that does not honour and remember its war heroes who sacrificed their lives falls short of fulfilling its duty as a nation-state. Why we are all gathered here today is to honour and remember a human being who sacrificed his life for our motherland. As the national security think tank, it is fitting that we can bring together both the military and civilians to honour this valiant military strategist.

I remember the fateful day of Gen. Kobbekaduwa's death, our family was in Kalawewa for my father's birthday and we had to rush back home because due to the untimely demise of his close friend and our neighbour, the late Brigadier Vijaya Wimalaratne. The next time I heard about

---

[w] Opening remarks by the author in his capacity as the Director General of the Institute of National Security Studies Sri Lanka (INSSSL) at the Annual Memorial Lecture Series in honour of Lieutenant General Denzil Lakshman Kobbekaduwa. The inaugural lecture in the series was delivered by General G H de Silva (Rtd.), on the '*Life and Times of Lt. Gen. Kobbekaduwa in the contemporary context*', on 8 December 2017.

[x] Lieutenant General Denzil Lakshman Kobbekaduwa was a Sri Lankan general. He led some of the most successful military operations in the early part of the Sri Lankan Civil War, such as Vadamarachchi Operation and Operation Balavegaya. He was mortally wounded and his commanders and staff killed when the Land Rover they were traveling in hit a land mine in the island of Kayts while making preparations for Operation Final Countdown, the proposed invasion of the Jaffna Peninsula. Lt. Gen Kobbekaduwa is much respected for his bravery and the humane qualities he showed during his tenure.

[y] Major General Vijaya Wimalaratne was a Sri Lankan army officer and one of the most distinguished generals in Sri Lanka.

Gen. Kobbekaduwa was through Dr. Colvin Samarasinghe, the neurosurgeon who put an X-ray in front of my face to show the damage caused to my own father[z] who was also a victim of the LTTE. I remember him saying, *"Son, this instance is similar to many lives that this war has claimed, including Gen. Kobbekaduwa — I think you are old enough to understand."* Thus, the pain of one individual is the same pain felt by all who have lost loved ones in our almost 30-year war. This tragically interconnects us all.

Our nation has suffered immensely; I am certain most in this audience are direct victims. Yet, today Sri Lanka stands as a proud nation, having defeated one of the most ruthless terrorist organisations in the world. We as a nation have not cowered away from this but rather most have celebrated our victory of eradicating the LTTE. Going forth, this nation will be built by the youth and therefore, it is left to us, the living, to advance the mission of the sacrificed war heroes, to fulfil that which they cannot. As the great poet Aeschylus reminds us: *"with pain and suffering we will discover wisdom"*.[85] To this I will add, what we need today is love, wisdom, and compassion towards one another and a feeling of justice for all. Gen. Kobbekaduwa waged war to achieve peace and believed in creating a harmonious society. This was evidenced by the way he led his life, a peace-loving general respected by all.

INSS, the national security think tank, with the leadership of the Secretary of Defence and advice from the military and civilian scholars, has achieved several important milestones. Today is another important day; the first civilian military security think tank will launch its annual lecture series, honouring a great military strategist loved by the entire nation. I am certain that in years to come they might not remember what we said here but will remember the great deed we launched today. The words of Shakespeare came to my mind: *"A breathing valiant man of an invincible unconquered spirit"*.[86]

---

[z] Oswin Abeyagoonasekera was a Member of Parliament and chairman and the leader of the Sri Lanka Mahajana Pakshaya or Party. He was assassinated by a female suicide bomber of the Liberation Tigers of Tamil Eelam (LTTE) while attending an election rally in support of Gamini Dissanayake, for the Presidential election of 1994.

Chapter 5

Democracy and Institution Building

"Members of Parliament would perform an important function, if they keep an unbiased eye on the working of the administration. But this too is a complex issue, since they too vary in quality and character. The worst situation is where public servants and Members of Parliament collaborate on doubtful enterprises, which also happens sometimes."

M.D.D. Pieris[a]

---

[a] In the Pursuit of Governance: A Memoir of Over Three and a Half Decades in the Public Service of Sri Lanka (2002), p. 636.

Death and Democracy[1]

"We cannot glorify death whether in the battlefield or otherwise. We, on the other hand, must celebrate life, and are fiercely committed to protecting and securing the sanctity of life, which is the most fundamental value without which all other rights and freedoms become meaningless."
— Neelan Tiruchelvam[2]

In 1991,[b] even when half a million American troops were a few hundred kilometres away from Baghdad, President George. H.W. Bush[c] resisted invading Iraq. This was a wise move on his part — to control Saddam Hussein's aggression by stopping the invasion of Kuwait and not completely dismantling Iraq. However, in 2003, after 9/11, the US operation '*Iraqi Freedom*'[d] deposed Saddam Hussein[e] on the grounds of possession of weapons of mass destruction (WMD) under the Presidency of George. W. Bush.[f]

The US intervention to overthrow Saddam Hussein created a situation that remains untenable for the people living in Iraq. An important question that needs to be addressed is whether the coalition of the US-led invasion had a plan to rebuild the country after dismantling Saddam's regime. The political climate worsened after the invasion and Iraq has been at the receiving end of innumerable suicide attacks. During Saddam Hussein's reign, radical and jihadist elements were not present and Shias and Sunnis co-existed.

---

[b] The Gulf War (2 August 1990–28 February 1991), codenamed Operation Desert Shield for operations leading to the build-up of troops and defence of Saudi Arabia and Operation Desert Storm in its combat phase, was a war waged by coalition forces from 35 nations led by the United States against Iraq in response to Iraq's invasion and annexation of Kuwait.

[c] George Herbert Walker Bush (George H.W. Bush) is an American politician who served as the 41st President of the United States from 1989 to 1993.

[d] The Iraq War was a protracted armed conflict that began in 2003 with the invasion of Iraq by a United States-led coalition that overthrew the government of Saddam Hussein. The 2003 invasion of Iraq was dubbed '*Operation Iraqi Freedom*' by the United States.

[e] Saddam Hussein was President of Iraq from 16 July 1979 until 9 April 2003. A leading member of the revolutionary Arab Socialist Ba'ath Party, and later, the Baghdad-based Ba'ath Party and its regional organisation, the Iraqi Ba'ath Party — which espoused Ba'athism, a mix of Arab nationalism and socialism — Saddam played a key role in the 1968 coup that brought the party to power in Iraq.

[f] George Walker Bush (George. W. Bush) is an American politician who served as the 43rd President of the United States from 2001 to 2009.

'*Jihadism*'[g] crept into Iraq when its borders were forced open from all directions. The consolidation of Al-Qaeda[h] thus paved the way for ISIS.

Since the US-led invasion in 2003, one of the deadliest attacks in Iraq was perpetuated just a few weeks ago in the Karrada district. It targeted innocent civilians and killed over 100 while injuring over 300.[3] The bombing happened when a lorry with explosives detonated while families were out in celebration of Ramadan. In July 2016, around the same time as the bombing, the Sir John Chilcot Report was released. The Chilcot Report[4] clearly stated that it was a mistake to disband Saddam's army and that this led directly to the insurgency, when there was no imminent threat from the then Iraqi leader. The report stated that the strategy of containment could have been adapted and continued for some time. It also categorically said that military action at that time was not a last resort. Finally, the report claimed that the Iraq invasion was made on the basis of flawed intelligence assessments and therefore should have been challenged.

Considering the findings of the report in a country with democracy at its helm, it can be argued that the then Prime Minister Tony Blair's[i] behaviour was clearly undemocratic, bordering on dictatorial. Looking at the chain of command and the decisions taken, there was no representative democratic practice evident. Such an instance is interesting to contrast with issues raised by Western governments on Sri Lankan war crimes.[5] These governments are keen to investigate the chain of command in the Sri Lankan war against terrorism. As the Iraq Inquiry's findings indicate a complete lack of democratic process, the British law firm, *Public Interest Lawyers,*[6] has already presented many cases of violation by the British forces before the International Criminal Court (ICC). The ICC, in its *Preliminary Examination Activities 2015*[7] report, stated that it had received 1,268 allegations of ill treatment and unlawful killings committed

---

[g] Jihadism is a 21st-century neologism found in Western languages to describe Islamist militant movements perceived as military movements "*rooted in Islam*" and "*existentially threatening*" to the West.

[h] Al-Qaeda is a militant Sunni Islamist multi-national organisation founded in 1988 by Osama bin Laden, Abdullah Azzam, and several other Arab volunteers who fought against the Soviet invasion of Afghanistan in the 1980s.

[i] Anthony Blair is a British politician who served as Prime Minister of the United Kingdom from 1997 to 2007 and Leader of the Labour Party from 1994 to 2007.

by British forces during the Iraqi invasion; of 259 alleged killings, 47 were said to have occurred when Iraqis were in British custody.

How do the US and the UK undo the damage done to Iraq and its people? It was evident that Iraq lacked a post-war strategy and an appropriate counter-insurgency strategy. Thousands of lives have been lost during and after the Iraq invasion. Iraq was a crucial lesson to some Western policy experts who believed that invasion and the dismantling of the state was a necessary last resort.

There are certain geopolitical values that are important and should be given the highest priority. In his 1918 work *The Decline of the West*,[8] German historian Oswald Spengler pointed out that the rise of urban Western civilisation and its transformation into a world civilisation would occur in a form increasingly divorced from the soil and this would have serious consequences. This is evident in the present day, with the rise of violent non-state actors and the economic inequality of an unjust world. What we see now are people appreciating their own civilisation, their own geography, their own values, and, to further quote Spengler, *"each springing with primitive strength from the soil of a mother-region to which it remains firmly bound*[9]*"*. A one-size-fits-all approach to overcoming geopolitical challenges will be unsuccessful; it is essential that home-grown solutions in partnership with local communities are seen as the way forward.

Riot and Responsibility: Governance[10]

One of the greatest Buddhist monks of Sri Lanka, Most Venerable Maduluwawe Sobitha,[j] who spoke fearlessly to overthrow the previous government to usher in a better political order, has passed away.[11] The entire nation mourns the loss of this great human being. In his speech at this author's first book launch, *Towards a Better World Order*,[12] a clear statement was made by the Venerable monk: *"politics in Sri Lanka is a direct ticket to hell."*[13]

---

[j] Maduluwawe Sobitha Thero was an influential Sinhalese Buddhist monk regarded for his nonviolent revolutionary leadership in Sri Lanka. The chief incumbent of the Kotte Naga Vihara, he was a prominent social-political activist and an independent thinker who endured to improve the positive and constructive aspects of Sri Lankan politics.

The first serious shock to the new government was the resignation of the former Minister of Law and Order, Hon. Thilak Marapana, over an issue about 'Avant Garde',[14] a floating armoury. While political stability should remain a priority, looking at the present state of the economy, Sri Lanka should spend time working towards the economic vision indicated by the Prime Minister in his economic policy statement.[15] With regards to further instability, in Colombo, 39 students from the Higher National Diploma in Engineering (HNDE) were arrested after an intense battle with the police.[16] The student protest was against privatisation of education, to increase levels of university intake, and to upgrade existing infrastructure. All these demands could have been discussed and peacefully worked out but unfortunately it turned into a violent police attack. The opposition and some members supporting the 18th Amendment to the Constitution are now requesting the National Police Commission to investigate the incident. Notably, it was the present government that re-instated the independent commissions, which were scrapped by the previous government.

It is important that the government address the students' issues. Unfortunately, the Education Ministry's portfolio is split across so many ministries that it will be difficult to take actionable policy measures. Still, the university student intake is to be increased to 40,000[17] and more still with adequate infrastructure. Our priority should be producing the most competent graduates who can contribute to the economy, just as Singapore did when it invested heavily to create a world-class labour pool under the aegis of Prime Minister Lee Kuan Yew. Investment in education and research and development is essential for a nation. In this regard, the right education policy is needed to introduce a single qualifications authority as a certifying body. These challenges have to be addressed by the government as student unrest can lead to serious complications if ignored. Sri Lanka has previously faced two youth insurrections before as a nation in 1971[k] and 1989.[l]

---

[k] The 1971 insurrection was the first unsuccessful armed revolt conducted by the communist Janatha Vimukthi Peramuna (JVP) against the Government of Ceylon under Prime Minister Sirimavo Bandaranaike. The revolt began on 5 April 1971 and lasted till June 1971.

[l] The 1987–89 JVP insurrection was the second unsuccessful armed revolt conducted by the Janatha Vimukthi Peramuna against the Government of Sri Lanka under President J. R.

Sri Lanka with its new administration also needs to fix many areas of the economy, which have been ignored by the previous government. As a nation, Sri Lanka is the only South Asian country that has moved to Stage 2 — an efficiency-driven economy — according to the Global Competitiveness Index report.[18] All other South Asian Nations are in Stage 1 — factor-driven — or in transition to Stage 2. This shows that Sri Lanka has done well compared to other South Asian countries in improving the basic factors of its economy. It is time to start competing with the East Asian economies; Sri Lanka should aim to achieve a per capita of over US$ 5500 in 2020.[19] To achieve such a target, several wheels of the economy need to be strengthened. Value-added exports need to be increased from its currently low percentage. Furthermore, Sri Lanka should aim to be a regional financial centre like Singapore and Dubai.

When a fearless voice dies, another is elevated to victory. This is epitomised by the fact that the late great priest Venerable Sobitha Thero and his desire for change helped instil good governance in society.

New Year Kokis to Luxury Permits[20]

"The world is a fine place, and worth fighting for" — *Hemingway*[21]

The Kokis[m] eaten on our traditional New Year hadn't had much time to digest when the news broke that luxury vehicle permits worth US$ 62500 were issued to all 225 Members of the Parliament of Sri Lanka — licenses they could sell for close to Rs. 20 million per permit.[22] Is this the change we voted for? Is this the culture we want to take forward?

It is notable that "Finance Minister Ravi Karunanayake mentioned during his long Budget speech that the Government would abolish all kinds of vehicle permits, including those given to Members of Parliament.[23]" Given the back-peddling of this statement, there was not

---

Jayewardene. Unlike the first unsuccessful JVP insurrection of 1971, the second insurrection was not an open revolt, but appeared to be a low intensity conflict that lasted from 1987 to 1989 with the JVP resorting to subversion, assassinations, raids, and attacks on military and civilian targets.

[m] Kokis is a sweet, crispy, deep-fried Sri Lankan dish made from rice flour and coconut milk. It is a traditional food served during the Sinhala/Tamil New Year in Sri Lanka.

much noise on the issue of permits from the political establishment. In addition, it was revealed that each Minister would receive Rs. 35 million for a Ministry vehicle and each Deputy Minister Rs. 28 million.[24] In contrast to the political elite, an office assistant in the government sector gets paid only Rs. 28,000[25] as a monthly salary and with this income has to not only look after his children and family but also cope with the rising cost of living. The political-economic situation has therefore not changed much for such an individual in the last ten years in this country.

With this exorbitant spending on our political elite, we are at the same time going with a begging bowl to the IMF asking for financial assistance to solve our financial crisis. Sri Lanka is requesting financial assistance of around US$ 1.5 billion from the IMF to sail over the current economic tide.[26] According to economists, the main conditions for the loan from the IMF are to reduce the nation's budget deficit, raise revenues, and bolster its foreign exchange reserves. Furthermore, the cost of many products will rise with the increase of Value Added Tax (VAT) to 15% from 2 May 2016,[27] an additional burden the common man must again take on to his life style. If the country is facing such an economic situation, why is it that the politicians are accepting luxury permits and getting separate permits for ministries?

The current state of affairs, with a Cabinet close to 100 ministers, was not the outcome that this author or the public hoped for when supporting the theme of good governance in the last election. A recent *Sunday Times* article held that around Rs. 5 million a month is the cost to maintain one individual minister.[28] While the politicians are asking the public to support their policies they are simultaneously robbing the public in daylight. Ideally, the state should be reducing permits and introducing affordable electric vehicles as pledged by President Sirisena at COP21[29] (the Conference of Parties 21), to create a better environment to reduce our carbon footprint. Many speak of such initiatives, with little evidence of implementation.

According to Central Bank reports, by 2020 Sri Lanka aims to reach a per capita of over US$ 5500[30] which is in another four years. Our current GDP per capita is US$ 3800.[31] Therefore, one should question the unfruitful lavish financial spending and the direction of the country's leaders who spend so. In this context, the media should educate the people on these shortcomings and support the public to create a better culture and environment. This was one reason why some journalists have given their lives to report the truth. Such incidents should never be resorted to again and should be at the forefront of good governance going forward.

I can only refer to George Orwell's 1945 political satire, *Animal Farm*,[32] which is a good example of today's political climate. When the animals decide to rebel against the existing establishment and restore a new and better order, they eventually understand that nothing much changes. In fact, after the animals take over they eventually get into a bigger mess and start missing the old ways. The farm, which was called '*Manor Farm*', was renamed as '*Animal Farm*', which didn't stick; eventually it was again renamed '*Manor Farm*'. There is still hope that the new government will rectify these issues and stick to the promises it made. The country we live is a fine place and worth fighting for. The state must restore a better order, because *"there is a calling that is yet above high office, fame, lucre and security. It is the call of conscience"*,[33] as stated by one of the greatest journalists we ever had in this island.

Disasters & Democracy: Facing Up To Reality in Following New Year Tragedy[34]

"The ultimate test of the value of a political system is whether it helps that society to establish conditions which improve the standard of living for the majority of its people." — Lee Kuan Yew[35]

Last year, an article titled '*New Year Kokis To Luxury Permits*'[36] was written for the *Colombo Telegraph*, highlighting that the kokis treats eaten on our traditional New Year didn't have the time to digest among us before luxury permits were issued to MPs. This very public who suffered last year from the burden of permits now has to face a colossal disaster.[37] This disaster has cost lives as the entire nation mourns rather than celebrates the New Year. The son who distributed kokis as a New Year tradition returned to see his parents buried by the garbage landslide which was stacked up owing to a systemic failure of standards and systems. This parable came true when a mountain of garbage stacked at Meethotamulla in Colombo District crashed, killing 30 and destroying more than 90 houses.[38] The last incident of a similar nature occurred in the East African nation of Ethiopia, killing 113 in March of this year (2017).[39]

Several reports by experts and public intellectuals on the garbage pile up were ignored by policymakers in the past. It is hoped that from now onwards, policymakers will have more respect for policy inputs from academia. We have become a reactive society rather than a proactive one. The reasons are clearly procrastination, rejection of solutions, and a cycle of blame. A systematic method to streamline and implement top priority projects that improve quality of life and ensure human security should be implemented by the Government without delay. The security of the individual and the security of the State should be a top priority. If the state takes the *Hobbesian choice*[n] of keeping chaos at bay, it would be fulfilling its duties toward its citizenry.

Notably, it is either best practice or tragedy that shapes policy. The former remains the ideal in order to avoid the loss of human lives. Unfortunately, many proposed projects for waste management, including waste conversion into energy plants, have been rejected by policymakers in Sri Lanka. In 2003, in Vijayawada,[o] India, this author witnessed how waste was converted into usable energy and supplied to the national grid. Let us hope we can start a similar project of this nature in Sri Lanka in the aftermath of our New Year's tragedy.

As reported by the World Economic Forum, Sri Lanka's economy is transitioning from being factor driven to efficiency driven.[40] Although certain segments of our society live a First World life, the headcount poverty index in Sri Lanka is 4.1%.[41,p] The author is of the opinion that those who belong to the First World segment (of which most are predominantly urban societies) educate their children overseas, with even healthcare obtained internationally. The country is at a $3,800[42]

---

[n] Thomas Hobbes was a 17th century English philosopher and political theorist writing about the balance between a secure civil society and democracy. He argued that the only way to have a secure civil society and avoid chaos is through universal submission to the absolute authority of a sovereign. The term 'Hobbesian Choice' is often used in modern parlance to indicate a choice between two extremes, usually equally unacceptable.

[o] Vijayawada is a city in the southeast Indian state of Andhra Pradesh.

[p] This figure is the official figure given by the Department of Census and Statistics. However, this figure does not account for overall poverty in the country, which is estimated to be much higher.

GDP per capita while our target according to the Central Bank is to achieve over $5,500 by the year 2020.[43] With the present economic climate this will be clearly unachievable. A nation like Singapore, which most of our politicians quote as an example for Sri Lanka to follow, is at a GDP per capita above $50,000.[44] To achieve this state, how long will Sri Lanka take? What best practices do we need to import and adapt? These remain among the larger questions we should be asking.

On the day of the disaster at Meethotamulla, this author was in Singapore talking to one of the young geopoliticians, Dr. Parag Khanna of the Lee Kuan Yew School, who authored the recent book *Technocracy in America*.[45] During the discussion we spoke about how important it is to have technical experts at the policy level and how nations like Singapore have achieved a level of technocracy while following the democratic model. Technocracy may be understood as a philosophy similar to the teachings of *Plato*.[q] The concept is about technical experts running the core institutions of a nation. Technocracy is evident in Singapore, South Korea, China, and even Rwanda.

The health of a political system is determined by the quality of its institutions. For more than a generation, citizens of Western societies have been steadily voicing their increasing dissatisfaction with their system of government, even directly challenging whether or not democracy is right for them. 49% of Americans now believe that experts should decide what is best.[46] Thus, the '*end of history*'[47] is being turned on its head, according to Parag Khanna. The cases of Switzerland and Singapore are both verifiably democratic and rigorously technocratic at the same time. They both have a high percentage of foreign-born populations, compulsory national military and civil service, strong linkages between education and industry, diversified economies, and massive state investment in research and development as well as innovation. They are both relentless in seeking self-improvement. Their only ideology is pragmatism. With the world's top-ranked civil service[48] (as measured by merit and autonomy), detailed scenarios and forecasts are used to strategize domestic priorities and international positioning. Crucially, both countries are also at the cutting

---

[q] Plato was a philosopher in Classical Greece and the founder of the Academy in Athens, the first institution of higher learning in the Western world.

edge of leveraging big data. In this regard, Switzerland has pioneering finance and technology companies, while Singapore has become a living lab for those innovations.

Thus, Sri Lanka should adopt technocracy. First, to change our political culture we should bring in technocrats in order to have a dramatic change over a short period of time. What we have currently are technical problems to which policymakers have failed to give solutions because they have no expertise on the subjects at hand. So technocrats should take up this work for the betterment of our country. The question hinges on the ability of a technocrat to get elected in a democratic system. Society cannot afford to get carried away during an election, especially on massive political spending. The public needs to be vigilant and evaluate each candidate purely on merit. The spending capacity of a candidate is not a qualification for their post and the general public must realise this. The national list should be used only for technocrats and not to satisfy losing candidates.

Given the current trajectory of our economy, with very small incremental changes year to year, it will take us a very long time to become a $22,000 per capita developed economy. This author's estimate is that at the present rate, it will take us till the year 2040 to achieve such a target. Technocracy is one solution we can introduce to fix the present underperforming governmental institutions and the relevant policymaking areas, especially to improve quality of life. To give an example, one could look at how the Singaporean government will soon introduce a five Singapore dollar health check to most citizens above the age of 40.[49] The health check will even include cancer screening. The idea is to detect health issues early and to improve public health.

From this perspective, it is important to consider the health implications on the quality of life in Sri Lanka, including the unmanaged recent dengue outbreak and the Meethotamulla garbage collapse. A sustainable political system should support society and improve people's living standards. If it does not, the political system has failed. If a democracy fails to bring discipline or development to society, then it is worth exploring the realities of moving towards a technocracy. In the words of Prime Minister Lee Kuan Yew: *"The exuberance of democracy leads to undisciplined and disorderly conditions which are inimical to development".*[50]

The Forgotten Professions: The Plight of a Nation[51]

"I hate victims who respect their executioners." — Jean-Paul Sartre[52]

The Sri Lankan public has become the unfortunate victim of the nation's health and sanitation crisis. Policymakers are being questioned by both the public and the media about their inability to manage the ongoing situation.

One of the world's most iconic cities, New York, was turned into a garbage dump in February 1968[53] due to the sanitation workers' refusal to collect garbage. After nine days, 100,000 tons of garbage had piled up and a state of emergency was declared. In Sri Lanka, garbage collection in Colombo and the surrounding areas has become a serious problem over the past few weeks.[54] Sabotage by sanitation workers and the relocation of the garbage dump, not to mention the ongoing blame game, has aggravated the situation. A record high of 100,000 dengue patients[55] is an indirect consequence of the situation. Hospitals have run out of beds, compounding the health crisis.

In this context it can be said that there does exist an increasing number of people who do jobs we can do just fine without — that is, even if they stop work, it would have a minimal impact. This, however, is not the case with garbage collectors. The sanitation of any city is an essential service. According to the *New Economic Foundation*,[56] a British think tank, for every pound earned by advertising executives, they destroy an equivalent of seven pounds in the form of pollution, stress, over-consumption, and debt; conversely, each pound paid to a trash collector creates an equivalent of twelve pounds in terms of health and sustainability.

While the public sector's essential services have many hidden benefits to society, they unfortunately go unrecognised and are not compensated enough. The agents of prosperity: teachers, law enforcement officers, nurses, and research scholars are paid poorly while unimportant and superfluous jobs are paid well. Rutger Bergman,[57] one of Europe's prominent young thinkers, describes the situation best as jobs of *"shifters"*. Instead of creating wealth, these jobs mostly just shift wealth around within the economy. David Graeber, an anthropologist at the London School of Economics, calls this *"Phenomenon for bullshit jobs."*[58] Innumerable people spend their entire life doing these jobs, which pays them well but does not create anything for society. A researcher in

Sri Lanka only gets an average salary of US$ 200–250 a month while the marketing executive gets ten times more.

A hefty pay check and a comfortable life do not mean one is producing something of great value. One could revisit Friedrich Engels, who explained this with the use of his term *"false consciousness"*,[r] to which the proletariat had fallen victim. For example, luxury vehicles imported by politicians with further supplementary budgets, was passed a few days ago by the Government in Sri Lanka.[59] It allows for the purchase of a few more vehicles and the maintenance of residences, but does not add any value to society. It only increases debt and public dissatisfaction. The proletariat is therefore misled by a segment of the society.

Sri Lanka's President recently (July 2017) pointed out that *"anyone watching TV feels there is no Government in the country"*[60] because development is not reported by the media. The President's development work tends to get overshadowed by public agitation, especially due to the multiple political voices of the Government, which confuse the polity. The Government should focus its energy on resolving and managing the ongoing crisis and strengthening the more productive sectors of the economy.

In addition, it has been reported that Sri Lanka will import 200,000 metric tons of rice from foreign nations such as Myanmar in July 2017.[61] Yet the country could become self-sufficient and even export rice if it properly manages this important area. Moreover, as an island nation, Sri Lanka still imports fish and coconut. On the other hand, Israel is one of the best examples of a technological revolution in their agricultural and dairy farming sector. For example, a cow produces on an average four litres of milk a day in Sri Lanka[62] while the corresponding quantity in Israel is 22 litres.[63] Annually, 10.5 tons of milk are produced in Israel,[64] much more than the milk production in the US, Australia, and Germany. In light of this, the Indian Prime Minister Narendra Modi's visit to Israel this month

---

[r] False consciousness is a term used by sociologists and expounded by some Marxists for the way in which material, ideological, and institutional processes in capitalist society mislead members of the proletariat and other class actors. These processes are thought to hide the true relations between classes and the real state of affairs regarding the exploitation suffered by the proletariat. Although Karl Marx frequently denounced ideology in general, there is no evidence that he ever actually used the phrase *"false consciousness"*. It appears to have been used — at least in print — only by Friedrich Engels.

focused on technology transfer between Israel and India.⁶⁵ This indicates a strategic direction taken by the Indian Prime Minister with regard to Israel. In fact, Israel's research and development expenditure is four per cent of its GDP,⁶⁶ a high amount that gives it the desired results. Certain countries, however, are uninterested in innovation and research; and all they focus is on quantity, profit, and short-term election goals.

The way things are in Sri Lanka right now should change; its political culture, economy, and universities can all be reinvented to generate real innovation and creativity. It is not necessary to wait patiently for a cultural change. The Sri Lankan government should introduce dramatic changes to all sectors and institutions, taking best practices even from small nations such as Bhutan that have introduced laws for Parliamentary candidates to have a formal degree qualification.⁶⁷ First, and foremost, policymakers should be in a position to understand the priorities and recognise the necessities of society.

Parliamentary Blows & the South Asian Buddha: The Case of Dignity in Sri Lanka⁶⁸

"On this World Press Freedom Day, I urge all governments, politicians, businesses, and citizens to commit to nurturing and protecting an independent, free media. Without this fundamental right, people are less free and less empowered. With it, we can work together for a world of dignity and opportunity for all." — Secretary-General Ban Ki-moon⁶⁹

World Press Freedom Day

The 3ʳᵈ of May marks World Press Freedom Day.⁷⁰ Among other factors, unimpeded violence against the press culminated in the *Silent Revolution* one year ago. This violence included injustice toward media giants and press freedom fighters such as Lasantha Wickrematungeˢ who were brutally assassinated. The contribution of Sri Lankan journalists over the decades of civil war and before remains immense. Despite manifold limitations to freedom they continued their work — a fact which needs to be appreciated.

ˢLasantha Wickrematunge was a Sri Lankan journalist, politician, and human rights activist who was assassinated in January 2009.

The author recalls the words of Ariyarathna Dombagahawatta, senior journalist and *Sunday Lankadeepa* editor, who said that during the insurrection in 1989 he fled the country to India as the assassins targeted him. He only returned when this horrific time was over.

According to the Freedom of the Press Report by *Freedom House*,[71] Sri Lanka is ranked at 64th place. This is not a positive rank in comparison to our neighbours, with India at 41st, Nepal 54th, Bangladesh 61th, Pakistan 64th and Afghanistan 62th place. Out of the *'Free'*, *'Partially Free'* and *'Not Free'* categories, as a country, Sri Lanka is categorized as *'Not Free'* when it comes to press. Nevertheless, the report comments on the progress made on this front: *"Unlike its neighbours, Sri Lanka experienced a marked improvement in press freedom conditions after a new Government took power in early 2015. Journalists faced fewer threats and attacks than in previous years, investigations into past violence made progress, a number of websites were unblocked, and officials moved toward the adoption of a right to information bill."*[72]

Another report on the subject at hand is the *Press Freedom Index*[73] by Reporters Without Borders, which ranks Sri Lanka at 141st place,[74] on par with Ethiopia but ranked lower than South Sudan. It is hoped that in next year's report Sri Lanka will rank higher, as the new Government is working hard to fully implement the RTI Act and also fully restore media freedom. After 14 months of careful study, a comprehensive report entitled *Rebuilding Public Trust — An assessment of media industry and profession in Sri Lanka*[75] was handed over to the Prime Minister, with 101 important recommendations to rectify the issues in our media industry by media experts and stakeholders. Hopefully we will see some progress in implementing these recommendations in the relevant institutions.

Health of the individual citizen

With the on-going increase in tax on private medical services,[76] the common people of Sri Lanka will find it difficult to obtain medical services, leading them increasingly to rely on the Government for its provision of free healthcare — which is perhaps ineffective. The Health Minister of Sri Lanka himself was admitted for medical treatment to Mount Elizabeth hospital (a popular hospital for VIPs of the Sri Lankan community) in Singapore, and having been impressed by the quality of service in Singapore said upon his return that he would build three hospitals as equal to Mount Elizabeth in Sri Lanka.[77] This is perhaps a good outcome and may improve our ailing medical service.

In a recent visit to Norway, the author learned about the high life expectancy and quality of life and health in the country. Life expectancy in Norway is 81 years compared to Sri Lanka at 77 years (which is arguably still a high figure for a South Asian nation).[78] Quality of life is essential in the modern era. The water and food you and your family consume should be of the highest quality to contribute to a long life. What we hear in Sri Lanka is not a positive story when it comes to our water, food, and the fertiliser used. Recently, trade stalls were seized by public health inspectors (PHIs) due to unsuitable food for human consumption being sold by vendors.[79]

In addition, the Chronic Kidney Disease (CKD) has killed 22,000 lives for the last two decades in Sri Lanka,[80] which is equal to the lives taken during our three-decade long civil war. The CKD is a serious concern in Sri Lanka, with the World Health Organization (WHO) reporting around 15%–22% of the population in the Anuradhapura, Polonnaruwa, and Badulla Districts being affected by the disease.[81] The WHO states that CKD is an environmental-exposure disease caused by multiple factors such as chronic exposure to kidney damaging pesticides, arsenic, lead, cadmium, poor diet, and genetic susceptibility to kidney failure.

The Sri Lankan President made a pledge at Paris COP21[82] to introduce smart solutions and we should believe in him. In this context, the Government should encourage the use of electric cars and other sustainable methods of generating electricity as well as improve the quality of food and water that we consume. With the economic crisis we are now facing as a nation, the status may further deteriorate. Thus, political leaders should make the correct policy decisions to improve quality of life in the country.

Violence against women and children

The tallest Buddha statue[t] in South Asia stands at 135 feet and was unveiled by President Sirisena in the town of Matugama.[83] The uneviling

---

[t] Buddharūpa is the Sanskrit and Pali term used in Buddhism for statues or models of beings who have obtained Buddhahood, including the historical Buddha.

was a great deed to spread the message of *Dhamma*[u] to a world which is in disorder and needs healing, particularly at a time when Buddha statues are being destroyed by ruthless terrorists such as the Taliban in Afghanistan.[84] Addressing the gathering, President Sirisena said, *"Buddhist philosophy has been instrumental in moulding a righteous society in the country and a moral society could be built based on Buddhist philosophy"*.[85] On the same day, due to the high number of cases reported in the country, the Task Force on Prevention of Violence Against Women and Girls[86] handed their Action Plan to the Prime Minister. The practice of Buddhism is more essential than its symbolism. A principal value of Buddhism is to respect and love women and children. Buddha once said, *"a nation can be judged on how they look after their women and children."*[87] Sri Lanka needs to invest in and practice this philosophy in its truest form.

The Buddhist philosophy also applies to the society at large. In this context, parliamentarians should work collectively bearing in mind the critical economic situation and social issues our country is facing. The Parliament ideally should be the most esteemed place to debate and implement the right policies. The place we send our representatives to safeguard our children's future has unfortunately come into disrepute due to the lack of respect and dignity of Parliamentarians for the institution; therefore, the course of this narrative must be changed to fit the teachings of the Buddha.

Economic Crime — A Sri Lankan Perspective[88]

This paper will examine two areas of economic crime in Sri Lanka. Firstly, it will examine the high level of political and financial corruption in society. Secondly, it will address the economic crimes committed by the Liberation Tigers of Tamil Eelam (LTTE), especially in terms of money laundering, during the three-decade long war that ravaged the country.

From the outset, the author can say that due to weak state institutions in many developing nations, including Sri Lanka, preventing and controlling economically motivated crime has become integral to supporting the nation state. If you take the latest CPI (Corruption

---

[u] In Buddhism, Dhamma means *"cosmic law and order"* and is also applied to the teachings of the Buddha.

Perception Index), Sri Lanka ranked 95 in 2016, dropping down the rank by 12 slots when compared to 2015.[89] Our deteriorating rank is a marked indicator of the importance of mitigating economic crime which is arguably fuelled by corruption.

Sri Lanka elected a new government in 2015. The central theme of President Sirisena's election manifesto was on fighting corruption and establishing good governance — which has become a huge challenge in our country during the last three years. Indeed, since coming into power, the Government has faced an increasing challenge to quell such corruption. One such incident is the Central Bank of Sri Lanka bond scam, which resulted in the former Governor of the Central Bank having to step down. According to media reports published,[90] it was alleged that the Governor had a conflict of interest, resulting in the Former Governor being privy to insider information. The evidence being established by the Commission of Inquiry that has been appointed by the President shows that the Governor took an active interest in the Public Debt Department of the Central Bank that is responsibility for government securities, purely for the benefit of his own interests. As a result of this economic crime, the Central Bank and the GOSL lost billions of rupees on the cost of government bonds.[91]

The Governor's actions and those of the Central Bank that supported him in this matter reflect the very poor standards of corporate governance at the Central Bank, which is the premier financial institution in the country and which bestrides the financial system of the country. It therefore has, perforce, to have people with impeccable integrity, to be able to maintain and sustain consumer and investor confidence in the financial system, which is paramount to being able to promote financial stability and economic growth in the country. Although the errant Governor has been removed and replaced, it is important that those responsible are held to account in order to sustain the fight against corruption in our country.

Another topical issue in Sri Lanka is the purchase of a Rs. 145 million (or US$ 1 million) luxury property from funds without original documents by the Foreign Minister of Sri Lanka.[92] This economic crime represents real estate propagation for money laundering. However, the President has been firm, stating that he would not tolerate corruption by anyone. Hence, on 10 August 2017, the Foreign Minister resigned due to the allegation against him.[93] This issue coupled with the bond scam has led to frustration, disillusionment, and loss of trust by the general public in the highest echelons of Government, in fighting economic crime and corruption.

Corruption in the government sector currently is at its highest as evidenced by the recent reported incidents. However, that is not to say that the former Government is not complicit in propagating economic crime and corruption. The former Government was accused of high level corruption and several key members are under investigation although no action has yet been taken against them. This is the crux of the problem in our country — for the last several decades, not a single high-level politician has ever been sent to jail in connection with bribery or corruption.

Political corruption is not exclusive to Sri Lanka. It can be seen all across the South Asian region from campaign funding, bribing for government tenders, non-declaration of assets etc., according to many participants at the CoCo 2014 conference[v] in Bangalore. The conference helped to bring out cross-border issues on corruption common to the South Asian Region. Notably, one of the biggest achievements Sri Lanka has made in combatting corruption was the full implementation of the Right to Information Act (RTI).[94] The Act will strengthen institutions and the general public's resolve to fight corruption and is part of the new Government's commitment to good governance.

Role of regulatory authorities

Having elaborated on the context in which corruption and economic crime occurs in Sri Lanka, let me now turn to the role of regulatory authorities. CIABOC,[95] the Bribery Commission of Sri Lanka, was re-commissioned many times with different Bribery Commissioners. It was Professor G.L. Peiris, as Minister of Justice in 1994, who was instrumental in introducing

---

[v] The CoCo 2014 was the inaugural session of the Coalition against Corruption (CoCo) conference co-hosted by the Center on Democracy, Development and the Rule of Law, Stanford University, Janaagraha Centre for Citizenship and Democracy, Bangalore, and Sunlight Foundation, Washington DC.

corruption as an offense in Sri Lankan law, as there was no such offense against corruption in the history of our country. Legal action prior to this was implemented only against a person accepting a bribe. The new Act brought about in 1994[96] formulated laws to penalise those who would also offer a bribe. The Act was also in line with the later 17th Amendment to the Constitution[97] and therefore did not solely vest the power to appoint officials to the Bribery Commission in the sitting government.

However, the former Government, under the 18th Amendment to the Constitution,[98] brought the Bribery Commission under the auspices of the President, thereby nullifying the independence of the Commission. This was done in the wake of the 2015 scandal, where the Speaker of the House of Parliament stated that he should be informed before MPs are summoned to the Bribery Commission,[99] thereby bringing up questions of the role of the Parliament and the Speaker as well as the Office of the President in influencing the Bribery Commission. This triggered much public agitation and media scrutiny. Thus, the task for the present Government should be on strengthening the independence of the Bribery Commission in fighting corruption and to make it a decentralized institution.

The Committee on Public Accounts[100] (CPA) has a role to play in this regard. The CPA is constituted under the Sri Lankan Parliament and probes the efficiency and financial discipline of the government, its ministries, departments, provincial councils, and local authorities. Thus, the CPA is an integral tool in fighting economic crime and corruption. Another tool in the tool kit is to strengthen the Auditor General's Department. This department is key to uncovering and investigating corruption and financial misappropriation in state institutions.

Contribution of whistle-blowers

The lynchpin of fighting economic crime and corruption in a democratic society with a free and responsible press is the contribution of whistle-blowers. Sri Lanka has just emerged from a period of governance that resorted to censorship and clamping down on democratic values. An unfortunate consequence of this period was that as a nation we lost one of our best journalists, Lasantha Wickramatunge,[101] who was a vocal and critical whistle blower on the past regime. He was brutally murdered and the investigation is still on-going to find the perpetrators. Similarly, the previous Government was also blocking content on many publishing sites including the Colombo Telegraph.[102] To fight this, people used to access these sites from proxy servers, as the Colombo Telegraph was one of the best online platforms which carried a lot of voices of the Sri Lankan polity.

To combat such pervasive corruption and to aid whistle blowers, websites such as *ipaidabribe.lk*[103] will become extremely powerful tools which are directly in the hands of the public. Unfortunately, such tools are still new to the Sri Lanka public and thus their utility is not commonplace in a society so entrenched with corruption and economic crime. The current Government and all other relevant institutes should support and promote these initiatives in order to overcome this challenge.

Terrorism and economic crime

Let us now delve into Sri Lanka's past and explore how the LTTE, who waged guerrilla warfare for over 25 years in our country, was crippled by the elimination of their financial arm. Since 1983, when Sri Lanka's economy came under the grip of terrorism, the largest expenditure of the GOSL was on the war, with its devastating effects on economic development. The 2004 tsunami provided the happy hunting grounds for terrorist financing in Sri Lanka. The post-tsunami revelation was that it opened the flood gates for terrorist financing to take on a human face. The largest inflow of tsunami relief came into the accounts of the Tamil Rehabilitation Organization (TRO),[104] deemed to be a registered NGO, but which was found to be the financing arm of the LTTE. The TRO waged all types of economic crimes in Sri Lanka that virtually brought this nation to a standstill.

The TRO, which had cleverly inveigled itself into the favours of the highest echelons of Sri Lankan politics, had also won over the Sri Lankan diaspora in the key capitals of the world — UK, the US, Australia and in Europe — to which many Sri Lankan Tamils had fled as economic and political refugees during the war. The TRO's use of extortion over the diaspora to mobilise funds for their use left the diaspora helpless to fight back. This was confirmed by the Swiss police about several members of the diaspora who had complained of terror tactics used by the TRO to extort money from them, but who were terrified of testifying in a court of law for fear of their lives. So no convictions could be brought against them by the Swiss police.[105]

The scale of the tsunami and its effects on Sri Lanka was such that the GOSL was desperately in need of funds to meet the humane needs of the tsunami victims. Where hitherto, foreign funds coming through the banking system would have been subject to close scrutiny and AML/CFT due diligence, funds purporting to be for tsunami relief were not subject to even the most basic scrutiny. Sri Lanka was in no position to question the sources or integrity of the funds that flowed into the country. However, the fact that it all came through the banking system gave the Central Bank the ability to collate data on these funds, their sources, and the recipients. The findings were indeed very revealing.

The largest inflow was to the TRO;[106] since 2003, the TRO had maintained bank accounts at seven systematically important banks in the country and was in receipt of large foreign remittances from across the world. At the time of its proscription, it had a network of 153 accounts at these seven banks, 148 of which were in the North and East.[107] The largest component of foreign currency remittances received by the TRO, accounting for 41%, came from the US.[108] These funds were received from the TRO office registered in Cumberland in the State of Maryland in the US, which was the entity being investigated by the US authorities with regard to arms purchases for the LTTE.[109] The largest individual contributor to the TRO from the US was Raj Rajaratnam[w] of the *Galleon Group* (36.3% of total remittances) who is now serving a jail sentence.

International NGOs had also transferred funds directly to the TRO for humanitarian projects.[110] It is interesting to note that economic crime can also be perpetuated by NGOs. We so often think of NGOs as connected to development and aid that we forget to consider the regulatory aspects. One of these foreign NGOs in Sri Lanka was found to be harbouring a LTTE airplane in one of its sites in the North.[111] The NGO Secretariat in Sri Lanka was very weak, or did not possess the mechanisms or processes to have these NGOs registered and their bona fides checked. They also

---

[w] Raj Rajaratnam is a Sri Lankan-American former hedge fund manager and billionaire founder of the Galleon Group, a New York-based hedge fund management firm.

escaped the scrutiny of Sri Lanka's overseas missions, which issued them the visas for entry into Sri Lanka. It was evident that everyone was capitalising on the vulnerability of the country in the aftermath of the tsunami. A symposium conducted in Colombo under the auspices of US Aid, to which countries from the region were also invited, revealed that this was a common occurrence in many countries which were fighting terrorism, where, in the aftermath of a natural disaster, an inflow of spurious NGOs was inevitable. I hope this case study has enlightened you on the fact that financing terrorism feeds economic crime and in turn impedes and devastates economic growth.

Conclusion

Professor Harold Laski of the London School of Economics (LSE) said: "*Eternal Vigilance is the Price of Liberty*".[112] The fight against economic crime cannot be accomplished if it is limited to the state. However, the litmus test of government failure is the inability to regulate corruption and economic crime, which is therefore an indicator of a failed state. Thus, the state must work in tandem with its citizens to be eternally vigilant in curbing the perpetuation of economic crime and corruption in society — for those who do not prevent crime when they can only foster it.

Chapter 6

Cyber Security and Foresight

"Pessimism should be stopped. It is a cowardly intellectual position."

Jerome C. Glenn[a]

---

[a] J.C. Glenn is the co-founder and Director of the Millennium Project, and inventor of Futures Wheel technique. He is the primary author of *State of the Future Report* and editor of *Futures Research Methodology*.

Unified Mechanism to Improve Cyber Security[1]

I congratulate the organisers — the Conference on Interaction and Confidence-building in Central Asia (CICA) — for choosing this apt and timely topic on cyber security, when the world is facing a serious cyber threat on this very same day of 28 June 2017.[2] The Institute of National Security Studies Sri Lanka (INSSSL), as the national security think tank, considers cyber security as a top priority. A few weeks ago, we as an institute had a thematic discussion[3] on the recent *WannaCry* attack and its effects to our region as well as how to prepare for future attacks. In this regard, it is notable that the Secretary to the Telecommunications Ministry has made efforts to establish a high level task force as an outcome of our discussion.

One of the speakers at today's forum,[4] Yang Jieming, stated that: *"we need an integrated security architecture but we have challenges and much complexity among our governments"*. In this regard, the founder of the World Wide Web, Tim Berners Lee said: *"The original idea of the web was that it should be a collaborative space where you can communicate through sharing information."*[5] Unfortunately, the collaborative space to advance our human goals has been misused. Therefore, all nations need to collaboratively find solutions for our challenges in the cyber domain.

Global threat

The global citizenry woke up to a very different world on Friday, 12 May 2017.[6] Within a day, more than 230,000 computers in over 150 countries were infected. Similarly, today we are witnessing the same sort of attack to most of the critical infrastructure in the Ukraine and many other places. In fact, one of the main underlying themes of the US and French Presidential elections, which continues to be a talking point even post-election, is the allegations of cyber-attacks on the election system.[7] Ms. Lang Ping, another speaker at today's forum, explained how terrorists use cyberspace to spread their ideology for recruitment and mobilization. This is true even in the Sri Lankan context, as the LTTE used the internet even back then to spread their ideology and post videos on social media.

Beyond borders

Clandestine intrusions into digital systems, including cybercrime and unsanctioned use of digital information that defy geographical and jurisdictional boundaries, seem to be growing and perpetrators seem undeterred by the cyber security countermeasures already in place to tackle the issue. The result is growing economic losses, many of which go unreported. There are intangible costs to society such as reputational damage, psychological trauma, general feelings of frustration, and insecurity. Beyond these costs, there are risks to national security. Cyber terror attacks can cripple the military, financial, and services sectors of advanced economies. The more developed and dependent on technology a country is, the more vulnerable its national infrastructure is to attacks against it. A disruptive, manipulative, or destructive cyber-attack can present a significant risk to economic and national security if lives are lost, property destroyed, policy objectives harmed, or economic interests affected.

This is why a significant responsibility lies in the hands of the global community as a whole on building cyber capabilities and organisations to defend the networks, systems, and information, as well as to defend national and collective interests against cyber-attacks. In the 21st century's wired world, our reliance on the confidentiality, availability, and the integrity of data stands in stark contrast to the general lack of adequate cyber security. Without wise and strong investments in cyber security and cyber defence, our data systems remain open and susceptible to even the most rudimentary and dangerous forms of exploitation and attacks. This is why cyber security needs to be more proactive and less reactive.

OBOR and SCO

Almost all of the One Belt, One Road (OBOR) projects will be imbued with operational, financial, legal and regulatory, and sovereign risks on account of the wide diversity in the countries involved, and their geographical, political, and economic situations. For a *"common cultural and civilizational threat that runs through Asia"*, a truly Asian connectivity needs to take into account not only institutional, regulatory, legal, financial, and commercial connections, but also digital connectivity.

Cyber security is one such area on which the realisation of OBOR depends heavily.

As Ren Xianliang,[8] the deputy head of the Cyberspace Administration[9] of China has stated, *"the use of the internet by terrorists, religious extremists, and extremist forces in certain areas has helped them infiltrate more areas."*[10] Economic infrastructure is therefore highly vulnerable to such attacks. As Mr. Ren reiterated, cyber security has become one of the key challenges for OBOR. Given that OBOR includes launching several development banks, including the multilateral Asian Infrastructure Investment Bank[11] (AIIB), the Silk Road Fund[12] and the BRICS New Development Bank,[13] between these three institutions there is a capital base of US$ 240 billion at stake. Therefore, one can envisage the e-banking infrastructure, which is at the heart of a project of this magnitude, throughout OBOR. Minimising vulnerabilities that exist in the cyber domain will ensure that e-banking and communications networks remain secure in this platform.

Therefore, it is apparent that the emerging political economy of OBOR will rely heavily on the cyber domain for communication, coordination, investment, and implementation. It is of utmost importance that proper digital communication channels remain unhindered, even in times of tension and hostilities. The cyber infrastructure of OBOR must therefore be carefully planned with a cohesive approach with inputs from all the partners and stakeholders so that all parties have an incentive to keep the infrastructure safe and sound. The cyber infrastructure must also have a higher level of legal immunity, especially in times of conflict. The infrastructure should not be abused by the participants who use its vulnerabilities for their own national interests. This way, the cyber security infrastructure of OBOR can act as a deterrent and create a safe space where e-commerce can flourish; for e-commerce is where the future of trade lies.

In recent years, Sri Lanka's greater dependence on critical infrastructure, industrial automation, and cyber based control systems has resulted in a growing unforeseen vulnerability to cyber-security threats. It is therefore crucial that cyber security professionals understand and have the knowledge to address these issues domestically, and that this is done in a shared forum. Nevertheless, as part of international forums, cyber-security cooperation is necessary. For example, the operational efficiency of OBOR is vulnerable and can be easily compromised if the networked participants do not have a uniformed approach to cyber security. Thus, cooperation among CERTs is essential among all OBOR nations. Notably, the Sri Lankan CERT[14] with its limited capacity is doing remarkable work to secure our cyber domain. By cooperating among CERTs we could strengthen and advance our capabilities to fight cybercrime against non-state actors.

On the other hand, the Shanghai Cooperation Organisation[15] (SCO) can also act as a platform to promote cyber security by coordinating and building resilience and skill competencies of the participants of OBOR. In this regard, Sri Lanka, being the maritime hub and a *"geostrategic super connector"* on the Maritime Silk Road (MSR), should seek full membership of the SCO. India and Pakistan have become full members this year (2017), marking a significant step.[16] A SCO membership wide forum, with a mandate to discuss cyber security issues and come up with Standard Operating Procedures and set benchmarks for security standardisation of critical infrastructure networks along OBOR is important in this regard.

The 2016 *Cyber Security Forum*[17] by the SCO is commendable for creating a platform to ensure shared cyber security in the international arena. However, this forum can go beyond and also draft a common legislative framework for the countries acceded to the SCO. Cyber security legislation in this regard must include prevention, detention and reaction. *Prevention* must be in the form of identifying and mitigating vulnerabilities; *Detection* in the form of simulating and analysing attack patterns and *Reaction* in the form of rapid response and recovery. A common cyber security policy as an outcome of this framework would be a turning point. If such a policy is to come about, all new strategies would become integrated and comprehensive, thereby approaching cyber security in a holistic manner — encompassing economic, social, educational, legal, law enforcement, technical, diplomatic, military, and intelligence related aspects. Yet if such a mechanism is to be implemented within the SCO or even more broadly within the OBOR, participant countries have to come to a consensus on what constitutes cybercrime, in order to have a unified approach. In sum, a unified understanding of cybercrime has to lead to a unified concept of criminalising cybercrime, in order to deter such crimes as well as to normalise the concept of a safe cyber domain.

A Collaborative Venture in the Age of 'Information Wars': Japan and Sri Lanka[18]

First let me thank the *National Institute for Defence Studies*[19](NIDS) in Japan for the kind invitation. I would like to begin with the famous speech made in San Francisco by the former President of Sri Lanka, then Minister of Finance, J. R. Jayewardene, in 1951, where he stated, *"We extend to Japan a hand of friendship, and trust that with the closing of this chapter in the history of man, the last page of which we write today, and with the beginning of the new one, the first page of which we dictate tomorrow, her people and ours may march together to enjoy the full dignity of human life in peace and prosperity."*[20]

From President Jayewardene to our current respective Presidents, H.E. Maithripala Sirisena and H.E. Mr. Shinzo Abe,[b] Prime Minister of Japan, there have been successful strong bilateral ties between Sri Lanka and Japan. This was exemplified in May 2016,[21] where the two nations showed that they have not only experienced a friendship that lasted over six decades, but also have steadfastly and resolutely stood by each other, both in good times and in testing times, in mutual assistance and cooperation. During the G7 Summit Outreach Meeting,[22] Prime Minister Abe offered Japan's support to Sri Lanka for economic development, maritime security, national reconciliation, and peace building.

Two countries that exhibit many facets of similarity, Japan and Sri Lanka are both island nations in Asia with unique cultural roots. However, in the post-war world order, Japan's developmental success as an East Asian miracle has created a watermark for aspiring South Asian nations to follow a path of development that was unique from the West, simultaneously setting an example for nations such as Sri Lanka to emerge as sustainable in the developmental journey. In the years that followed 1952, Sri Lanka has been a beneficiary of the friendly arm Japan has extended to its Asian peers in terms of developmental aid and assistance. I have witnessed this first-hand, when I was the Chairman of the *Ceylon*

---

[b] Shinzō Abe is a Japanese politician serving as the 57th Prime Minister of Japan and Leader of the Liberal Democratic Party since 2012, and previously from 2006 to 2007. He is the third-longest serving Prime Minister in post-war Japan.

Fisheries Harbour Corporation,[23] during the post-Asian tsunami[c] period, where reconstruction aid was given to Sri Lanka by Japan to rebuild its fishery harbours. Japan accounts for 40 per cent of Sri Lanka's bilateral aid packages.[24] In this regard, Japan has undertaken an important role in times of tension, not only for Sri Lanka, but also for other countries in the South Asian region. This benevolence of the Japanese nation envisages dreams of new opportunities, granting further assistance and collaboration to the developing countries of South Asia. In his visit to Japan in October 2015,[25] our Prime Minister, Ranil Wickremesinghe, proposed a framework for collaboration in five fields, which specifically included Security.

In the present information age, predominated by drivers of globalisation and its inherent information flows, the regional security dimensions of South Asia are capitulated in the age of what can be termed as an *'information war'*. With the evolution of security threats from interstate war to intra-state insurgencies, transnational terrorism and climate security issues, *'information'*, in the current context, plays a pivotal role in ensuring regional security as well as accountability and transparency of domestic institutions, which are also the imminent political goals of the current Sri Lankan National Government.

In this regard, *'Soft Power'*[d] emerges as an essential constituency in combating the evolving security threats in the era of the *'information wars'*. As the Prime Minister noted in 2015, collaboration and connectivity are the key elements in this venture.[26] Accordingly, collaboration in terms of utilising the Japanese expertise in science and technology was outlined to be paramount, especially in terms of collaboration between existing institutions, especially to strengthen education, human security, and to counter climate change.

However, *Soft Power* and its collaborative imperative is not the panacea to the novel security issues that trend at the break of dawn. The

---

[c] The 2004 Indian Ocean earthquake occurred on 26 December with the epicentre off the west coast of Sumatra, Indonesia. It is the third-largest earthquake ever recorded on a seismograph. The earthquake and resulting tsunami affected many countries in Southeast Asia and beyond, including Indonesia, Sri Lanka, India and Thailand, the Maldives, Somalia, Myanmar, Malaysia, Seychelles, and others.

[d] Soft Power is a persuasive approach to international relations, typically involving the use of economic or cultural influence.

lessons from the Japanese success story iterates a strong narrative of an ardent political culture and cogent democratic institutions, which are equally vital at the face of the security issues brought forth by variegated information flows. This is because a weak political culture is often followed by weak institutions which are obsolete against the evolving security dynamics. The *Fragile States Index*[27] of 2016, compiled and published by the *Fund For Peace*[28] non-profit think tank, and the *Foreign Affairs*[29] magazine highlighted the weak security apparatuses of states in South Asia, including Sri Lanka, which can lead to state fragility, a threat to regional as well as sustainable security. In this regard, H.E. President Sirisena, accentuated his commitment to transparency, accountability and the rule of law, and his determination to wipe out corruption, in his statement on '*Stability and Prosperity in Asia*'[30] at the Outreach Sessions of the G7 Summit in May 2016 in Japan, which draws a new light on the future of our institutions and political culture.

Thus, in this collaborative venture, think tanks emerge as essential, both to ensure *soft power* diplomacy and to sustain a strong political culture and institutions. Firstly, think tanks can ensure the successful discharge of Track II diplomacy[e] and build regional as well as international partnerships at state and non-state levels, which can be utilised to share knowledge and expertise. Secondly, collaboration between think tanks can improve regional security by producing scholarly thematic papers and discussion which could serve as advisory templates and utilise the ideational processes that supplement governments. In essence, it is important to reminiscence that, in the age of the '*information wars*', any pockets of will to collaborate are valuable; for the dispersion of information can create strong security infrastructure that is resilient to novel security issues of the post-cold war international system. Since South Asia is a region terrorised by transnational security threats in the post-ISIS age, the connectivity and collaboration of research institutions are indispensable.

On this note, The Institute of national Security Studies Sri Lanka (INSSSL) was founded in July 2016, where H.E. President Sirisena noted the vitality of a premiere national Defence think tank in understanding the

---

[e] Track II diplomacy is the practice of non-governmental, informal and unofficial contacts and activities between private citizens or groups of individuals, sometimes called non-state actors.

security environment of the region. The INSSSL's ability to inaugurate joint research and policy discussions in the evolving security debate of South Asia renders it an important actor in pursuing a collaborative ventures and also serving as a link between the region and in this context, with Japan, in security research and analysis.

As Atifete Jahjaga, the former Kosovo President, stated, *"Democracy must be built through open societies that share information. When there is information, there is enlightenment. When there is debate, there are solutions. When there is no sharing of power, no rule of law, no accountability, there is abuse, corruption, subjugation and indignation."*[31] In this light, undoubtedly, collaboration is the best solution to the emerging security threats in the era of information wars, and the prowess of Japan as a nation is none other than a resource to a developing region such as South Asia, in restructuring its security architecture to be more resilient and synergetic to the evolving security threats.

Cyber Security Threats to Sri Lanka[32]

"A computer based attack on the national infrastructure could cripple the nation more quickly than a military strike." — Robin Cook[33]

Cyber security in Sri Lanka and the world beyond

Is cyber security part of our National Security Strategy? If so, are we ready to face the biggest security threat the entire world is facing, in a domain that was not explored traditionally via land, sea, or air? It is an essential component when formulating the defence policy today and the type of complexity escalates when we are talking about cyber warfare.

On Friday, 12 May 2017, within the span of a day, more than 230,000 computers in over 150 countries were infected by the *WannaCry* ransomware attack.[34] We witnessed the same sort of attacks to critical infrastructure on energy firms in Ukraine, the NHS in the UK, and many other places on the 27 June. In Ukraine, workers were forced to manually monitor the radiation level at the old Chernobyl[f] nuclear plant as

---

[f]The Chernobyl disaster was a catastrophic nuclear accident. It occurred on 25–26 April 1986 in the No. 4 light water graphite moderated reactor at the Chernobyl Nuclear Power Plant.

computers failed.[35] In addition, one of the main underlying themes of the US and French presidential elections, which continues to be a talking point even post-election, are the allegations of cyber-attacks on the election system. The Sri Lankan President's website and the Sri Lankan Health Ministry's website were also attacked by hackers.

As the national security think tank, the Institute of National Security Studies Sri Lanka (INSSSL) has cyber security as a top priority. An important roundtable discussion was held by INSSSL on the recent *WannaCry* cyber-attack,[36] on its effects worldwide as well as Sri Lanka and the need for preparedness, while also looking at the larger implications of cyber security. As a direct outcome of the aforementioned roundtable, the Secretary of the Ministry of Telecommunications and Digital Infrastructure, Mr. Wasantha Deshapriya, has established a high-level task force to prepare the National Cyber Security Strategy for our nation.

The new cyber domain and its implications

"The original idea of the web was that it should be a collaborative space where you can communicate through sharing information,"[37] affirmed by Tim Berners Lee, the founder of the World Wide Web. Yet regrettably, this collaborative space to advance our human goals has often been misused. Thus, I must stress the importance of all nations collaborating to find common solutions to common challenges in the cyber domain.

Many cyber security experts pointed out the NSA's non-disclosure of the underlying vulnerability and their loss of control of the *Eternal Blue*[g] cyber-attack tool, in the aftermath of the *WannaCry* cyber-attack. According to the distinguished British cyber security expert Graham Cluley, *"some culpability on the part of the US intelligent services"*[38] must not be brushed aside for *"they could have done something ages ago to get this problem fixed and they didn't do it."*[39] This not only highlights the danger of cyber-attacks and the underlying vulnerability of our military,

---

[g] *Eternal Blue* is an exploit developed by the U.S. National Security Agency (NSA) according to testimony by former NSA employees. It was leaked by the Shadow Brokers hacker group on 14 April 2017, and was used as part of the worldwide *WannaCry* ransomware attack on 12 May 2017.

economic, and social infrastructure to such attacks, but also highlights the imagined and imaginable risks that come with it.

South Asia's financial sector faces a dual threat. First, there are cyber-criminals who are looking to steal money. Second, advanced threat actors are seeking sensitive financial information to gain a business advantage. A few weeks ago at Cambridge University, I was privy to the threat of economic crime in the cyber domain and this was cast as a serious issue for many who are in the financial sector. Another example is the second conference of the CICA Non-Governmental Forum in Beijing, 28 June 2017, where I spoke at a Cyber Security panel, with experts on the subject from Ukraine, China, East Asia, and many others. I proposed that the operational efficiency of OBOR is vulnerable and can be easily compromised if the networked participants do not have a uniform approach to cyber security. Cooperation among Computer Emergency Readiness Teams (CERT) is essential among all OBOR nations. Sri Lankan CERT, even with its limited capacity, is doing remarkable work to secure our cyber domain. By cooperation among CERTs we could strengthen and advance our capabilities to fight cybercrime.

Clausewitz and parallel warfare in cyberspace

To truly understand the ramifications of a cyber-attack, I would like to draw your attention to a concept called Clausewitz's *Trinitarian Warfare*.[42] The trinity is composed of three dominant tendencies: the military, the government, and the people.[43] These tendencies interact with each other and their interactions and inter-relationships have changed over time. Even if one tendency is attacked, the other two have the resilience to revive and sustain the trinity. Today these tendencies are heavily dependent on digital information. From personal mobile phones to military systems, they are all operating on information systems. Therefore, this concept speaks to the susceptibility of the military-industrial complex and strategic warfare.

If all three tendencies are simultaneously attacked — that is, parallel warfare, with regards to cyberspace — the victim nation will suffer immense damage and destruction. To understand parallel warfare, one has to understand the three tendencies and how they will affect the whole system. Nations need to build resilience and anti-cyber warfare and cyber security capabilities to overcome or mitigate parallel warfare in cyberspace.

Challenges Sri Lanka faces

To face these critical challenges, Sri Lanka requires cyber security experts with capacity, but we do not have enough experts in this field. Planning, funding, and training a defence force for future cyber security threats should be considered a top priority. Based on our intelligence mechanism, how we handle uncertainty by scenario planning should be carefully executed.

There is no research and development into cyber security, nor any adequate monetary investment on this front. Setting up cyber training institutes in the country is essential. Such a lack of investment has meant that there are no incentives for companies in Sri Lanka to engage in the cyber domain or to invest in cyber security. However, this year's (2017) annual budget will most probably provide us with some incentive to develop this sector.

In terms of critical infrastructure, it was brought to light that Sri Lanka's critical infrastructure is not safeguarded in terms of cyber security. This makes our economy very vulnerable to cyber-attacks. Similarly, in terms of vendor products, it was discussed that Sri Lanka should invest in designing indigenous products instead of procuring them externally. Our own algorithms should be developed for high-level security applications. For such initiatives, government, military, and academia should work together. Lastly, the initial cyber platform should be created on a national level so that in a few years we can show some form of progress. The above areas are avenues that should be pursued in order for Sri Lanka to build a comprehensive cyber security platform.

Forecast 2016: A Roadmap for Sri Lanka[44]

"Our objective is to make Sri Lanka the most competitive nation in the Indian Ocean and to develop the island as a mega city for the region that will go between Singapore and Dubai, thus make it competitive and the time has come for us to think how we are going to do it." — Ranil Wickremesinghe[45]

A year since the victory of incumbent Sri Lankan President Maithripala Sirisena, the rainbow coalition has not delivered on its huge promises of reform. However, to its credit, it has managed (with some success) to introduce newer and more outward-looking policies. First, freedom of expression has been fully restored. The trend of blocking media sites has ended, and the safety of media personnel re-established. Second, independent commissions such as the Commission to Investigate Allegations of Bribery or Corruption (CIABOC) have been fully reinstated. Third, a foreign policy rebalance between the West and China is in the process of being rebuilt.

Economy

The January 2016 Sri Lanka Economic Forum[46] brought with it some excellent thoughts from global leaders such as Ricardo Hausmann, Joseph Stiglitz, and George Soros to the forefront. Prime Minister Wickremesinghe stated, *"Sri Lankans who voted for the change and those who didn't vote should unite to build this nation to the height achieved by nations like Singapore."*[47] Soros said that Sri Lanka should lower its expectations as there is a clear sign of a global economic slowdown this year (2017). The US$27 billion Soros Fund Management (SFM) is looking to invest US$300 million initially in the economy — a good start at the beginning of the year.[48] However, economist Montek Singh Ahluwalia said that revenue as per GDP was 12 per cent when it should be 20 per cent.[49] Therefore, comprehensive tax reforms are needed to increase revenue to 18 to 20 per cent of GDP in the next few years.

Containing the fiscal deficit to five per cent of the GDP[50] should continue to stabilise the economy. To reduce fiscal deficit, it is important to focus on increasing revenue and decreasing government expenditure — a difficult task to undertake in the present political context. Losses incurred by public enterprises are a huge fiscal burden that needs to be addressed. Politicians who offer employment merely to satisfy the electorate should be stopped. An example of that is the Ceylon Fishery Harbours Corporation,[51] which had a little over 800 employees in 2009. Today, 1800 people are employed for the same lot of harbours. Once a profitable corporation, it is currently incurring losses with its large number of employees. In the same way, a large cabinet with nearly 100 ministers leads to the wastage of state resources.

It was against this socio-political and economic backdrop that Wickremesinghe participated in the World Economic Forum in Davos — a conference where he could interact with top minds, investors, and political leaders — to plan his strategic economic agenda for the country. For the first time in 10 years, Sri Lanka had high-level political representation at Davos. In fact, this author, during two visits to Davos, was the only government representative from Sri Lanka, without much support from the government. The tide has changed, and for the better.

Standard of living

The government should focus on improving citizens' quality of life by providing the best possible solutions to problems, instead of discussions about unfruitful political gossip. Unfortunately, most of Sri Lanka's headlines have been to the contrary. For instance, 2,700 people, i.e. an average of 7.5 people every day, were killed in road accidents in 2015 — an increase compared to 2014.[52] On the other hand, given how there were numerous references to Singapore at the Sri Lanka Economic Forum, an example from Singapore is in order. On 25 December 2015, the Prime Minister of Singapore, Lee Hsien Loong,[h] opened the Downtown Line 2 (DLT2),[53] an extension to Singapore's existing public rail network that is set to ease traffic. As Lee stated, *"with a new MRT line and extension to be opened next year onwards the network will double to 360 km by 2030. It will be comparable to London, New York and Tokyo, this means 8 in 10 homes will be within a 10 minute radius."*[54] This is just one example of several important lessons and practices Sri Lanka could import from Singapore.

The World Economic Forum has categorised Sri Lanka as an efficiency-driven economy (Stage 2) in this year's (2017) Global Competitiveness Index.[55] This is an achievement, for Colombo has moved up from factor-driven (Stage 1). Almost all South Asian countries are still in Stage 1 or in transition. Sri Lanka should aim to move from efficiency-driven to the next

---

[h] Lee Hsien Loong is a Singaporean statesman serving as the 3rd and current Prime Minister of Singapore since 2004.

stage of transition, and then to innovation-driven by 2030. A goal to double GDP per capita by 2020 and to improve all sectors of the economy should be set. Given its tremendous human resource potential, Sri Lanka has the capacity to carry this out. However, in order to become the region's top workforce not just in terms of size but also quality, this valuable resource requires training. Investment in research and development and improvement in educational systems and universities should be the government's priority.

Governance

Improving transparency and strengthening mechanisms to fight corruption are important areas that require focus. Optimising the productivity of the government's loss-making institutions, strengthening and encouraging the private sector to expand, combating sexual abuse, and enforcing child protection rights are among the neglected areas that should be addressed. The Government will soon announce the new Constitutional Assembly[56] to draft the new Constitution with public participation. After this, it will be sent for approval, and then referendum. It is a task that will reset several core areas of the present governance structure; and therefore, should ideally be undertaken after debate and dialogue with the public. However, there is room for malicious campaigns to create fear; therefore, the Government should steer through this carefully with stakeholder participation.

In addition, the recent surge in nationalism resulting from a *'Sinha Le'* (Sinhalese blood) campaign that has gone viral on the internet is definitely not a positive sign, as it could manifest in the worst form of nationalism. Instead, nationalism should be used to preserve one's language. This sort of appreciation for languages will create interest among the younger generations to learn and appreciate a language such as Sinhala — a dying language, according to the UN.[57]

Reconciliation

As a nation, Sri Lanka has suffered tremendously in the past, and should now move towards uniting all ethnic groups via a genuine reconciliation processes. President Sirisena demonstrated a sincere sign of reconciliation on the day he completed a year in office: he pardoned the LTTE assassin,

Sivaraja Jenivan, who had attempted to assassinate the President in 2006. The pardon was an act of remembering the past but also forgiveness in order to create a better future. This is a great deed and signals the commencing of brave and genuine efforts towards the reconciliation process.

Overview

Sri Lanka possesses the potential to achieve great heights. With the correct processes in place, and a collective effort to create a better political culture, the country could spur its economic growth to overcome its challenges, both internal and external.

Crisis and Foresight Analysis[58]

The dawn of the fourth industrial revolution brings with it the promise of further human advancement. Yet, while humanity should be aspiring for a better life, disturbing events like the terrorist attacks in Manchester,[59] London, and the Philippines,[60] and the recent white phosphorus attack in Raqqa,[61] Syria, point to humanity's burial of its own journey toward a better world. The 17th century philosopher Blaise Pascal[i] rightly explained, *"Humanity is great, because it knows itself to be wretched."*[62] Is there then, with advanced human intellect, still hope of creating a better world and preventing or minimising the loss of human life? Machiavelli[j] said in this regard: *"It is necessary not only to pay attention to immediate crisis, but to foresee those that will come and to make every effort to prevent them."*[63]

In Sri Lanka this year (2017), over 200 lives were lost and half a million affected by the torrential rainfall that caused floods and landslides[64]; it was the same cycle of rain with a different magnitude than last year. The nation's vulnerability to such natural disasters in the near future and years ahead should be taken into the highest consideration. The attitude of a

---

[i] Blaise Pascal was a French mathematician, physicist, inventor, writer, and Catholic theologian.

[j] Niccolò Machiavelli was an Italian diplomat, politician, historian, philosopher, humanist, and writer of the Renaissance period. He has often been called the father of modern political science.

reactive response to crisis situations in the country should change in this regard. A proactive methodology designed to minimise casualties should be considered. When considering Sri Lanka's vision for 2050, the 100 ministries within Sri Lanka and the newly created ones currently project vagueness and uncertainty.

Sri Lanka's future will depend on the choices that are created today for a better tomorrow. For this, it is important to question the reference template used to make such choices — is it out dated or still a relevant template? For example, in the last budget,[65] the Sri Lankan government increased taxes on electric vehicles. However, at the United Nations Framework Convention on Climate Change (UNFCCC) COP 21 in Paris, the President pledged to the sustainability project, followed by supporting remarks from the Prime Minister in New York[66] on the same subject. This is a relevant template. The question then is how to bridge the gaps in policymaking?

Sri Lanka could play a significant role in the next few decades due to its pivotal geo-strategic positioning. Therefore, it is very important to identify and discuss the national challenges for the next 25 to 50 years, and even beyond. Demographic shifts, urbanization, population ratios, and the challenges that Sri Lanka could face from within and from outside powers are some salient points to be considered. For this, there is a need to prepare foresight maps for the nation, its institutions, and ministries for the long term, a 50-year horizon, and with the correct methodology, so that the nation can be easily steered from regime to regime and mandates can be identified by a scientific method. This does not happen in Sri Lanka at present.

In Sri Lanka, line ministries have been arbitrarily put together and yet the Government claims that this has been done scientifically. For instance, the Ministry for Education and Highways[67] has been cobbled together; similarly, the Ministry for Finance and Media[68] has been merged as well. There is no connection among the subject areas of these 'scientifically' amalgamated ministries. Additionally, the ministries' mandates are allocated in an ad-hoc manner, leading to overlaps and duplications of work. When institutes are created or structured this way, they lose their strategic direction and focus. Therefore, it appears that the quality of governance has been replaced by quantity. In any country, the grand strategy is spelled out by its leaders and the strategy has to be justifiably adjusted to accommodate changes in this context. If it cannot be justified, the government should not create new entities that will burden its budget and could even derail the grand vision.

With regards to the Millennium Project,[k] *"the decision support software and foresight systems are constantly improving: for example, big data analytics, simulations, collective intelligence systems, indexes and e-governance participatory systems."* Integrating foresight systems into a society is a priority and many governments have already done so. In 2016, the Sri Lanka Foresight Initiative[69] was launched by this author, in collaboration with the Millennium Project, which operates in over 60 countries to improve policymaking and strategic narratives on key priority areas by engaging the government and other stakeholders in society.

Unfortunately, since its launch in May 2016, there has not been a single inquiry or request to implement this methodology. The powerful *Delphi platform* that is used has benefited many countries and the Sri Lanka can only stand to gain in this regard. The Sri Lankan Millennium Node could visit ministries and institutes to assist and train the officers to develop a context specific foresight map. According to futurist Dr. Puruesh Chaudhary, who operates the Pakistan node for Millennium Project, *"Futures thinking facilitates the process of institutionalized decisions amongst the leadership corridors improving learning faculty and increases the quality of policy inputs and strategic outcomes."*[70] She eloquently explains the importance of inculcating future studies in to Government policy making, in her latest paper *'The Big Idea: Next Generation of Leadership in Pakistan needs a 'New-Think'.*'[71]

For a country like Sri Lanka which aspires to be the *'Miracle'* or *'Wonder of Asia'*, its leaders should craft the foresight map that takes the country to the aspired destination.

Forecast 2017: Sri Lanka[72]

It was less than half a million votes that restored democratic order in Sri Lanka and set the nation in the correct direction three years ago.[73]

---

[k] The Millennium Project is an independent non-profit think tank composed of futurists, scholars, decision-makers, and business planners, which focuses on the future. It publishes its State of the Future report annually.

8 January 2015[74] saw the dawn of good governance locally and a recalibration of the island's foreign policy. The draconian 18th amendment[75] to the Sri Lankan Constitution was scrapped by an (extra) ordinary man who took on the challenge to topple the existing government. Expectations were and are high to change the existing political culture. The adoption of new ways is difficult for individuals who deeply believe in a set of values because it represents a shift from an established zone of comfort and influence. Fresh recommendations, new methods of fighting corruption, and much more have to be absorbed and proven instead of rejected out of hand.

On the economic front, Sri Lanka began 2016 with the visit of George Soros.[1, 76] While his visit did not bring with it the anticipated investment, Professor Riccardo Hausmann from Harvard University shared valuable insights when in Sri Lanka.[77] In addition, the appointment of the new governor to Sri Lanka's Central Bank was appreciated by many due to the controversy surrounding the former governor.[78] In terms of the political landscape, the bipartisan unity Government with deep differences in political ideologies experimented with different methods of working together throughout 2016 but failed to deliver on many promises. However, the effort to work together with those differences must be appreciated. The biggest challenge is in finding a common ground to execute differing ideas. Civil society experts could perhaps educate the government on bipartisan methods and models instead of destroying the new model. The nation will have only one choice if the present model is reset. The Sri Lankan governance model is evolving towards a technocracy. People expect a technocratic rule by technical experts to deliver results in areas such as infrastructure, clean air, water management, reliable transportation, public safety, ease of conducting business, good schools, quality housing, freedom of expression, access to jobs, etc.

President Sirisena's third year

At a ceremony to mark the beginning of a third year in office, Sri Lanka's President Maithripala Sirisena invited Chandrababu Naidu, Chief Minister

---

[1]George Soros is a Hungarian-American investor, business magnate, philanthropist, political activist, and author. Soros is one of the world's most successful investors.

of India's Andhra Pradesh State, as his special guest.[79] The visiting chief minister shared lessons learnt from the technological development of Andhra Pradesh's economy, particularly on water and power management. According to President Sirisena, unaccounted poverty in Sri Lanka stands much higher than the recorded percentage. This is ample reason to declare 2017 as the year to eradicate poverty[80] — a challenging task given the present economic situation.

Looking back, in the past two years, there has been an improvement in the human rights situation in the country, particularly with regard to media freedom. There has not been a single incident of murder or of journalists departing the nation due to fear, during President Sirisena's time in office. However, the perpetrators of the murder of veteran journalist Lasantha Wickramatunge, who was killed on 8 January 2009, have yet to be brought to justice. Social media comments regarding this delay raise questions as to whether this investigation would meet the same fate as that of Richard de Zoysa,[81] another veteran journalist who was assassinated in 1990. Not all solutions can be found in 24 months but the media is highlighting the people's frustrations.

Cybercrime and threats to state security via this domain is another pertinent issue for the Government in 2017. The hacking of the President's website[82] and the recent hacking of the Health Ministry website[83] are incidents the Government should immediately take action against. There have been multiple incidents of cybercrime all across South Asia but these were a first in Sri Lanka. Thus, the rise of violent non-state actors in the cyber domain has become a complex geopolitical problem that threatens many countries today.

Sri Lanka and the new world order

China's rising naval power has built one of the largest submarine fleets.[84] Their fleet is causing a tense situation in the IOR, with regard to their port calls in the region, which are set to heighten tensions especially in the South China Sea. In this global power tapestry, Sri Lanka has to find its path to gain the best geopolitical and economic benefit; but this is a challenge, because of the strategic interests of the global powers. According to Professor Indra de Soysa, *"Our strategic position is likely to be of great political interest to great powers that will be tempted to meddle in the internal politics of Sri Lanka. This means that Sri Lankan policy must synchronize with regional and extra-regional powers with an interest in the region. On this count, Sri Lanka could potentially take a lead role in establishing a movement that demilitarizes and de-securitizes the Indian Ocean by building a regime for peaceful cooperation."*[85]

Challenges in 2017

In 2017, the Sri Lankan nation will face three key challenges:

First is the country's debt crisis. FDI remains at a very low rate compared to last year. In addition, two global reports were unfavourable towards Sri Lanka: Bloomberg[86] ranked it among the highest risk countries in the world for investors; and the Corruption Perception Index (CPI) placed the island-state at 95th place,[87] up from 94th place in the previous year. Therefore, the primary focus should be on the economic crisis the nation is facing.

The second challenge is the human rights issue that the Government has had to face in March 2017. According to the UN Special Rapporteur on Torture, Juan Mendez, there are credible reports to show white van abduction have taken place under the Sirisena Government as well.[88] However, it is this author's opinion that international pressure via these baseless allegations against Sri Lanka is perpetuated by the same individuals, who are also accusing Sri Lanka of not undertaking structural reforms to tackle systemic failures of the justice machinery. The Sri Lankan government needs to effectively counter these challenges. The Consultation Task Force on Reconciliation Mechanisms[89] (CTFRM), appointed by the Government, recommended a hybrid court with foreign judges, and was endorsed by the Global Tamil Forum (GTF) and the Tamil National Alliance (TNA). Reportedly, the President expressed his displeasure towards the idea of a hybrid model.

The third challenge is the upcoming local government elections and the drafting of the new Constitution, with internal political pressure created by former President Mahinda Rajapaksa. The recent political rally and protest by the villagers and the Joint Opposition Members of

Parliament at the opening ceremony of the Sri Lanka–China Industrial Zone in Hambantota is a clear indication of the same.[90] The Government's decision to lease 15000 acres of land[91] to a Chinese company was viewed as a serious threat to the nation's sovereignty. Yet the project is moving forward despite the protest. Clearly, the island holds substantial strategic value due to its geographical position and this deal has resulted in the Sri Lankan government owing Beijing $8 billion (more than 12 per cent of its total $64.9 billion debt).[92]

To conclude, 2017 began with the loss of one of the country's most eminent jurists and visionaries for peace. Justice C.J. Weeramantry[m] was instrumental in introducing peace education to the world and although he was a recipient of the UNESCO Prize for Peace Education,[93] he failed to introduce the same to his own country. Peace education and global dignity are programmes that are operational in over 60 countries. Such programmes should be introduced to Sri Lanka. Given the right set of values, the country may yet have hope to achieve good governance.

Sri Lanka drops 14 places: World Economic Forum GCI report[94]

"Sri Lanka cannot become a hub by building infrastructure alone, liberal trade and investment policies are key." — Dr. Saman Kelegama[95]

From the first email sent in 1971 to the tenth anniversary of the iPhone today, it is clear that we all live in the fourth industrial revolution. Many nations need to compete with different sets of strengths and sophistication in this world. There have been impressive developments in many fields such as artificial intelligence, synthetic biology, big data and on-demand technologies. More economically competitive nations will be more productive and will provide the most social benefits whilst creating the best innovation ecosystems.

While economic growth is important it is also necessary to work toward the social aspirations of a society. With the ongoing geopolitical

---

[m] C.J. Weeramantry was a Sri Lankan lawyer who was a Judge of the International Court of Justice (ICJ) from 1991 to 2000, serving as its Vice-President from 1997 to 2000. Weeramantry was a Judge of the Supreme Court of Sri Lanka from 1967 to 1972.

uncertainty and many global challenges, including natural disasters, world leaders need to focus on better political and economic policies.

In 2017, the Global Competitiveness Index (GCI) report[96] measured the performance of 140 nations. The GCI report is a comprehensive and deep analysis of economic competitiveness among nations that is produced yearly by the World Economic Forum (WEF).[97] WEF has been measuring economic competitiveness of nations from 1979. *"It assesses the factors and institutions identified by empirical and theoretical research as determining improvements in productivity, which in turn is the main determinant of long-term growth and an essential factor in economic growth and prosperity. The Global Competitiveness Report hence seeks to help decision makers understand the complex and multifaceted nature of the development challenge; to design better policies, based on public-private collaboration; and to take action to restore confidence in the possibilities of continued economic progress."*[98]

The GCI report shows that Sri Lanka has slipped from 71st place last year to 85th place in 2017.[99] According to the report, this is *"due to a deteriorating institutional environment, lower goods markets efficiency and infrastructure that is assessed as less well developed."*[100] The ranking comes as a shock since Sri Lanka has dropped further in ranking when compared to its place in 2015, when it was at rank 68.[101] However, when looking at South Asia overall, many nations including Bhutan (up 15 places), Nepal (up 10 places), Pakistan (up seven places), and Bangladesh (up seven places) have improved in competitiveness.[102]

According to the report, the most problematic factors for doing business in Sri Lanka have been the inefficient government bureaucracy, poor work ethic in the national labour force, and policy instability. Furthermore, many South Asian nations such as Bangladesh and India face corruption as their topmost problem factor. Of the 12 pillars of assessment (Figure 1), four pillars of basic requirement monitor institutions, infrastructure, macroeconomic environment, health, and primary education. The other six pillars are the efficiency enhancers which include higher education and training, goods markets efficiency, labour market efficiency, financial market development, technological readiness and market size. The final two pillars are business sophistication and innovation.

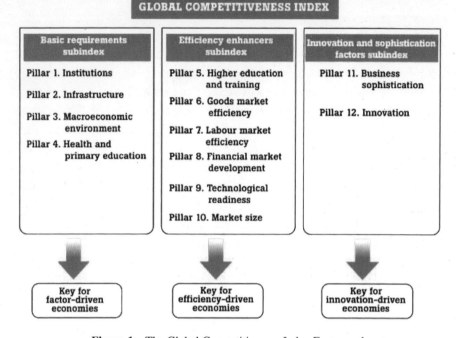

Figure 1 The Global Competitiveness Index Framework

When compared with last year, Sri Lanka has done worse in all 12 pillars,[103] excepting a slight improvement in two pillars, namely macroeconomic environment and market size. In comparison, Bangladesh[104] has performed exceptionally well when compared to last year, especially in the innovation and sophistication sub-index, moving from 116 to 106 — a ten rank improvement. In addition, Pakistan,[105] when compared to last year, has seen tremendous improvement in all three sub-indexes and most of the 12 pillars. As many South Asian nations have had significant improvements in all 12 pillars of competitiveness, the question remains: Why has Sri Lanka done worse in 2017 (Figure 2)? This report should thus be a concern for our economic policy makers.

According to the report Sri Lanka's *"macroeconomic stability needs to remain a priority for the Government, as the country continues to cope with high levels of debt and tries to restore a sound macroeconomic environment. The Government managed to decrease the deficit and*

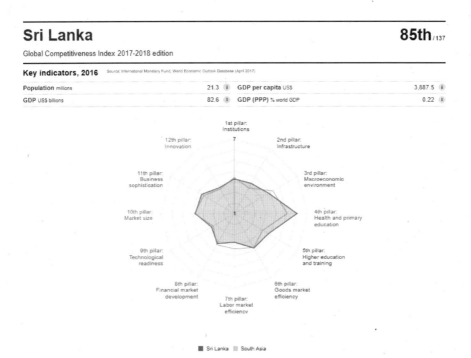

Figure 2 Sri Lanka's Ranking in Global Competitiveness Index

stabilize debt after the country entered assistance program by the IMF in 2016. Yet, the burden of interest on debt remains high and currently amounts to most of the revenue collected by Government. Inflation also increased and forced the authorities to tighten monetary policy, with negative effects on credit. Business confidence has been declining over the past two years."[106] Despite the report showing that we have performed worse than most South Asian nations, the Prime Minister at the recent inauguration of Middle Class Housing Scheme explained: "Total debt exceeds the revenue. However, the revenue is higher than the debt today but we will have to borrow more. Some thought the Government will not be able to manage the economy. However, we successfully managed the economy and increased the revenue."[107] Due to weak economic planning and miscalculations resulting from beautification projects and massive infrastructure loans, the mega projects have failed to create revenue or create decent jobs to strengthen the economy. The Central Bank projection was to achieve a GDP per capita of over US$ 5,500 by 2020.[108] It is clear that in this present state we will not achieve this target.

Sri Lanka has not managed to expand its value-added exports and tap into global value chains. As cautioned by the young economist, Kithmina Hewage, at a recent Asian Development Bank forum, *"goods included in the export basket of Sri Lanka that was setup in 1995 and 2015 were almost identical after 20 years. Vietnam made a decision on its exports and changed its priority structure which helped them to reach export revenue of $185 billion in 2015 from $5 billion in 1995, but sadly for Sri Lanka that did not change its perspective of exports which ended at $10 billion in 2015 from $3 billion in 1995. Sri Lanka failed to implement economic liberalization policies for trade and investment as well as establish a stable environment to attract investments which support plugging into regional value chains."*[109] This same message was echoed by Harvard professor Ricardo Hausmann,[110] who stated that while Vietnam added 48 new products to its export basket, Sri Lanka only added seven from the years 2000–2015. Sri Lanka's seven products did not create much value according to Professor Hausmann (Figure 3).

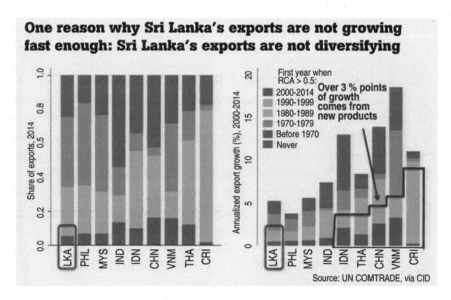

Figure 3 Sri Lankan Export Basket Compared to Other Asian Nations

Thus, Sri Lanka is facing a serious economic situation. If it is not immediately addressed with the right set of economic policy prescriptions, the country's condition will further deteriorate. It is unclear if the investment in more mega infrastructure projects and a reset of the Constitution will create a headwind towards further instability or whether it is the right kind of prescription at the right time for strengthening the economic environment.

Endnotes

Chapter 1

1. Published 14th November 2017 by the Institute of Peace and Conflict Studies (IPCS). See: http://www.ipcs.org/article/india/the-geopolitics-of-floating-bases-and-the-new-world-order-5391.html.
2. Mahan, A.T. (2016) *The Influence of Sea Power upon the French Revolution and Empire 1793–1812* (*Complete*), Library of Alexandria, 428 pp.
3. Mahan, A. T., (1949) *The Influence of Sea Power Upon History 1660–1783*, Boston: Little Brown.
4. From the US embassy in Sri Lanka's website: https://lk.usembassy.gov/uss-nimitz-visit-sri-lanka-first-u-s-aircraft-carrier-since-1985/
5. *Foreign Naval Visits to Sri Lanka from the Years 2010–2017.* Exact Total = *Source*: Sri Lanka Naval Database.
6. *Indian Express* news article: http://indianexpress.com/article/india/to-counter-china-india-sri-lanka-joint-military-exercise-in-pune-from-oct-13-4884495/ (Accessed: 18th December 2017).
7. *The Hindu* news article: http://www.thehindu.com/news/international/INS-Vikramaditya%E2%80%99s-maiden-overseas-port-call-to-Colombo/article14012153.ece (Accessed: 27th December 2017).
8. http://www.bbc.com/news/av/world-us-canada-41934951/china-President-trump-v-candidate-trump.
9. "Secure a Decisive Victory in Building a Moderately Prosperous Society in All Respects and Strive for the Great Success of Socialism with Chinese Characteristics for a New Era," In *Delivered at the 19th National Congress of the Communist Party of China*, October 18, 2017.
10. Statistics from *Ibid*.
11. *Ibid*.

12. https://www.britannica.com/event/Russian-Revolution-of-1917 (Accessed: 28th December 2017).
13. Published 22nd August 2017 by the Institute of Peace and Conflict Studies (IPCS). See: http://www.ipcs.org/article/india/sri-lanka-leveraging-the-politics-of-geography-a-href-5343.html.
14. *Leonard Woolf*, BBC News. 23 May 2014. http://www.bbc.com/news/magazine-27518833 (Retrieved 27 February 2015).
15. Woolf, L., *A Village in the Jungle*.
16. *Ibid.*
17. Mackinder, H. J. (1943) "The Round World and the Winning of the Peace," *Foreign Affairs*, Vol. 21, No. 4, pp. 595–605.
18. See: https://history.state.gov/departmenthistory/short-history/kennan.
19. See IISS biography: http://en.iiss.pku.edu.cn/fg/researcher/person/content?column_id=126&id=18.
20. https://www.weforum.org/agenda/2016/11/america-s-dominance-is-over/.
21. See: http://www.satp.org/satporgtp/countries/shrilanka/document/actsandordinance/13th_amendment.pdf.
22. See: https://peacemaker.un.org/sites/peacemaker.un.org/files/IN%20LK_870729_Indo-Lanka%20Accord.pdf.
23. Annual Report on the Development of the Indian Ocean Region (2015) *21st Century Maritime Silk Road*, eds. R. Wang and C. Zhu, Singapore: Springer.
24. http://www.island.lk/index.php?page_cat=article-details&page=article-details&code_title=176829.
25. Published 15th May 2017 by the Institute of Peace and Conflict Studies (IPCS). See: http://www.ipcs.org/article/india/steering-co-operation-across-oceans-5284.html.
26. *President Xi Jinping delivering speech at World Economic Forum* (Davos 2017).
27. http://www.independent.co.uk/news/world/americas/us-politics/donald-trump-north-korea-aircraft-carrier-sailing-opposite-direction-warning-a7689961.html.
28. Kissinger, H. (1960). "Limited War: Conventional or Nuclear? A Reappraisal," *Daedalus*, Vol. 89, No. 4, pp. 800–817.
29. https://www.reuters.com/article/us-usa-asia-pence/u-s-vice-President-to-visit-south-korea-japan-indonesia-australia-hawaii-idUSKBN17821J.
30. http://www.theaustralian.com.au/national-affairs/foreign-affairs/pence-turnbull-agree-to-raise-pressure-on-pyongyang/news-story/42d3be3752a3484edef5bbc0edeed176.
31. *Ibid.*

32. https://thediplomat.com/2011/10/chinas-overhyped-submarine-threat/.
33. https://economictimes.indiatimes.com/news/international/world-news/sri-lankan-pm-ranil-wickramasinghe-sees-huge-potential-in-cooperation-with-china/articleshow/51764287.cms.
34. *Ibid.*
35. https://timesofindia.indiatimes.com/india/arun-jaitley-raises-sovereignty-concern-over-one-belt-one-road/articleshow/58567348.cms.
36. See: Institute of National Security Studies Sri Lanka website: http://www.insssl.lk/preview.php?id=57.
37. See Endnote 26.
38. Published 14th September 2016 by the Institute of Peace and Conflict Studies (IPCS). See: http://www.ipcs.org/article/south-asia/oceans-of-distrust-5126.html.
39. https://www.britannica.com/biography/Albert-Camus.
40. http://www.lki.lk/publication/take-aways-ban-ki-moon/.
41. *Ibid.*
42. http://www.lki.lk/.
43. Dallaire, R. (2003) *Shake Hands with the Devil: The Failure of Humanity in Rwanda*, Toronto: Random House.
44. Rohde, D. (1998) *Endgame: The Betrayal and Fall of Srebrenica, Europe's Worst Massacre Since World War II*. Boulder, CO: Westview Press.
45. Gunaratne, K. (2016) *Road to Nandikadal: True Story of Defeating Tamil Tigers*, Colombo: Kamal Gunaratne.
46. *Ibid.*
47. http://www.dailymirror.lk/115218/SL-Ambassador-attacked-in-Malaysia.
48. http://www.thehindu.com/news/national/sri-lankan-monk-assaulted/article4516524.ece.
49. http://www.defseminar.lk/.
50. SinhaRaja Tammita-Delgoda (2005) *The World of Stanley Kirinde*, Stamford Lake.
51. http://www.indiafoundation.in/indian-ocean-conference-2016/.
52. http://www.frontpage.lk/page/Indian-Ocean-Conference-is-necessary-Prime-Minister-Ranil-Wickramasinghe-/12812.
53. *Ibid.*
54. https://thediplomat.com/2015/10/interview-francis-fukuyama/.
55. "Geo-strategy in the Indo-Pacific," presentation made by author at the Observer Research Foundation (ORF) Dialogue "Indo-Pacific Region: Converging India-Japan Interest," 13-02-2017 Leela Palace, New Delhi. See: http://www.orfonline.org/research/indo-pacific-region-converging-india-japan-interests/.
56. https://www.stratfor.com/.

57. https://worldview.stratfor.com/article/big-power-little-sri-lanka-india-china-rivalry.
58. See Endnote 3.
59. *Ibid.*
60. Spykman, N. J. (1944) *The Geography of the Peace*, New York: Harcourt, Brace.
61. https://www.weforum.org/agenda/2017/01/chinas-xi-jinping-defends-globalization-from-the-davos-stage/.
62. https://thediplomat.com/2015/12/chinas-one-belt-one-road-initiative-outlook-for-obor-and-the-us-rebalance/.
63. Bhatia, R. K. and Sakhuja, V. (eds.) (2014) *Geostrategic Imperative of the Indo-Pacific Region Emerging Trends and Regional Responses Saroj Bishoyi Indo-Pacific Region: Political and Strategic Prospects*, New Delhi: Vij Book and Indian Council of World Affairs, xvi+185 pp.
64. http://www.icwa.in/crarcfour.html.
65. See Endnote 57.
66. World Port Rankings (2011) American Association of Port Authorities, http://aapa.files.cms.
67. *Ibid.*
68. http://www.ft.lk/article/569163/India-anchors-SL-confidence-in-Colombo-port.
69. http://www.hcicolombo.org/pdf/hb-india-sl.pdf.
70. https://www.weforum.org/agenda/2016/09/what-makes-south-asia-the-fastest-growing-region-in-the-world/.
71. http://dailynews.lk/2017/12/15/local/137426/poverty-free-sri-lanka-2030.
72. http://www.sundayobserver.lk/2017/10/29/news/aims-wiping-out-poverty.
73. http://www.island.lk/index.php?page_cat=article-details&page=article-details&code_title=178444.
74. https://www.cia.gov/library/readingroom/docs/CIA-RDP88T00096R000300340001-2.pdf.
75. President Jayewardene's San Francisco speech: https://www.youtube.com/watch?v=e0FTwGA9H0E.
76. http://www.insssl.lk/preview.php?id=34.
77. http://www.pressreader.com/india/the-new-indian-express/20120822.
78. Speech delivered by Author at TMC "Members Meet," The Management Club at Galadari Hotel, 14th November 2017. See: http://www.ft.lk/other-sectors/-Sri-Lanka-facing-the-geo-political-game-in-the-Indian-Ocean--lecture-by-Asanga-Abeyagoonasekera-at-M/57-643646.
79. https://www.globalsecurity.org/military/world/sri-lanka/history-taprobane.htm.

80. *Ibid.*
81. http://www.go-lanka.com/sri-lanka/geography.html.
82. *Ibid.*
83. http://www.fao.org/3/a-i1820e.pdf.
84. World Oil Transit Chokepoints, U.S. Energy Information Administration, November 2014, https://www.eia.gov/beta/international/regions-topics.cfm?RegionTopicID=WOTC.
85. "Indian Ocean Tsunami: Then and Now," BBC News, 25 December 2014.
86. Myanmar: Cyclone Nargis 2008 Facts and Figures, International Federation of the Red Cross and Red Crescent Societies, 3 May 2011.
87. https://www.silkroadstudies.org/resources/pdf/Monographs/1006Rethinking-4.pdf.
88. Kaplan, R. D. (2010) *Monsoon: The Indian Ocean and the Future of American power*, New York: Random House.
89. http://www.ft.lk/article/69932/Commemorating-Zheng-He--the-greatest-navigator-to-visit-Sri-Lanka-from-China.
90. Patnaik, S. and Haldar, S. K. (1980) "Sino-Sri Lanka Economic Relations: An Appraisal," *China Report*, Vol. 16, No. 6, pp. 19–31. https://doi.org/10.1177/000944558001600603.
91. *Ibid.*
92. See Endnote 88.
93. *Ibid.*
94. Quote from Prime Minister Ranil Wickremesinghe's speech at the Indian Ocean Conference, Colombo, 2017.
95. *Ibid.*
96. Brewster, D. (2017) "Silk Roads and Strings of Pearls: The Strategic Geography of China's New Pathways in the Indian Ocean," *Geopolitics*, Vol. 22, No. 2, pp. 269–291.
97. ShenDingli, "Don't Shun the Idea of Setting Up Military Bases Overseas," January 28, 2010, (http://www.china.org.cn/opinion/2010-01/28/content_19324522.htm.
98. *Ibid.*
99. https://www.foreignaffairs.com/articles/china/2011-02-20/chinas-search-grand-strategy.
100. https://www.ft.com/content/88d584a2-385e-11e7-821a-6027b8a20f23.
101. See Endnote 20.
102. http://foreignpolicy.com/2016/09/03/the-legacy-of-obamas-pivot-to-asia/.
103. *Ibid.*
104. https://www.foreign.senate.gov/imo/media/doc/SRI.pdf.

105. Alice Wells quoted in: https://economictimes.indiatimes.com/news/international/business/us-concerned-over-unsustainable-debt-burdens-to-lanka-by-china/articleshow/60425371.cms.
106. https://www.narendramodi.in/pm-modi-at-the-international-fleet-review-2016-in-visakhapatnam-andhra-pradesh-413019.
107. http://mea.gov.in/SpeechesStatements.htm?dtl/28907/Address+by+External+Affairs+Minister+at+the+2nd+Indian+Ocean+Conference+August+31+2017.
108. *Ibid.*
109. Ghosh, P. K. (2014) "Maritime Security Trilateralism: India, Sri Lanka, and the Maldives," *Strategic Analysis*, Vol. 38, No. 3, pp. 283–288.
110. Bhabani Sen Gupta (ed.) (1986) *Regional Co-operation and Development in South Asia*, Vol. 1, New Delhi: Centre for Policy Research.
111. See K. Subrahmanyam in Brewster, D. (2014) *India's Ocean: The Story of India's Bid for Regional Leadership*, Routledge Security in Asia Pacific Series, Taylor & Francis.
112. Guang, L. L. (1992) "India's Role in South Asia: A Chinese Perspective," In *India's Role in South Asia*, eds. V. L. B. Mendis. Colombo: Bandaranaike Centre for International Studies.
113. http://indianexpress.com/article/india/india-sri-lanka-military-exercise-named-mitra-shakti-concludes-4907334/.
114. Ganguly, A., Chauthaiwale, V. and Sinha, U. K. (eds.) (2018) *The Modi Doctrine: New Paradigms in India's Foreign Policy*, Wisdom Tree.
115. https://www.reuters.com/article/us-sri-lanka-china-submarine/chinese-submarine-docks-in-sri-lanka-despite-indian-concerns-idUSKBN0IM0LY20141102.
116. http://indiatoday.intoday.in/story/sri-lanka-President-mahinda-rajapaksa-blames-india-raw-for-his-election-defeat/1/423763.html.
117. See Endnote 50.
118. http://www.newsweek.com/india-defense-arms-trade-narendra-modi-pakistan-china-modi-f-35-564542.
119. https://economictimes.indiatimes.com/news/defence/indian-navy-aiming-at-200-ship-fleet-by-2027/articleshow/48072917.cms.
120. http://www.iora.net/en.
121. http://ions.gov.in/about_ions.
122. http://www.censusindia.gov.in/2011census/dchb/DCHB_A/33/3309_PART_A_DCHB_ERODE.pdf.
123. Gunaratne, R. "Sri Lanka Tamil Insurgency," http://www.sudaytimes.lk/970119/plus4.html.
124. *Ibid.*

125. Menon, S. (2016) *Choices: Inside the Making of India's Foreign Policy*, Washington: Brookings Institution Press.
126. http://www.frontpage.lk/page/JR-was-forced-to-into-deal-with-India-CIA-papers-reveal-/18684.
127. https://www.ndtv.com/india-news/prime-minister-narendra-modi-reaches-sri-lanka-first-indian-pm-to-visit-in-28-years-746237.
128. http://www.bbc.com/news/world-asia-india-31865470.
129. See Endnote 74.
130. https://www.weforum.org/reports/the-global-competitiveness-report-2017-2018.
131. Indra de Soysa, INSSSL Defence Review 2017.
132. Harsh V Pant, https://www.gepoloticalmonitor.com/the-new-battle-for-sri-lanka-3956/.
133. *Ibid*.

Chapter 2

1. Published 4th December 2017 by the Institute of Peace and Conflict Studies (IPCS). See: http://www.ipcs.org/article/south-asia/changing-political-horizons-in-sri-lanka-5402.html.
2. Hilton, J. 1900–1954 (1950–1959) *Lost Horizon*, New York: Decca.
3. *Ibid*.
4. https://www.iss.europa.eu/content/espas-report-%E2%80%98global-trends-2030-citizens-interconnected-and-polycentric-world%E2%80%99
5. http://www.lankabusinessonline.com/shangri-la-hotel-colombo-declared-open-by-President-pm/.
6. https://www.forbes.com/sites/wadeshepard/2016/09/30/sri-lankas-debt-crisis-is-so-bad-the-Government-doesnt-even-know-how-much-money-it-owes/#230867234608.
7. https://www.weforum.org/reports/the-global-competitiveness-report-2017-2018.
8. http://www.pmdnews.lk.
9. Orwell, G. (1996) *Animal Farm: A Fairy Story*, *New York*, NY: Signet Classics.
10. http://www.sundaytimes.lk/180204/columns/local-council-polls-outcome-would-decide-govts-future-279862.html.
11. Published 4th December 2017 by the Institute of Peace and Conflict Studies (IPCS). See: http://www.ipcs.org/article/south-asia/monuments-over-mortality-5380.html.

12. http://www.insssl.lk/preview.php?id=122.
13. http://www.island.lk/index.php?page_cat=article-details&page=article-details&code_title=15457.
14. https://www.reuters.com/article/us-sri-lanka-corruption/sri-lanka-foreign-minister-resigns-over-corruption-charges-idUSKBN1AQ0Y5.
15. Shakespeare, W. and Hubler, E. (1987) *The Tragedy of Hamlet, Prince of Denmark*, New York, NY: Penguin Books. Act 3, Scene 4, p. 7.
16. http://www.dailymirror.lk/article/Sri-Lanka-s-dubious-honour-at-Washington-corrupt-quartet-142440.html?src=ilaw.
17. http://www.crimesymposium.org/index.html.
18. http://www.dailymirror.lk/article/Asanga-speaks-at-Cambridge-th-Int-l-Symposium-on-Economic-Crime--136573.html.
19. https://www.sbs.ox.ac.uk/programmes/execed/amlp/tim-morris-transformational-leadership-change.
20. http://www.who.int/mental_health/resources/suicide_prevention_asia.pdf.
21. Published 20th April 2017 by the Institute of Peace and Conflict Studies (IPCS). See: http://www.ipcs.org/article/south-asia/sri-lanka-national-interests-in-a-globalised-world-5274.html.
22. https://www.nbcnews.com/news/other/inside-job-cia-suspect-some-jfks-killing-f2D11627219.
23. https://tradingeconomics.com/sri-lanka/gdp-per-capita.
24. http://www.statistics.gov.lk/poverty/Poverty%20Indicators_2016.pdf.
25. http://www.dailymirror.lk/126907/Repeating-the-Ginger-for-Chillies-error.
26. http://www.lankabusinessonline.com/sri-lanka-economy-expected-to-grow-6-3-pct-in-2017-cb/.
27. http://www.President.gov.lk/President-returns-after-most-beneficial-russian-visit/.
28. http://www.sundaytimes.lk/article/1019011/putin-gifts-president-kandyan-era-sword.
29. http://www.adaderana.lk/news.php?nid=38511.
30. Published 10th November 2016 by the Institute of Peace and Conflict Studies (IPCS). See: http://www.ipcs.org/article/south-asia/securing-sri-lankas-national-interests-5173.html.
31. http://www.dailymirror.lk/118678/Thank-you-for-the-music-for-the-songs-we-are-singing.
32. https://www.Parliament.lk/uploads/comreports/1478667396060758.pdf.
33. http://www.defence.lk/new.asp?fname=President_confers_gallantry_medals_20161028_01.
34. https://www.Parliament.lk/budget-2018.

35. https://www.nasaspaceflight.com/2018/01/indias-pslv-launches-cartosat-2f/.
36. https://www.isro.gov.in/spacecraft/list-of-communication-satellites.
37. https://directory.eoportal.org/web/eoportal/satellite-missions/content/-/article/irnss.
38. https://thediplomat.com/2017/01/japan-plans-first-military-communications-satellite-launch/.
39. Spykman, N. J. and Rollins, A. A. (1939) "Geographic Objectives in Foreign Policy I," *American Political Science Review* Vol. 33, No. 3, pp. 391–410.
40. https://america.cgtn.com/2017/01/17/full-text-of-xi-jinping-keynote-at-the-world-economic-forum.
41. https://www.theatlantic.com/magazine/archive/2013/08/the-real-meaning-of-ich-bin-ein-berliner/309500/.
42. Kaufmann, E. (2013) "Robert D. Kaplan: The Revenge of Geography: What the Map Tells Us about Coming Conflicts and the Battle against Fate," *Population and Development Review*, Vol. 39, 347–350; doi:10.1111/j.1728-4457.2013.00596.x.
43. *Ibid.*
44. Mackinder, H. J. (1919/1942) *Democratic Ideals and Reality*, New York: Norton.
45. http://foreignpolicy.com/2017/07/20/trump-nato-hybrid-warfare-hybrid-defense-russia-putin/.
46. http://www.cn.undp.org/content/china/en/home/ourwork/povertyreduction/overview.html.
47. https://www.transparency.org/news/feature/corruption_perceptions_index_2016#table.
48. http://global-is-asian.nus.edu.sg/index.php/no-longer-in-thrall-to-western-democracy-asia-turns-to-technocrats-for-answers/.
49. http://thehill.com/policy/national-security/316435-trump-waterboarding-isnt-torture.
50. https://thewire.in/115872/sri-lanka-conflict-areas-yasmin-sooka.
51. http://webarchive.nationalarchives.gov.uk/20171123123237/http://www.iraqinquiry.org.uk/.
52. http://www.ft.lk/news/President-reiterates-stance-on-foreign-judges--says-there-are-enough-local-judges-with-knowledge/56-645600.
53. https://worldview.stratfor.com/article/big-power-little-sri-lanka-india-china-rivalry.
54. *Ibid.*
55. http://www.defence.lk/new.asp?fname=Sri_Lanka_celebrates_69th_Independence_Day_20170204_02.

56. Published 7th April 2016 by the Institute of Peace and Conflict Studies (IPCS). See: http://www.ipcs.org/article/south-asia/politics-of-promise-between-sirisena-and-rajapaksa-5012.html.
57. Rousseau, J.-J. (1968) *The Social Contract*, Harmondsworth: Penguin.
58. https://edition.cnn.com/2016/03/27/asia/pakistan-lahore-deadly-blast/index.html.
59. http://www.bbc.com/news/world-europe-35869985.
60. https://www.reuters.com/article/us-sri-lanka-politics/sri-lankas-new-president-names-100-day-cabinet-before-polls-idUSKBN0KL1NT20150112.
61. http://www.ft.lk/opinion/mahinda-rajapaksa-and-the-bribery-and-corruption-commission-inquiry/14-412263.
62. Published 8th September 2015 by the Institute of Peace and Conflict Studies (IPCS). See: http://www.ipcs.org/article/south-asia/sri-lanka-moving-towards-a-higher-collective-outcome-4910.html.
63. http://www.dailymirror.lk/86153/hallenges-has-to-be-overcome-with-dilig.
64. https://www.un.org/sg/en/content/sg/statement/2015-03-31/secretary-generals-opening-remarks-humanitarian-pledging-conference.
65. https://www.theguardian.com/world/2015/sep/02/shocking-image-of-drowned-syrian-boy-shows-tragic-plight-of-refugees.
66. See Endnote 64.
67. http://www.adaderana.lk/general-election-2015/index.php.
68. *Ibid.*
69. *Ibid.*
70. *Ibid.*
71. http://www.democracyspeaks.org/blog/local-Government-elections-test-sri-lanka%E2%80%99s-national-unity-Government.
72. http://www.dailymirror.lk/137339/Is-the-UNHRC-Resolution-on-Sri-Lanka-legal-1.
73. http://www.un.org/en/sc/ctc/specialmeetings/2012/docs/United%20Nations%20Security%20Council%20Resolution%201373%20(2001).pdf.
74. https://www.news.lk/news/sri-lanka/item/198-sri-lanka-signs-unsc-resolution-proscribing-16-ltte-organizations.
75. Lutfey Siddiqi, Adjunct Professor, National University of Singapore.
76. Published 11th August 2015 by the Institute of Peace and Conflict Studies (IPCS). See: http://www.ipcs.org/article/south-asia/the-importance-of-electing-the-best-to-our-nations-Parliament-4905.html.
77. Quote from: http://www.island.lk/index.php?page_cat=article-details&page=article-details&code_title=129822.
78. See Endnote 67.

79. http://srilankabrief.org/2017/03/94-mps-in-sri-lanka-Parliament-has-failed-o-level-exam-only-25-out-of-225-are-graduates/.
80. http://www.cbsl.gov.lk/pics_n_docs/10_pub/_docs/efr/annual_report/AR2015/English/content.htm.
81. http://www.sundaytimes.lk/150419/news/nec-recommendations-to-reduce-ol-maths-failures-to-be-presented-to-ms-145237.html.
82. Unconfirmed tabloid source: http://gossip.hirufm.lk/english/374/2015/08/sri-lankan-house-maid-for-sale-onsaudi-arabian-web-site-riyal-25000.html.
83. Lee, K. Y. (1998) *The Singapore Story: Memoirs of Lee Kuan Yew*, Singapore: Prentice-Hall.
84. https://www.timeshighereducation.com/student/best-universities/best-universities-singapore.
85. https://www.csmonitor.com/World/Global-News/2015/0728/Obama-to-African-leaders-No-one-should-be-president-for-life.
86. Published 9th June 2015 by the Institute of Peace and Conflict Studies (IPCS). See: http://www.ipcs.org/article/south-asia/sri-lanka-brain-drain-connection-culture-and-national-development-4887.html.
87. https://www.biography.com/people/john-quincy-adams-9175983.
88. Piketty, T. and Goldhammer, A. (2014) *Capital in the Twenty-first Century*, Cambridge, MA: The Belknap Press of Harvard University Press.
89. *Ibid*.
90. https://www.reuters.com/article/us-asia-migrants/myanmar-says-persecution-not-the-cause-of-migrant-crisis-idUSKBN0OK11320150605?virtualBrandChannel=11563.
91. Private conversation between author and unnamed politician.
92. Private conversation between author and unnamed individual.
93. http://freakonomics.com/2012/06/21/would-paying-politicians-more-attract-better-politicians/.

Chapter 3

1. Published 26th December 2016 by the Institute of Peace and Conflict Studies (IPCS). See: http://www.ipcs.org/article/south-asia/sri-lankan-foreign-policy-diaspora-and-lobbying-5209.html.
2. Kissinger, H. (1994) *Diplomacy*, New York: Simon & Schuster.
3. https://www.american.edu/sis/faculty/aacharya.cfm.
4. Acharya, A. (2014) "Global International Relations (IR) and Regional Worlds: A New Agenda for International Studies," *International Studies Quarterly*, Vol. 58, No. 4, pp. 647–659; https://doi.org/10.1111/isqu.12171.

5. https://www.theguardian.com/us-news/2016/dec/03/trump-angers-beijing-with-provocative-phone-call-to-taiwan-president.
6. http://www.sundaytimes.lk/090830/FunDay/fundaytimes_1.html.
7. http://www.ft.lk/article/539559/Sri-Lanka-s-foreign-policy-under-President-Maithripala-Sirisena.
8. https://en.wikipedia.org/wiki/Sri_Lankan_diaspora.
9. Mearsheimer, J. J., Walt, S. M. and Rogers, D. (2007) *Spotswood Collection*, The Israel lobby and U.S. Foreign Policy.
10. *Ibid.*
11. https://factfinder.census.gov/faces/tableservices/jsf/pages/productview.xhtml?pid=ACS_16_5YR_B02015&prodype=table.
12. Published 11th July 2016 by the Institute of Peace and Conflict Studies (IPCS). See: http://www.ipcs.org/article/india/the-island-and-the-mainland-impact-of-fisheries-on-indo-5076.html.
13. https://www.narendramodi.in/pm-modi-president-of-sri-lanka-jointly-dedicate-newly-renovated-duraiappah-stadium-in-jaffna-484582.
14. http://www.srilanka.travel/adam's-bridge.
15. *Ibid.*
16. http://southasiajournal.net/katchatheevu-should-be-brought-back-to-indian-control-in-order-to-ensure-safe-fishing-by-indians/.
17. http://www.thehindu.com/news/national/tamil-nadu/sri-lankas-bottom-trawling-ban-indias-deep-sea-fishing-all-you-need-to-know/article19396217.ece.
18. https://www.greenpeace.org.uk/what-we-do/oceans/overfishing/bottom-trawling/.
19. https://roar.media/english/life/in-the-know/sri-lankas-bottom-trawling-ban-implemented-or-not.
20. http://www.gc.noaa.gov/gcil_maritime.html.
21. http://extwprlegs1.fao.org/docs/pdf/srl161856.pdf.
22. http://www.sundaytimes.lk/150215/news/fishing-dispute-high-on-agenda-at-sirisena-modi-talks-tomorrow-135842.html.
23. http://dailynews.lk/2016/02/08/features/fishing-solutions-palk-strait.
24. http://www.mfa.gov.lk/index.php/en/media/statements/1396-the-maritime-boundary-between-sri-lanka-and-india-stands-settled-minister-bogollagama.
25. http://indianexpress.com/article/india/sri-lanka-50-percent-drop-in-poaching-by-indian-fishermen-in-lankan-waters-4435974/.
26. https://fs.fish.govt.nz/Page.aspx?pk=81.
27. http://www.agc.gov.my/agcportal/uploads/files/Publications/LOM/EN/Act%20317%20-%20Fisheries%20Act%201985.pdf.

28. See Endnote 19.
29. Published 13th June 2016 by the Institute of Peace and Conflict Studies (IPCS). See: http://www.ipcs.org/article/india/new-delhi-tamil-nadu-relations-and-indias-sri-lanka-policy-5058.html.
30. Sri Salman Kuhrshid, Indian External Affairs Minister Speaking at the Asian Relations Conference held in 2013 at the Indian Council for World Affairs, New Delhi. See: http://icwadelhi.info/asianrelationsconference/images/stories/Keynoteaddresseam.pdf.
31. https://timesofindia.indiatimes.com/india/India-votes-against-Sri-Lanka-at-UNHRC-DMK-slams-govt-for-diluting-resolution/articleshow/19109157.cms.
32. http://www.ft.lk/news/jayalalithaa-assures-dual-citizenship-to-sl-tamils-in-tamil-nadu/56-540468.
33. http://www.tamilguardian.com/content/we-will-fight-attain-independent-eelam-jayalalitha.
34. https://thewire.in/58125/devolution-the-only-solution-northern-provinces-vigneswaran-on-tamil-ties-with-the-sri-lankan-state/.
35. https://www.state.gov/j/ct/rls/crt/2016/272233.htm.
36. https://www.wsws.org/en/articles/2014/11/10/slch-n10.html.
37. http://www.nuclearsuppliersgroup.org/en/about-us.
38. Published 13th May 2016 by the Institute of Peace and Conflict Studies (IPCS). See: http://www.ipcs.org/article/south-asia/remembering-tagore-in-turbulent-times-5028.html.
39. https://www.gutenberg.org/ebooks/33525.
40. https://edition.cnn.com/2016/06/20/asia/bangladesh-new-isis-hotspot/index.html.
41. https://www.theatlantic.com/magazine/archive/2015/03/what-isis-really-wants/384980/.
42. See Endnote 35.
43. https://www.youtube.com/watch?v=3NKOZPq8YZw.
44. *Ibid.*
45. https://www.gov.uk/Government/topical-events/anti-corruption-summit-london-2016.
46. https://www.transparency.org/news/feature/corruption_perceptions_index_2016.
47. http://www.worldbank.org/en/topic/governance/brief/anti-corruption.
48. Published in South Asia Journal 14 Jan 2018, http://southasiajournal.net/trumpism-and-the-diplomatic-dragon balancing-interests-in-the-new-year/.
49. Published by the IPCS, New Delhi for Dateline Colombo, http://www.ipcs.org/article/south-asia/sri-lanka-the-new-regime-and-the-revolution-5432.html.

50. Lecture was delivered at Ministry of Foreign Affairs of France, Quai d'Orsay on 6th March 2018 followed by a roundtable discussion Chaired by Dr. Frédéric Grare who is the Chargé de mission Asia, officials at Ministry of Foreign Affairs and Ministry of Defence.
51. Kaplan, R. D. (2012). *The Revenge of Geography: What the Map Tells Us About Coming Conflicts and the Battle Against Fate*. First edition, New York: Random House.
52. Dorpalen, A. (1942) *The World of General Haushofer: Geopolitics in Action*, Farrar & Rinehart, Incorporated.
53. The Official Website of the President of Sri Lanka, Policy Statement delivered by President Maithripala Sirisena addressing the 8th Parliament of Sri Lanka on September 1, 2015, http://www.president.gov.lk/policy-statement-delivered-by-president-maithripala-sirisena-addressing-the-8th-parliament-of-sri-lanka-on-september-1-2015/.
54. Robert D. Kaplan on China's Port Expansion in the Indian Ocean (Agenda), *Stratfor,* 2012, https://worldview.stratfor.com/article/robert-d-kaplan-chinas-port-expansion-indian-ocean-agenda.
54. Pant, H. V. (2016) *Indian Foreign Policy: An Overview*. Manchester University Press.
55. Ibid.
56. Ptolomy's World Map. The British Library, http://www.bl.uk/learning/timeline/item126360.html.
57. Arasaratnam, S. (1958) *Dutch Power in Ceylon 1658–1687*, Djambatan.
58. Australian Institute of International Affairs, *India's Monroe Doctrine is Dead*, Mar 21st 2016, http://www.internationalaffairs.org.au/australianoutlook/indias-monroe-doctrine-is-dead/
59. Ganguly, A. Chauthaiwale, V. Sinha, U. K. (2018) *The Modi Doctrine: New Paradigms in India's Foreign Policy*, Wisdom Tree.
60. Reuters, *China to Take 70 Percent Stake in Strategic Port in Myanmar — official*, Oct 17th, 2017, https://www.reuters.com/article/china-silkroad-myanmar-port/china-to-take-70-percent-stake-in-strategic-port-in-myanmar-official-idUSL4N1MS3UB.
61. Khurana, G. S. (2008) "China's 'String of Pearls' in the Indian Ocean and Its Security Implications," *Institute for Defence Studies & Analyses — Strategic Analysis,* Vol. 32, No. 1.
62. Reuters: *Chinese Submarine Docks in Sri Lanka Despite Indian Concerns*, Nov 2nd, 2014, https://www.reuters.com/article/sri-lanka-china-submarine/chinese-submarine-docks-in-sri-lanka-despite-indian-concerns-idINKBN0IM0LU20141102.

63. Nehru, J. (1985) *Selected Works of Jawaharlal Nehru*, Vol 3, Series 2, Jawaharlal Nehru Memorial Fund.
64. Brewster, D. (2014) *India's Ocean: The Story of India's Bid for Regional Leadership*, Routledge.
65. Institute of Peace and Conflict Studies, *Gujral Doctrine Security Dimensions of the Gujral Doctrine*, Aug 2nd, 1997, http://www.ipcs.org/article/india-the-world/gujral-doctrine-security-dimensions-of-the-gujral-doctrine-2.html.
66. See Endnote 64.
67. Jane's 360 Magazine.
68. Economic Times, *Indian Navy Aiming at 200-Ship Fleet by 2027*, Jul 14th, 2015, https://economictimes.indiatimes.com/news/defence/indian-navy-aiming-at-200-ship-fleet-by-2027/articleshow/48072917.cms.
69. US Embassy in Sri Lanka, *Remarks by Adm. Harry Harris, Commander, U.S. Pacific Command at Galle Dialogue,* https://lk.usembassy.gov/remarks-adm-harry-harris/.
70. India Foundation, *Indian Ocean Conference 2016*, http://www.indiafoundation.in/indian-ocean-conference-2016/
71. Lanka Business Online, *Sri Lanka's PM Addresses Indian Ocean Conference 2017*, Sept 1st, 2017, http://www.lankabusinessonline.com/sri-lankas-pm-addresses-indian-ocean-conference-2017/.
72. United Nations Press Release, *Ad Hoc Committee on Indian Ocean Adopts Report to General Assembly,* Jul 26th, 2005, https://www.un.org/press/en/2005/gaio4.doc.htm.
73. http://www.worldlii.org/int/other/%20UNGARsn/1972/89.pdf.
74. Council for Security Cooperation in the Asia Pacific, http://www.cscap.org/.

Chapter 4

1. Published 19 March 2018 by the Institute of Peace and Conflict Studies (IPCS). See: http://www.ipcs.org/comm_select.php?articleNo=5451.
2. Published 21st March 2017 by the Institute of Peace and Conflict Studies (IPCS). See: http://www.ipcs.org/article/south-asia/re-building-sri-lanka-an-island-at-a-crossroads-5250.html.
3. Gandhi, M. (1989) *Hind Swaraj, Or, Indian Home Rule*, Ahmedabad: Navajivan Publishing House.
4. Professor Andrew Porter, *Review of Empire: How Britain Made the Modern World* (Review no. 325), http://www.history.ac.uk/reviews/review/325 Date accessed: 16 February, 2018.
5. http://www.dailymirror.lk/article/-leaders-in-freedom-struggle-declared-as-national-heroes-136503.html.

6. *Ibid.*
7. http://www.dailynews.lk/2017/02/28/local/108992/sri-lanka-assures-unhrc-commitment-accountability-and-reconciliation.
8. https://www.hrw.org/news/2017/03/03/sri-lanka-un-official-calls-progress-worryingly-slow.
9. http://www.island.lk/index.php?page_cat=article-details&page=article-details&code_title107986.
10. *Ibid.*
11. *Ibid.*
12. https://www.reuters.com/article/us-sri-lanka-rights-un/sri-lanka-divided-as-panel-backs-foreign-judges-to-probe-war-crimes-idUSKBN14P2CP.
13. http://www.economynext.com/Sri_Lanka_President_rejects_foreign_judges_in_war_probe-3-7490.html.
14. http://www.interpeace.org/.
15. http://www.scrm.gov.lk/consultations.
16. http://www.mfa.gov.lk/index.php/media/news-archive/3186-inaugural-national-reconciliation-conference-today.
17. Lewis, B. (1995) *The Middle East: A Brief History of the Last 2000 Years*, New York, NY: Scribner.
18. Published 13th October 2016 by the Institute of Peace and Conflict Studies (IPCS). See: http://www.ipcs.org/article/south-asia/understanding-our-blindspot-to-make-peacebuilding-comprehensive-5152.html.
19. Emily, D. In a letter to a mentor, TW Higginson, seeking an honest evaluation of her talent (1862), https://www.theatlantic.com/magazine/archive/1891/10/emily-dickinsons-letters/306524/.
20. https://www.apartheidmuseum.org/.
21. http://www.dailymirror.lk/116325/-Eluga-Tamil-demonstration-in-Jaffna.
22. https://implicit.harvard.edu/implicit/takeatest.html.
23. http://blindspot.fas.harvard.edu/.
24. *Ibid.*
25. Katz, D. and Braly, K. W. (1933) "Racial Stereotypes of One-Hundred College Students," *Journal of Abnormal and Social Psychology*, Vol. 28, pp. 280–290.
26. *Ibid.*
27. *Ibid.*
28. https://www.weforum.org/agenda/authors/miniya-chatterji/.
29. *Ibid.*
30. https://www.britannica.com/biography/Albert-Camus.
31. http://www.bbc.com/news/world-europe-30708237.
32. https://edition.cnn.com/2015/11/13/world/paris-shooting/index.html.

33. *Ibid.*
34. Russian flight carrying passengers from Shyam el Shek was bombed.
35. https://edition.cnn.com/2015/11/16/middleeast/beirut-explosions/index.html.
36. Huntington, S. P. (1997) *The Clash of Civilizations and the Remaking of World Order*, New York: Touchstone.
37. https://www.huffingtonpost.com/bernardhenri-levy/andre-glucksmann-in-his-v_b_6190944.html.
38. http://g20.org.tr/.
39. Awan, I. and Blakemore, B. (2012) *Policing Cyber Hate, Cyber Threats and Cyber Terrorism*, London: Ashgate Publishing.
40. https://www.brookings.edu/testimonies/isis-in-the-pacific-assessing-terrorism-in-southeast-asia-and-the-threat-to-the-homeland/.
41. https://www.csis.org/programs/transnational-threats-project/foreign-fighter-project.
42. https://rcss.org/events/nesa-strategic-studies-summit/.
43. http://g20.org.tr/.
44. Published 12th October 2015 by the Institute of Peace and Conflict Studies (IPCS). See: http://www.ipcs.org/article/south-asia/sri-lanka-and-the-world-terrorism-and-effective-reconciliation-4922.html.
45. https://www.cbsnews.com/news/vladimir-putin-addresses-russias-intentions-in-syria/.
46. http://www.syriahr.com/en/.
47. http://www.mfa.gov.lk/index.php/en/media/media-releases/6207-pres-unga2015.
48. http://www.ohchr.org/EN/pages/home.aspx.
49. http://www.ohchr.org/EN/HRBodies/HRC/Pages/OISL.aspx.
50. http://www.mfa.gov.lk/index.php/en/media/ministers-statements/6758-ispd-stockholm.
51. https://www.lawnet.gov.lk/wp-content/uploads/2016/11/010-SLLR-SLLR-2002-3-IN-RE-THE-EIGHTEENTH-AMENDMENT-TO-THE-CONSTITUTION.pdf.
52. http://groundviews.org/2013/01/10/a-legal-primer-the-impeachment-of-the-chief-justice-in-sri-lanka/.
53. See Endnote 49.
54. Published 6th July 2015 by the Institute of Peace and Conflict Studies (IPCS). See: http://www.ipcs.org/article/south-asia/sri-lanka-toward-a-diaspora-re-engagement-plan-4896.html.
55. http://archives.sundayobserver.lk/2015/10/04/pol05.asp.

56. http://www.elections.gov.lk/.
57. http://www.ft.lk/news/tna-gtf-mangala-in-confidence-boosting-talks-in-london/56-430901.
58. http://colombogazette.com/wp-content/uploads/2014/04/1854_41-E.pdf.
59. http://www.un.org/en/sc/ctc/specialmeetings/2012/docs/United%20Nations%20Security%20Council%20Resolution%201373%20(2001).pdf.
60. http://www.dailymirror.lk/77795/govt-wants-to-review-ban-on-tamil-diaspora-organizations-listed-as-terrorists.
61. http://www.thesundayleader.lk/2017/02/26/attempt-to-topple-govt-this-year-vasudeva-nanayakkara/.
62. http://www.island.lk/index.php?page_cat=article-details&page=article-details&code_title=127068.
63. https://www.youtube.com/watch?v=LMX2NjyJ1oQ.
64. http://www.lki.lk/wp-content/uploads/2017/09/Countering-Youth-Radicalization.pdf.
65. http://dailynews.lk/2016/01/13/features/forgiveness-virtue-brave.
66. http://www.nytimes.com/2003/01/14/world/masters-of-suicide-bombing-tamil-guerrillas-of-sri-lanka.html.
67. Narayan Swamy, M. R. (2010) *The Tiger Vanquished: LTTE's Story*, New Delhi: Thosand Oaks; California, Sage.
68. https://www.hrw.org/reports/2004/srilanka1104/2.htm.
69. *Ibid*.
70. https://www.hrw.org/report/2006/03/14/funding-final-war/ltte-intimidation-and-extortion-tamil-diaspora.
71. http://www.jvpsrilanka.com/english/.
72. http://www.dailynews.lk/2017/04/05/features/112482/sanguinary-memories-jvp-insurgence-1971.
73. http://bcgr.gov.lk/.
74. *Ibid*.
75. https://www.isdglobal.org/programmes/research-insight/publications/.
76. http://www.pmdnews.lk/president-sirisena-sends-best-wishes-crown-prince-norway-10th-anniversary-global-dignity/.
77. http://www.defence.lk/english.asp.
78. http://www.nirmin.gov.lk/.
79. http://www.defence.lk/new.asp?fname=Conference_on_the_Role_of_Youth_in_Reconciliation_held_20171212_04.
80. See Endnote 16.
81. Mukherjee, S. (2016) *The Gene: An Intimate History*, Simon & Schuster, Inc.

82. https://www.genome.gov/12011238/an-overview-of-the-human-genome-project/.
83. *Ibid.*
84. http://www.bbc.com/news/world-asia-35265792.
85. Aeschylus, (1848) *The Agamemnon Of Aeschylus*, London: J. W. Parker.
86. Shakespeare, W., Cox, J. D. and Rasmussen, E. (2001) *King Henry VI: Part 3*, London: Arden Shakespeare.

Chapter 5

1. Published 9th August 2016 by the Institute of Peace and Conflict Studies (IPCS). See: http://www.ipcs.org/article/peace-and-conflict-database-early-warning-and-conflict-alert/death-and-democracy-5097.html.
2. Dr. Neelan Tiruchelvam, In his last parliamentary speech relating to the Emergency Debate (June 15,1999). See: http://www.island.lk/2003/07/25/featur01.html.
3. https://edition.cnn.com/2016/07/04/middleeast/baghdad-car-bombs/index.html.
4. http://webarchive.nationalarchives.gov.uk/20171123123237/http://www.iraqinquiry.org.uk/.
5. http://www.bbc.com/news/world-south-asia-13158916.
6. https://www.globalresearch.ca/icc-investigates-allegations-of-abuses-by-british-forces-in-iraq-but-not-tony-blair/5535352.
7. See: p. 9 in https://www.icc-cpi.int/iccdocs/otp/OTP-PE-rep-2015-Eng.pdf.
8. Spengler, O. 1880–1936 (1928) *The Decline of the West*, New York: A. A. Knopf.
9. *Ibid.*
10. Published 17th November 2015 by the Institute of Peace and Conflict Studies (IPCS). See: http://www.ipcs.org/article/south-asia/riot-and-responsibility-governance-in-sri-lanka-4934.html.
11. https://www.newsfirst.lk/2015/11/nation-mourns-loss-of-most-ven-maduluwawe-sobitha-thero/.
12. Abeyagoonasekera, A. (2015) *Towards a Better World Order: Selected Writings and Speeches.*
13. http://www.dailymirror.lk/article/asanga-presents-towards-a-better-world-order-to-president-99203.html.
14. https://www.newsfirst.lk/tag/avant-garde/.
15. http://www.pmoffice.gov.lk/download/press/D00000000009_EN.pdf?p=7.
16. www.ft.lk/news/ranil-wants-report-on-student-police-clash/ -490323.

17. https://www.parliament.lk/uploads/documents/paperspresented/annual-report-university-of-colombo-2014.pdf.
18. https://www.weforum.org/reports/the-global-competitiveness-report-2016-2017-1.
19. http://www.lankabusinessonline.com/sri-lanka-economy-expected-to-grow-6-3-pct-in-2017-cb/.
20. Published by Author on 19th April 2016. See: https://www.colombotelegraph.com/index.php/new-year-kokis-to-luxury-permits/.
21. Hemingway, E. (1940). *For Whom the Bell Tolls*, Charles Scribner's Sons, Chapter 30.
22. http://www.thesundayleader.lk/2016/08/28/vehicle-permits-for-mps-grossly-abused/.
23. Archives: Daily News editorial 25th November 2015. See: http://www.dailynews.lk/editorial.
24. See Endnote 22.
25. https://salary.lk/home/salary/public-sector-wages.
26. https://www.ft.com/content/c2238d7a-0df9-11e6-b41f-0beb7e589515.
27. http://www.ird.gov.lk/en/publications/Value%20Added%20Tax_Acts/VAT_Act_No._20_2016_E.pdf.
28. http://www.sundaytimes.lk/160417/index.html.
29. https://www.un.int/srilanka/news/sri-lanka-signs-paris-agreement-climate-change.
30. See Endnote 19.
31. https://tradingeconomics.com/sri-lanka/gdp-per-capita.
32. Orwell, G. (1996) Animal Farm: A Fairy Story New York, NY : Signet Classics.
33. http://www.thesundayleader.lk/20090111/editorial-.htm.
34. Published by author on 2nd May 2017. See: https://www.colombotelegraph.com/index.php/disasters-democracy-facing-up-to-realities-in-following-new-year-tragedy/.
35. https://edition.cnn.com/2015/03/28/opinions/singapore-lee-kuan-yew-graham-allison/index.html.
36. See Endnote 20.
37. http://dailynews.lk/2017/04/17/features/113310/meethotamulla-tragedy-consequences-negligence-and-lethargy.
38. *Ibid*.
39. https://edition.cnn.com/2017/03/15/africa/ethiopia-trash-landslide-death-toll/index.html.
40. See Endnote 18.

41. http://www.statistics.gov.lk/poverty/Poverty%20Indicators_2016.pdf.
42. https://tradingeconomics.com/sri-lanka/gdp-per-capita.
43. See Endnote 19.
44. See Endnote 31.
45. Khanna, P. (2017) *Technocracy in America: Rise of the Info-State*, CreateSpace Independent Publishing Platform.
46. https://www.geopoliticalmonitor.com/interview-dr-parag-khanna-on-how-to-fix-the-us-political-system/.
47. Fukuyama, F. (1992) *The End of History and the Last Man*, New York: Free Press.
48. https://www.bsg.ox.ac.uk/sites/www.bsg.ox.ac.uk/files/documents/6.3440_IFG_InCISE_Report_Main_WEB.PDF.
49. http://www.straitstimes.com/singapore/health/5-health-screening-for-18-million-singaporeans-letters-out-from-august.
50. http://www.nas.gov.sg/archivesonline/data/pdfdoc/lky19921118.pdf.
51. Published 24th July 2017 by the Institute of Peace and Conflict Studies (IPCS). See: http://www.ipcs.org/article/south-asia/the-forgotten-professions-the-plight-of-a-nation-5332.html.
52. Sartre, J.-P. (1966) *Loser Wins* (*Les Séquestrés D'Altona: A Play in Five Acts*), London: H. Hamilton.
53. https://untappedcities.com/2015/02/11/today-in-nyc-history-the-great-garbage-strike-of-1968/.
54. https://www.newsfirst.lk/2017/04/disposal-colombo-garbage-obstructed-tragedy-meethotamulla/.
55. https://www.newsfirst.lk/2017/08/122000-cases-dengue-reported-island-wide/.
56. http://neweconomics.org/.
57. Metcalf, B. (2017) "Utopia for Realists: And How We Can Get There by RutgerBregman (review)," *Utopian Studies* Vol. 28, No. 3, pp. 685–688.
58. https://libcom.org/library/phenomenon-bullshit-jobs-david-graeber.
59. http://srilankabrief.org/2016/06/govt-to-spend-rs-1175-mn-for-luxury-vehicles-for-ministers/.
60. http://www.dailymirror.lk/article/No-Government-in-the-country-No-country-in-the-Government--132272.html.
61. http://www.sundaytimes.lk/170709/business-times/sri-lanka-to-urgently-import-200000-mt-rice-248683.html.
62. http://www.daph.gov.lk/web/index.php?option=com_content&view=article&id=63&Itemid=218&lang=en.
63. http://www.icba-israel.com/cbase/2012.pdf.

64. https://www.ciwf.org.uk/media/5235182/Statistics-Dairy-cows.pdf.
65. https://www.hindustantimes.com/india-news/trade-start-ups-agro-tech-focus-of-israeli-pm-netanyahu-s-india-visit/story-z5kWnG7yDod09tFFVybv4I.html.
66. https://data.worldbank.org/indicator/GB.XPD.RSDV.GD.ZS.
67. http://www.ecb.bt/?p=5470.
68. Published by author on 5th May 2016. See: https://www.colombotelegraph.com/index.php/parliamentary-blows-the-south-asian-buddha-the-case-of-dignity-in-sri-lanka/.
69. https://www.un.org/press/en/2016/sgsm17719.doc.htm.
70. https://en.unesco.org/wpfd.
71. https://freedomhouse.org/report/freedom-press/freedom-press-2016.
72. *Ibid*.
73. https://rsf.org/en/world-press-freedom-index.
74. https://rsf.org/en/ranking.
75. https://www.mediasupport.org/wp-content/uploads/2016/05/Rebuilding-Public-Trust-English-final-version-advance-copy-1-May-20162.pdf.
76. http://www.economynext.com/Sri_Lanka_value_added_tax_on_healthcare_is_unconscionable-3-4933-2.html.
77. http://dailynews.lk/2016/03/31/local/78012.
78. https://ourworldindata.org/life-expectancy.
79. https://www.news.lk/news/sri-lanka/item/12866-raids-conducted-to-find-unhealthy-food.
80. https://www.ncbi.nlm.nih.gov/pmc/articles/PMC5102238/.
81. *Ibid*.
82. See Endnote 29.
83. http://dailynews.lk/2016/04/20/local/79358.
84. http://www.bbc.com/news/world-asia-31813681.
85. https://www.youtube.com/watch?v=8lcX2dxV3-0.
86. https://www.scribd.com/document/330396082/Task-Force-Recommendations-FINAL-24-03-16-1-2.
87. http://www.vipassana.co/discourses/Buddha-The-Super-Scientist-of-Peace.
88. The Author Speaking at the *Thirty-Fifth International Symposium on Economic Crime*, Jesus College, Cambridge, 4th September 2017. See: http://www.transcrime.it/wp-content/uploads/2017/08/35-International-Symposium-on-Economic-Crime.pdf.
89. https://www.transparency.org/news/feature/corruption_perceptions_index_2016#table.
90. http://srilankabrief.org/tag/bond-scam/.

91. https://www.parliament.lk/uploads/comreports/1478667396060758.pdf.
92. https://www.colombotelegraph.com/index.php/penthouse-ravi-offers-public-super-luxury-house-through-lottery/.
93. https://www.reuters.com/article/us-sri-lanka-corruption/sri-lanka-foreign-minister-resigns-over-corruption-charges-idUSKBN1AQ0Y5.
94. https://www.rti.gov.lk/.
95. http://www.ciaboc.gov.lk.
96. http://www.commonlii.org/lk/legis/num_act/ctiaoboca19o1994704/.
97. https://www.parliament.lk/constitution/amendments-upto-the-seventeenth-amendment.
98. https://www.parliament.lk/constitution/eighteenth-amendment.
99. http://www.ft.lk/front-page/speaker-says-bribery-commission-should-inform-him-before-summoning-mps/44-409757.
100. http://www.parliament.lk/en/component/committees/commitee/showCommittee?id=8.
101. https://www.newsfirst.lk/2017/10/fate-lasantha-wickramatungas-murder-case/.
102. https://www.colombotelegraph.com/index.php/sri-lanka-blocks-colombo-telegraph/.
103. http://www.ipaidabribe.lk/#gsc.tab=0.
104. Records of the Financial Intelligence Unit of the Central Bank of Sri Lanka (classified).
105. *Ibid.*
106. *Ibid.*
107. *Ibid.*
108. *Ibid.*
109. *Ibid.*
110. *Ibid.*
111. *Ibid.*
112. Laski, H. J. (1948) *Liberty in the Modern State*, London: Allen & Unwin.

Chapter 6

1. Speech made by Author on 28th June 2017, "Unified mechanism to improve Cyber Security," at the 2nd Conference on Interaction and Confidence-building in Central Asia (CICA) Non-Governmental Forum.
2. http://www.bbc.com/news/technology-40416611.
3. http://www.ft.lk/article/617118/INSSSL-threat-lens-on-%E2%80%98Cyber-Security:-The-Evolving-Threat-Landscape-in-Sri-Lanka%E2%80%99.

4. http://www.cica-china.org/eng/.
5. Berners-Lee, T. (2000) *Weaving the Web: The Original Design and Ultimate Destiny of the World Wide Web by its Inventor*, New York: HarperCollins Publishers.
6. https://www.theguardian.com/technology/2017/may/12/global-cyber-attack-ransomware-nsa-uk-nhs.
7. https://www.mpg.de/11357138/W001_Viewpoint_010-015.pdf.
8. http://www.wuzhenwic.org/2016-10/12/c_58722.htm.
9. https://uk.practicallaw.thomsonreuters.com/8-618-2325?transitionType=Default&contextData=(sc.Default)&firstPage=true&bhcp=1.
10. See Endnote 8.
11. https://www.aiib.org/en/index.html.
12. http://www.silkroadfund.com.cn/enweb/23773/index.html?previePc=true.
13. https://www.ndb.int/.
14. http://www.slcert.gov.lk/.
15. http://eng.sectsco.org/.
16. https://thediplomat.com/2017/06/its-official-india-and-pakistan-join-shanghai-cooperation-organization/.
17. http://infoshos.ru/en/?idn=8349.
18. Speech made by Author on 26th November 2016, at the National Institute for Defence Studies (NIDS). See: http://www.insssl.lk/preview.php?id=10.
19. http://www.nids.mod.go.jp/english/.
20. President Jayewardene's San Francisco speech: https://www.youtube.com/watch?v=e0FTwGA9H0E.
21. http://www.mofa.go.jp/files/000160708.pdf.
22. *Ibid*.
23. http://www.cfc.gov.lk/.
24. http://www.dailymirror.lk/90565/precious-sri-lanka-japan-relations.
25. http://www.dailymirror.lk/89877/ranil-abe-meet-in-japan.
26. *Ibid*.
27. http://fundforpeace.org/fsi/.
28. http://global.fundforpeace.org/.
29. https://www.foreignaffairs.com/.
30. http://www.president.gov.lk/steer-econ-growth-to-sustain-well-being-of-asia-president-sirisena-calls-on-g-7/.
31. http://www.president-ksgov.net/?page=2,6,2377.
32. Speech made by Author on 15th September 2017, "Cyber Security Threats Made to Sri Lanka", at the 35th National IT Conference (NITC). See: http://www.nitc.lk/2017/.

33. https://www.theguardian.com/technology/2001/apr/19/hacking.security.
34. Weatherford, M., (May 15, 2017) "How Trump's Executive Order Could Prevent Future Ransomware Attacks," http://fortune.com/2017/05/15/ransomware-wannacry-virus-microsoft-patch-cyber-attack-bug/.
35. Perlroth, N., Scott, M. and Frenkel, S., (June 27, 2017) "Cyber-attack Hits Ukraine Then Spreads Internationally," https://www.nytimes.com/2017/06/27/technology/ransomware-hackers.html
36. See Endnote 3.
37. See Endnote 5.
38. Anand, M. (May 17, 2017) "Wanna Cry?," https://reflections.scit.edu/?p=3688.
39. Fox-Brewster, T. "Microsoft Just Took: A Swipe at NSA Over the Wanna Cry Ransomware Nightmare," https://www.forbes.com/sites/thomasbrewster/2017/05/14/microsoft-just-took-a-swipe-at-nsa-over-wannacry-ransomware-nightmare/#397313323585.
40. AFCEA Cyber Committee (October 2013) "The Economics of Cybersecurity: A Practical Framework for Cyber security Investment," https://www.afcea.org/committees/cyber/documents/EconomicsofCybersecurityFinal10-24-13.pdf.
41. Scientific Advice Mechanism High Level Group of Advisors, Cybersecurity in the European Digital Single Market, March 2017, p. 12.
42. Clausewitz, C., Howard, M., Paret, P. and Brodie, B. (1984) *On War*, Princeton, NJ: Princeton University Press.
43. *Ibid*.
44. Published 31st January 2016 by the Institute of Peace and Conflict Studies (IPCS). See: http://www.ipcs.org/article/south-asia/forecast-2016-a-roadmap-for-sri-lanka-4978.html.
45. Sri Lankan Prime Minister speaking at the Sri Lanka Economic Forum 2016. See: http://srilankaeconomicforum.org/.
46. http://srilankaeconomicforum.org/.
47. *Ibid*.
48. *Ibid*.
49. http://archives.sundayobserver.lk/2001/pix/PrintPage.asp?REF=/2016/02/14/fin12.asp.
50. http://www.treasury.gov.lk/documents/10181/12876/2017/360b3514-d267-4836-9890-713ce8955b70.
51. http://www.cfhc.gov.lk/.
52. http://www.sundaytimes.lk/160103/news/road-deaths-reach-record-high-of-2-700-in-2015-177260.html.

53. http://www.pmo.gov.sg/newsroom/pm-lee-hsien-loong-opening-downtown-line-2-26-december-2015.
54. *Ibid.*
55. https://www.weforum.org/reports/the-global-competitiveness-report-2017-2018.
56. http://english.constitutionalassembly.lk/.
57. http://www.unesco.org/languages-atlas/index.php.
58. Published 20th June 2017 by the Institute of Peace and Conflict Studies (IPCS). See: http://www.ipcs.org/article/south-asia/crisis-and-foresight-analysis-5302.html.
59. http://www.bbc.com/news/uk-england-manchester-40008389.
60. https://edition.cnn.com/2017/06/25/asia/philippines-marawi-isis/index.html.
61. https://www.nytimes.com/2017/06/10/world/middleeast/raqqa-syria-white-phosphorus.html
62. Pascal, B. (1909–1914/2001) *Thoughts, Translated by W. F. Trotter. Vol. XLVIII, Part 1. The Harvard Classics*, New York: P.F. Collier & Son, Bartleby.com, www.bartleby.com/48/1/.
63. Machiavelli, N. and Wootton, D. (1995). *The Prince*, Indianapolis: Hackett Publishing Co.
64. https://reliefweb.int/report/sri-lanka/sri-lanka-floods-and-landslides-situation-report-2-5-june-2017.
65. http://www.treasury.gov.lk/budget-estimates-2016.
66. https://www.dgi.gov.lk/news/latest-news/1238-prime-minister-s-speech-at-un-ocean-conference.
67. http://www.mohsl.gov.lk/web/index.php?lang=en.
68. http://www.treasury.gov.lk/minister-of-finance.
69. http://www.ft.lk/article/550837/Sri-Lanka-Foresight-Initiative--SL-is-the-60.
70. http://www.issi.org.pk/the-big-idea-next-generation-of-leadership-in-pakistan-needs-a-new-think/.
71. *Ibid.*
72. Published 18th February 2017 by the Institute of Peace and Conflict Studies (IPCS). See: http://www.ipcs.org/article/south-asia/forecast-2017-sri-lanka-5237.html.
73. http://www.parliament.lk/en/election-2015.
74. https://www.ft.com/content/254cbce0-97a5-11e4-be9d-00144feabdc0.
75. https://www.lawnet.gov.lk/wp-content/uploads/2016/11/010-SLLR-SLLR-2002-3-IN-RE-THE-EIGHTEENTH-AMENDMENT-TO-THE-CONSTITUTION.pdf.

76. http://www.sundaytimes.lk/92408/billionaire-george-soros-wants-to-invest-in-sl.
77. http://www.investsrilanka.com/news/story/4147/Guest-lecture-by-prof-Ricardo-Hausmann-highlights-the-importance-of-technology-and-know how-in-fostering-economic-development-Harvard-Kennedy-School-of-Government.
78. http://www.adaderana.lk/news.php?mode=beauti&nid=35897.
79. http://www.dailymirror.lk/article/MS-invites-Andhra-Pradesh-CM-for-nd-anniversary-of-Unity-govt-121291.html.
80. http://www.presidentsoffice.gov.lk/?p=3723.
81. https://www.colombotelegraph.com/index.php/richard-was-murdered-22-years-ago-remembering-richard/.
82. http://dailynews.lk/2016/11/18/local/99473.
83. http://www.dailymirror.lk/article/Health-Ministry-website-hacked-121615.html.
84. https://www.globalfirepower.com/country-military-strength-detail.asp?country_id=china.
85. https://www.ntnu.edu/employees/indra.de.soysa.
86. https://www.bloomberg.com/graphics/global-risk-briefing/.
87. https://www.transparency.org/news/feature/corruption_perceptions_index_2016.
88. https://daccess-ods.un.org/TMP/1556047.49917984.html.
89. https://www.newsfirst.lk/2017/01/consultation-task-force-reconciliation-mechanisms-completes-final-report/.
90. https://www.aljazeera.com/news/2017/01/protest-hambantota-port-deal-turns-violent-170107080155843.html.
91. http://www.bbc.com/news/world-asia-40761732.
92. https://www.nytimes.com/2017/12/12/world/asia/sri-lanka-china-port.html.
93. http://portal.unesco.org/en/ev.php-URL_ID=33068&URL_DO=DO_TOPIC&URL_SECTION=201.html.
94. Published by Author on 14th December 2017. See: http://www.dailymirror.lk/article/SL-drops-places-WEF-GCI report-142157.html.
95. http://www.dailymirror.lk/113636/Charting-a-course-for-hub-status-1.
96. See Endnote 56.
97. https://www.weforum.org/.
98. *Ibid.*
99. *Ibid.*
100. *Ibid.*
101. http://reports.weforum.org/global-competitiveness-report-2015-2016/.
102. See Endnote 56.

103. http://reports.weforum.org/global-competitiveness-index-2017-2018/countryeconomy-profiles/#economy=LKA.
104. http://reports.weforum.org/global-competitiveness-index-2017-2018/countryeconomy-profiles/#economy=BGD.
105. http://reports.weforum.org/global-competitiveness-index-2017-2018/countryeconomy-profiles/#economy=PAK.
106. *Ibid.*
107. https://www.pressreader.com/sri-lanka/daily-mirror-sri-lanka/20170929/.
108. http://www.lankabusinessonline.com/sri-lanka-economy-expected-to-grow-6-3-pct-in-2017-cb/.
109. http://www.ips.lk/wp-content/uploads/2017/09/Hewage_ADB_Overview-of-Sri-Lankan-Economy.pdf.
110. https://www.hks.harvard.edu/faculty/ricardo-hausmann.

Index

ad-hoc committee, 88, 89
Alfred Mahan, 4, 7, 17, 27
Al-Qaeda, 100, 110, 119
Arun Jaitley, 12
Asian Infrastructure Investment Bank, 6, 144
Asian foreign policy, 15
Asia-Pacific Trade Agreement, 20
Atifete Jahjaga, 149

balance of power, 8, 18
Ban Ki-moon, 13, 59, 130
Barack Obama, 32, 63, 102
Belt and Road Initiative, 6, 7, 31
Bay of Bengal Initiative for Multi-Sectoral Technical and Economic Cooperation (BIMSTEC), 20
blue-water navy, 10, 31
brain drain, 62, 64, 65, 70
Bribery Commission, 57, 135, 136
Buddha, 11, 49, 92, 130, 132, 133

Carl Vinson, 9, 12
Central Bank, 46, 50, 52, 83, 97, 123, 126, 134, 159, 166
Chronic Kidney Disease, 132

C.J. Weeramantry, 162
Cold War, 8, 54, 68, 148
collective security, 4, 89
Colvin Samarasinghe, 115
Committee on Public Accounts, 136
cyber security, 142–144, 149, 150

David Brewster, 30
David Graeber, 128
Denzil Kobbekaduwa, 114
Donald Trump, 5, 10, 30, 33, 49, 55, 68, 77

ethnic conflicts, 13, 107
European Union (EU), 44, 83, 85
European Union Institute for Security Studies, 44

fake news, 93, 94
Francis Fukuyama, 15
Friedrich Engels, 129
Free Trade Agreement (FTA), 20

geopolitical, 5, 11, 15–19, 21, 24, 27, 29, 31, 35, 36, 38, 40
George. H.W. Bush, 118
George Kennan, 7

George W. Bush, 118
geo-strategic, 16, 17, 19–22, 30, 50, 157
Global Competitiveness Index, 41, 44, 154, 163
G.L. Peiris, 15, 135
governance, 55, 58, 59, 62, 76, 83, 122, 155
Great October Revolution, 6
Gwadar port, 6, 30, 35, 79

Halford Mackinder, 7, 27
Hambantota Port, 6, 7, 29, 79, 84
Henry Kissinger, 10
Hillary Clinton, 52
human rights, 14, 39, 55, 73, 95, 102, 103

Ibrahim Sahib Ansar, 14
Indian Ocean Conference, 15, 88
Indian Ocean Naval Symposium, 37, 87
Indian Ocean Region (IOR), 4, 15, 24, 29, 33, 40, 41, 83, 88, 160
Indian Ocean Rim Association, 37, 87
Indo-Sri Lankan Accord, 8
Institute for National Security Studies Sri Lanka (INSSSL), 12, 112, 114, 142, 150
International Criminal Court, 119
International Monetary Fund (IMF), 123, 165
Islamic State (IS), 59, 75, 101

James Hilton, 44
Jawaharlal Nehru, 34
J. Jayalalitha, 71, 74
John F Kennedy, 49
J. R. Jayewardene, 33, 146

Kamal Gunaratne, 13
Kanti Bajpai, 32
Kitty Hawk, 11

Lakshman Kadirgamar, 11, 22, 41
Lalith Athulathmudali, 45, 76
Lasantha Wickramatunge, 130, 136, 160
Lawrence W. Prabhakar, 19
Lee Kuan Yew, 32, 45, 62, 121, 124, 126, 127
Leonard Woolf, 7
Liberation Tigers of Tamil Eelam (LTTE), 97, 103, 105, 107, 108, 110, 115, 133, 137, 138, 142, 155
local government elections, 82, 161
Lotus Tower, 47, 49, 80, 86

Mahinda Rajapaksa, 36, 51, 57, 105, 161
Maithripala Sirisena, 4, 8, 16, 21, 39, 41, 44, 46, 50, 52, 56, 58, 94–96, 98, 103, 107, 111, 113, 123, 132, 134, 146, 148, 153, 155, 159, 161
Malcolm Turnbull., 10
manifest destiny, 35, 87
Mattala Rajapaksa International Airport, 9
Meethotamulla, 124, 126, 127
Michael J. Delaney, 14
Mike Pence, 10
Ministry of Defence, 44, 112
Monroe Doctrine, 34, 85, 87
multi-polar world, 68, 70

Narendra Modi, 11, 22, 33, 36, 39, 71, 85, 129
Neelan Tiruchelvam, 13, 118
Nicholas Spykman, 17, 54

Nick Rankin, 7
Nimitz, 4, 37
Nisha Biswal, 15
Non-Aligned Movement, 68
North Atlantic Treaty Organization (NATO), 14, 18, 55

One Belt, One Road, 6, 11, 29, 143
Oswald Spengler, 120

Parag Khanna, 55
P.K Balachandran, 23
Prisoner's Dilemma, 60
Puruesh Chaudhary, 158

Raj Rajaratnam, 138
Ranil Wickremesinghe, 11, 15, 58, 59, 88
reconciliation, 98, 102, 104, 106, 146, 155, 161
rehabilitation, 1, 101, 109, 137
Ren Xianliang, 144
Ricardo Hausmann, 153, 166
Right to Information Act, 57, 135
Robert Kaplan, 29, 84
Rutger Bergman, 128

Saddam Hussein, 118
Shanghai Cooperation Organisation, 145
Shen Dingli, 31
Shinzo Abe, 146
Silent Revolution, 81, 82, 130
Silk Road, 6, 8, 11, 16, 20, 29, 30, 32, 144, 145
Sirimavo Bandaranaike, 14, 68, 89, 121
Sobitha Thero, 45, 106
soft power, 12, 14, 15, 33, 147

South Asian Association for Regional Cooperation (SAARC), 22, 85
South Asian Free Trade Area (SAFTA), 20
South China Sea, 10, 18, 19, 55, 160
Strait of Hormuz, 27, 30
Strait of Malacca, 27, 30
Suresh Mehta, 19
Sushma Swaraj, 33

Tamil diaspora, 41, 69, 103
Tamil political aspirations, 40
Temple of the Sacred Tooth Relic, 92
terrorism, 27, 34, 56, 61, 92, 100, 101, 103, 107, 119, 137, 139, 147
Tim Berners Lee, 142, 150
tsunami, 22, 137, 138, 147

United Nations Framework Convention on Climate Change, 157
United Nations Human Rights Council (UNHRC), 95, 96, 103
United Nations High Commissioner for Refugees (UNHCR), 60

Velupillai Prabhakaran, 13, 73, 108
Vladimir Ilyich Ulyanov, 6
Voice of America, 33, 47

Wang Jisi, 8, 31
William Shakespeare, 24, 48
World Economic Forum, 8, 20, 32, 41, 44, 83, 125, 154, 162
World Health Organization, 49, 132

Xi Jinping, 7, 9, 12, 54, 81

About the Author

Professor Asanga Abeyagoonasekera is the Director General of the National Security Think Tank of Sri Lanka (INSSSL) under the Ministry of Defence. He is a visiting professor for Geopolitics (Northern Kentucky University), International Security (University of Colombo) and International Political Economy (University of London RIC). Asanga is a columnist for the Institute of Peace and Conflict Studies and the South Asia Journal. He has authored many academic journal articles and presented in defence and foreign policy think tanks, universities and government ministries including Quai d'Orsay in Paris. His major field of interest is the geopolitics of South Asia, the Indian Ocean Region and regional security in South Asia.

He has 13 years of experience in the government, served as the former Executive Director of the government foreign policy think tank — the Kadirgamar Institute, and was Advisor to the Minister for External Affairs from 2012–2015. He was educated at Harvard Kennedy School, the Jackson Institute for Global Affairs (Yale University), Lee Kuan Yew School of Public Policy (National University of Singapore), University of Oxford, and Edith Cowan University (Western Australia).

Asanga was recognised as a Young Global Leader for the World Economic Forum. He is author of Towards a Better World Order (2015). Asanga is an alumnus of the U.S. Department of State's International Visitor Leadership Programme, the Asia-Pacific Center for Security Studies (Hawaii), and the National Defense University (Washington).